HARVARD ECONOMIC STUDIES

VOLUME CVI

The studies in this series are published by the Department of Economics of Harvard University. The Department does not assume responsibility for the views expressed.

NORWAY

The Planned Revival

By

ALICE BOURNEUF

HARVARD UNIVERSITY PRESS

Cambridge, Massachusetts

1958

© 1958, by the President and Fellows of Harvard College

Distributed in Great Britain by Oxford University Press, London

Library of Congress Catalog Card Number 58–10397

Printed in the United States of America

TO MY MOTHER

Preface

I first became interested in the Norwegian economy when I had the opportunity of working under Mr. A. E. Staley, Jr., Mission Chief of the Economic Corporation Administration in Norway, in 1948.

My continued interest in Norwegian postwar economic policies, and my gradual progress toward an understanding of them, were largely due to the patient cooperation of government officials with the staff of the Mission during my stay in Norway. The Ministry of Commerce was the department responsible for relations with the Mission. Minister of Commerce Erik Brofoss, who is now Governor of the Bank of Norway, and Director Eivind Ericksen of the National Budget Office, who is now Undersecretary in the Ministry of Finance, made every effort to give the economic staff of the Mission the benefit of their keen understanding of and insights into Norwegian economic problems and policies.

It would be impossible to name all the other officials who were helpful. Truls Glesne, now Director of the National Budget Office, Jahn Halvorsen, Johan Cappelan, Knut GetzWold, Dagfin Juel, and Helge Seip, all of whom were in the Department of Commerce during the years 1948 to 1951, were generous enough to try to meet the almost insatiable demands of the Mission for detailed explanations of economic developments and masses of statistical material.

Governor Gunnar Jahn, Governor of the Bank of Norway when I was in Norway, was also kind enough to discuss Norwegian problems with me on several occasions. Minister Arne Skaug, who was in Paris when I was working on Scandinavian problems there from 1951 to 1953, was also most helpful.

Some of these Norwegian officials were good enough to read an earlier draft of this book and give me the benefit of their criticisms. Director P. J. Bjerve of the Central Bureau of Statistics also commented on an earlier draft. Mr. Skanland of the National Budget Office pointed out a number of errors and misconceptions. Mr. John

Sheahan of Williams College read over an early draft very carefully also and made some valuable suggestions for rewriting.

The main work was done at Harvard University while I had a Littauer School of Public Administration Fellowship in 1953–54. Professors Arthur Smithies, James Duesenberry, and Seymour Harris, who was responsible for my original interest in economics from my student days at Radcliffe, gave me good advice in the early stages. Professor Alvin Hansen discussed some of the problems with me. The study was presented as a doctoral thesis at Radcliffe.

It was due to the encouragement and very thoughtful criticism of Professor J. K. Galbraith that I tackled the job of trying to make the doctoral thesis into a book. He recommended a major reorganization of the material in the thesis, read over the manuscript several times, and gave me good suggestions on many important points.

Miss Dorothy Wescott was kind enough to edit the entire manuscript and make it much clearer and more readable than it was.

Needless to say, in spite of all the helpful comments of Norwegian and American economists, any mistakes, misunderstandings, and shortcomings are mine.

Berkeley, California

A. B.

January 1, 1958

Contents

List of Tables

NORWAY

The Planned Revival

1

Norway's Postwar Problems

Norway's balance-of-payments position was critical at the time of liberation after World War II, and inflationary pressures that had built up during the occupation created a precarious financial situation. War losses were heavy and were concentrated in export sectors, on which Norway was dependent for procuring essential foods and raw materials. But while balance-of-payments deficits and inflationary pressures continued for several years, they were not unmanageable and did not seriously interfere with the program for both restoring the prewar level of output and developing and expanding productive capacity. The proportion of total output devoted to investment year after year since the war has been higher than in any other Western democratic country.

A number of external factors contributed to Norway's recovery. The fact that there was no serious slump in United States employment and income after the war helped to maintain prosperous conditions throughout the world. The Marshall Plan and the programs of European economic cooperation set up under the Plan played a vital role in Europe's postwar program. Western European progress was more rapid on the whole than after World War I, and Marshall Plan aid to Norway arrived just in time to forestall a sharp cut in the original postwar program.

Probably the most important difference between Norway and other Western European countries in the recovery period has been the extent to which Norway has relied on economic planning and direct controls. In contrast to such countries as Germany and Belgium, where recovery has been attributed partly to the speedy elimination of controls and to tight money policies,[1] rapid progress in Norway has been due at least in part to policies that are quite the opposite.

[1] See, for example, Henry C. Wallich's *Mainsprings of the German Revival* (New Haven: Yale University Press, 1955).

Norway's experience provides a case study of comprehensive planning designed to achieve a rapid rate of economic growth in the face of serious limiting factors. Before the war, Norway had been less fully industrialized than some of the other Western European countries. Her greatest resource, hydroelectric power potential, had only begun to be exploited. The country was not underdeveloped in the sense of having a very low level of per capita income or of having political, institutional, or educational barriers to economic growth; but there were important possibilities for expanding productive capacity and raising the level of income. Many other countries in similar circumstances today are consciously trying to speed up their rate of economic growth. Norway's experience with comprehensive planning therefore deserves careful study.

Economic planning and direct controls did not lead to interference with political or civil liberties. The character of the Norwegian people suggests that such interference would not be tolerated. Nor were recovery and development achieved at the expense of the lower income groups. The heavy investment program went hand in hand with expanded welfare and social security programs, and also with a considerable redistribution of income within the wage earning group.

The aim of this study is to give a general account of Norway's postwar economic plans and of how they were carried out. It does not try to consider every phase of the country's economic policy. Attention is focussed primarily on plans for resource uses, how closely the results corresponded with the plans, and how the actual results were achieved. In addition, considerable attention is given to monetary, fiscal, and price-wage policies. Although resource plans, the direct measures used to implement them, and monetary, fiscal, and price-wage policies are closely interrelated, they are discussed and explained to some extent in separate chapters; without such separate treatment it is impossible to give a clear history of the development of policy decisions and instruments and of the actual course of economic events.

Norway's postwar problems must be considered against the background of her prewar economic position, the effect of the war on the economy, and the main problems that the Government faced after the liberation in May 1945. An outstanding feature of the prewar period was the dependence on foreign trade and shipping. Exports of pulp and paper, fish, and shipping services paid for necessary imports of food, raw materials, fuels, manufactured goods, and ships. It is not surprising, however, that Norway is so dependent on foreign trade and shipping. Over 70 per cent of the country's area is waste land — barren mountain plateaus and lakes; one quarter is forest land, and only 3 per cent is suitable for farming or grazing. Mineral deposits are limited.

Imports of goods and services in 1938 equalled 26 per cent of gross national product, exports 29 per cent.[2] Per capita imports were higher than in any other country in the world except New Zealand. The most important single source of foreign-exchange earnings was the merchant fleet, net earnings from shipping paying for about one third of total imports. Among commodity exports, the most important were pulp and paper and fish, which accounted for over 40 per cent of the total.

About one fourth of Norway's foreign trade before the war was with the United Kingdom, one fifth with Germany, and one seventh with the Western Hemisphere, mostly the United States. A substantial sterling surplus was used to meet deficits with Germany and continental Europe. Freight receipts in sterling from countries all over the world explained the sterling surplus. Almost two thirds of dollar imports were paid for with dollar shipping earnings, and there was a slight dollar surplus.

In the early decades of the twentieth century, Norway had built up its industrial capacity. Expansion of foreign-exchange earnings had been necessary to support a rapidly increasing population. Despite emigration of almost a million persons, the population rose by almost 1 million, or by 40 per cent, between 1900 and 1938, when it totaled 2.9 million persons.

The economy in 1900 was primarily agricultural, with timber and coastal fishing supplying the main exports; but by 1938, dependence on agriculture, fishing, and forestry had been reduced substan-

---

[2] Imports were relatively low because of substantial unemployment. The principal imports were bread grains, feeding stuffs, sugar, coal, petroleum, iron and steel products, cars and trucks, textiles, and machinery. Norway depended on imports for 85 per cent of bread grain consumption, 50 per cent of concentrated feedstuffs, 75 per cent of iron and steel, coal and coke, cars and trucks, sugar and petroleum, cotton, rubber, hides and leather. The principal commodity exports were fish and fish products (19 per cent), paper and pulp (22 per cent), ores and metals (8 per cent), oils and fats (mostly whale oil), and fertilizers.

tially. It is true that manufacturing industries, such as pulp and paper and canned fish, which are based on fishing and forestry, were developed; yet of greater importance was the exploitation, from 1910 onward, of Norway's hydroelectric power resources, and the development of industries based on the heavy use of power, the electrochemical and electrometallurgical industries. There was also a rapid growth of the merchant fleet; from 1910 to 1938 the fleet doubled, to become the fourth largest in the world. The whaling fleet, including large floating factory ships, expanded in the twenties until Norway became the world's largest producer of whale oil.

Foreign capital helped to finance the development of the export industries. Foreign companies had begun to build pulp and paper mills in Norway in the 1870's and they were active later in the electrochemical and electrometallurgical industries. Purchases of ships built abroad were financed with the help of foreign loans. There was a net import of capital in most of the years from 1850 to 1900, and in every year from 1900 to 1932. Only in the later thirties did capital imports cease. The small export surplus in those years was due largely to high unemployment and a resulting low level of commodity imports.

Table 1. Gross domestic product by industrial origin,
percentage distribution, 1910, 1930, and 1938

	1910	1930	1938
Agriculture	14	7	8
Forestry	6	4	4
Fishing	3	2	2
Whaling	1	4	1
Mining	1	1	1
Manufacturing	21	23	23
Construction	3	4	5
Electricity, gas, and water	1	3	2
Wholesale and retail trade	16	14	15
Shipping	8	8	10
Inland transport	3	5	5
Community and business services	4	6	6
Government services	2	2	2
Personal services	6	5	4
Ownership of buildings	9	10	9
Other	2	2	2
Total[a]	100	100	100

Source: Central Bureau of Statistics. Data for 1910 and 1930 are from *National Accounts, 1900–1929* (Oslo, 1953); those for 1938 are from *National Accounts, 1938 and 1948–1953* (Oslo, 1954). Data are at current market prices.

[a] Details may not add up to 100 per cent because of rounding.

The changes in the composition of output in the decades up to World War II were substantial (Table 1), and most of the changes had taken place by 1930. Agriculture fell from 14 per cent of total output in 1910 to 8 per cent in 1938; forestry from 6 to 4 per cent; and fishing from 3 to 2 per cent.[3] Much of the manufacturing output, however, was based on the product of the forests, the fisheries, and the whaling fleet. As shown in Table 1, output rose relatively in shipping, manufacturing, construction, electric power, inland transport, and services. The rise in total manufactured output was relatively small, but within the manufacturing sector there was a sharp shift from handicraft and small-scale cottage industry to factory output.[4]

As industries were developed, labor moved from the farms and the forests, and by 1938 only 31 per cent of total employment was in agriculture and forestry, compared with 41 per cent in 1900 and 55 per cent in 1875 (Table 2). While the percentage for employment

Table 2. Employment in principal sectors, percentage distribution, 1875–1938

	Agriculture and forestry	Fishing and whaling	Industry, handicrafts, mining, and construction	Trade, finance, hotels, restaurants, etc.	Transport	Housework	Other	Total[a]
1875	55	4	19	4	7	8	2	100
1890	48	7	22	6	7	7	3	100
1900	41	6	27	8	8	7	4	100
1910	42	5	25	9	8	8	4	100
1920	37	5	28	11	8	7	5	100
1930	35	6	25	12	9	8	5	100
1938	31	5	26	13	8	10	7	100

Source: Central Bureau of Statistics. Data before 1938 from *Economic Survey, 1900–1950*. Data for 1938 are not strictly comparable; they are rough calculations based on full-time equivalent employment data in *National Accounts, 1938 and 1948–1953*.
[a] Details may not add up to 100 per cent because of rounding.

in industry, handicrafts, mining, and construction as a group did not rise after 1900, there was a shift from handicrafts and cottage

[3] Comparable data are not available for 1900.
[4] See *Economic Survey, 1900–1950* (Oslo: Central Bureau of Statistics, 1955).

industry into the other three sectors. The largest increases were in trade, finance, the service industries, and the "all other" sector.[5]

The rapid pace of industrial development before the war is brought out even more clearly by changes in the volume of production in the principal new industries. Output in the ore and metal industries in 1939 was thirty-four times and that in the chemical industries eighteen times the 1900 level. Electrochemical and electrometallurgical plants, producing almost entirely for export, accounted for most of the expansion. Pulp and paper output, already substantial in 1900, increased five times from 1900 to 1939.[6]

At the end of the thirties, Norway had not by any means exhausted the possibilities for economic development. Only a small fraction of the potential hydroelectric power had been exploited; further expansion of electrochemical and electrometallurgical industries awaited only additional power development; and there were unexploited low-grade iron ore deposits and large pyrite deposits. Presumably, more labor could be drawn from the farms and the forests without reducing output in those sectors.

The war, however, caused severe losses. Not only was development brought to a standstill, but a substantial part of the country's capital stock was destroyed. There was widespread destruction in northern and western Norway. Not one building remained standing in the "scorched earth" area in northern Norway. The one big iron ore mine, in northern Norway, was flooded, and every building, pier, and installation demolished. A number of west coast towns were completely destroyed by bombing in 1940. Several manufacturing concerns in western Norway were badly damaged. About 22,000 houses in all were destroyed, and virtually no houses were built during the five years of occupation.

During the occupation, the Central Bureau of Statistics in Oslo made a study of the prewar economy and of the effects of the war on the economy in terms of the first national accounts estimates for Norway covering the period 1935–1943. These data, though rough when compared with later calculations, made it possible to evaluate

[5] The increase in employment in housework in 1938 reflected large-scale industrial unemployment.

[6] See *Economic Survey, 1900–1950.*

the effect of the war on Norway. Primarily using this material, Odd Aukrust and Petter Jakob Bjerve made an analysis of the cost of the war, which was published in May 1945.[7]

According to this study, the war had destroyed almost one fifth of Norway's total capital stock as of 1939. The destruction was about 25 per cent greater than the total output of 1939[8] and about 50 per cent greater than output in late 1944 and early 1945. Total output in early 1945 was estimated at 4 billion 1939 kroner, or slightly over 80 per cent of 1939 output.[9] The loss of capital was reckoned at between 5.5 billion and 6 billion kroner at 1939 prices. The bare minimum of net investment needed to restore productive capacity to the prewar level was estimated at 3 billion 1939 kroner. Since 1941, net output was believed to have been well below that in prewar years, and the Germans had taken over a third of total output year after year for war purposes.[10]

The cost of restoring prewar productive capacity estimated in the 1945 study later proved to be too high for certain sectors; in some sectors it was possible to restore output quickly with a relatively small amount of investment. But the cost of restoring capacity in the major export sectors, notably shipping, whaling, and fishing, was probably underestimated. The prices of imported ships and imported equipment rose sharply compared with the prices of Norwegian exports. On balance, then, the estimate that was made of the total cost of the war to Norway may not have been excessive.[11]

The losses of the merchant, whaling, and fishing fleets were overwhelming in view of Norway's dependence on the foreign-exchange

[7] *Hva krigen kostet Norge* (Oslo: Dreyers Forlag, 1945). The account of war losses in the present text relies heavily on this study.

[8] Output in 1939 was estimated at 4.8 billion kroner, or about $1 billion.

[9] Or about 6.4 billion 1945 kroner.

[10] Estimates of total output, and output compared with prewar, later proved to be much too low. The share of output taken by the Germans was estimated on the basis of German expenditures and German requisitioning, offset to some extent by net imports from Germany.

[11] It is impossible to make any precise comparison of these estimates of war costs with actual investment in 1945 and 1946, or with the actual cost of restoring prewar productive capacity. Total output is now estimated to have been above prewar by 1946, but the composition of output was entirely different from prewar, and the actual war damage and losses, particularly in major export sectors, had not been restored.

earnings of these sectors to pay for needed imports. Because about 90 per cent of the merchant fleet was in overseas waters when war broke out, it escaped the occupation authorities and was in the service of the allies during the war; therefore half of it was lost. Over 70 per cent of the whaling fleet was lost, including nine out of ten of the huge floating factories, also in the service of the allies. About 40 per cent of the fishing fleet was demolished. To rebuild these fleets, especially the merchant fleet, would mean a huge drain on foreign-exchange reserves, since most of the ships had to be constructed in foreign shipyards. Although Norway had accumulated considerable claims in sterling from ship earnings and insurance during the war, it was not clear how far these claims would go toward replacement of the fleets.[12]

The effect of the war and of the occupation on Norway was not limited to actual physical losses and war damage. The virtual cutting off of imports during the occupation, except for certain minimum supplies from Germany, seriously weakened the economy.[13] In 1942 and 1943 the volume of imports was about one third the 1938 level, in 1944 one fifth. Private consumption, not allowing for quality deterioration, declined to about 60 per cent of that in prewar years. Consumption depended largely on imported food, feedstuffs, raw materials, and manufactured goods. Agricultural output fell partly because of a lack of fertilizers and feedstuffs. Both the timber cut and fish catch were far below prewar. Industrial production fell to about half the prewar rate. Output per worker declined sharply. Consumer and household stocks, as well as business stocks, were depleted.

Also of great importance was the effect on the price-wage structure and monetary system. Serious inflationary pressures had been built up during the occupation. The Germans financed their expenditures by direct borrowing from the Norges Bank, the Norwegian central bank. The huge monetary expansion was not allowed to lead to comparable price and wage increases. A complete system of price controls,

[12] The total claims on sterling of the wartime shipping agency, Nortraship, were over 2 billion kroner.

[13] Imports from Germany exceeded exports to Germany during the occupation. Imports were largely bread grain and sugar, and exports were mostly fish. Food imports were permitted partly to support the large occupation forces in Norway.

wage freezes, allocations, import controls, rationing, and even direct production and labor controls had been developed in the course of the occupation.

Between the fall of 1939 and the spring of 1940, there were several general price regulations and price adjustments. Wages were frozen in principle in the fall of 1939, but certain cost-of-living adjustments were granted. In April 1940, prices were frozen at the levels of April 8, 1940, except for such changes as might be approved by the Price Directorate. Rents were frozen at 10 per cent below 1940 levels. Interest rates above 3½ per cent were reduced. Dividends were limited to 5 per cent for most companies and to 8 per cent for others. In May, wages also were frozen at April 1940 levels. At that time, however, both prices and wages were substantially above the 1939 levels; for example, wholesale prices were about one-third higher than in August 1939.

Further increases in both prices and wages were approved after April 1940. Price increases were allowed to cover rising costs of materials and to stimulate output in agriculture, the forests, and fishing. Wage increases were approved for hired farm labor, foresters, and fishermen, all of whom had been among the lowest paid workers in Norway before the occupation. Substantial wage increases were necessary to keep labor from moving to more highly paid work in the cities and on German fortifications, at a time when the output of the farms and fisheries was essential to maintain food and fuel consumption. Higher prices were paid to farmers and fishermen also, but they were offset to some extent by consumer subsidies.[14]

At the end of the occupation, the cost of living was about 50 per cent and wholesale prices about 75 per cent above the 1938 level. An increase in 1940 of the general sales tax on all purchases to 10 per cent accounted for some of the rise in the cost of living. Hourly earnings in industry were only 20 to 30 per cent above 1938 earnings. On the other hand, wages paid to construction workers and wages in farming, forestry, and fishing were about double the prewar wages.

The rise in wages and prices was not at all in proportion to the increase in the money supply. The Germans to some extent offset the

[14] Subsidies rose steadily to an annual sum of about 225 million kroner by the time of liberation.

inflationary effects of direct borrowing from the central bank by high taxes, budget surpluses, and borrowing from private banks and the public.[15] The government debt, excluding the debt to the Norges Bank, approximately doubled. The long-term interest rate was raised to 3.5 per cent. In spite of such measures, the cash assets of the private banks and the public increased enormously; at the time of liberation, private bank reserves in cash and deposits at the Norges Bank were about fifty times the prewar level, notes in circulation outside the banks more than seven times the prewar level, and time and demand deposits in the hands of the public twice the prewar level. The total money supply (notes plus time and demand deposits) in the hands of the public was almost three times that in 1938.[16] Direct controls kept prices at less than twice the prewar level in spite of this much greater increase in the money supply.

Long before the liberation, government economists and officials, whether in Oslo, in London with the government in exile, or in Washington, were considering the problems that Norway would face after the war. One of the most basic decisions would be concerned with the rate at which productive capacity should be restored and developed. There would clearly be a conflict between rapid restoration of the prewar standard of living and rapid restoration of prewar productive capacity. Foreign-exchange reserves and even foreign loans could be used to bring quick relief to the Norwegian people after years of a grossly inadequate diet and of a virtual dearth of manufactured consumer goods, or they could be used to buy ships, whaling factories, fishing gear, and machinery. Domestic labor and materials could be used for housing and cinemas, or for further power development and factory construction.

The fact that the population had grown by about 7 per cent during

---

[15] Direct borrowings from the Norges Bank amounted to 11.3 billion kroner. Taxes and borrowings from the private banks and from the public were used to pay off 2 billion of the debt to the Norges Bank and to accumulate 2 billion in deposits at the Norges Bank. The 7 billion kroner net expansion was reflected in a 4-billion increase in private bank reserves, and a 2.5-billion increase in notes in circulation outside the banks. See Aukrust and Bjerve, *Hva krigen kostet Norge,* for a full account of occupation financial policies.

[16] The precise figure is about 2.7 times. For data on the prewar money supply and the money supply after the monetary reform, at the end of 1945, see Table 3, Chapter 2.

the war, to 3.1 million, suggested that more than prewar productive capacity and the prewar level of exports would be needed to purchase food, materials, and manufactured goods. A return to the prewar rapid rate of economic development would add to the immediate postwar problems. The diversion of resources to both reconstruction and continued economic development would make it all the more difficult to restore prewar living standards. But continued development was necessary to secure rising living standards for a growing population.

The amount of foreign capital that Norway should try to raise would necessarily depend on prospects for further expansion of exports. If renewed economic development was to be carried on after the liberation, one of the big problems would be to find the industries capable of earning additional foreign exchange. For physical reasons, the timber cut and whale catch could not be expanded much beyond the results in prewar years. The possibilities of increasing the fish catch seemed uncertain. The pulp and paper industry was overexpanded in relation to the potential domestic supply of timber. Most of the limited mineral deposits had been exploited before the war. Power and industries based on power presumably offered the best prospects for expansion. And, eventually, the merchant fleet might be expanded.

Special attention would have to be given to developing dollar earning capacity. In the early postwar years, Germany could not be counted on as a large supplier, and it was unlikely that sterling could be used to meet deficits with the Continent. Because of the heavy reconstruction needs and the low output in most of Europe, it appeared that Norway and the rest of Europe would have to rely on the United States as a supplier much more than before the war.

Actually, the greatest immediate problem was the inflationary pressure. Even before liberation, government officials were convinced that the only short-run solution was to maintain price controls and to make certain price and wage adjustments. But the problem of how to handle the situation in the longer run was more difficult.

Should an effort be made to eliminate the excess liquidity of the banks and the public? A strict monetary reform could sterilize or block bank reserves and also notes and deposits in the hands of the public. Temporarily, at least, forced savings out of current income could be required. Or should active inflation be permitted to eliminate the suppressed inflation and reduce consumption pressure? Or should the government try to stabilize prices and wages and, over a period of years, gradually work off the inflationary pressures?

The decisions reached on monetary and price-wage policy would have important effects on carrying out any program for resource uses. Inflationary pressure for a period of years would imply continued heavy reliance on direct controls over both investment and consumption. Active inflation would lead to a wage-price spiral, to strikes, and to loss of output. A strict monetary reform to wipe out the excess liquidity of the banks and the public would avoid these problems, but would require positive action to achieve the appropriate expansion of credit to finance reconstruction and development.

The problem of dealing with the financial situation would have to be considered in the light of balance-of-payments implications. A postwar exchange rate must be determined. If Norway were experiencing active inflation, would it be possible to choose a rate which would not interfere with export prospects? With price and wage stability would it be easier to ensure the competitive position of Norwegian exporters? Even if foreign capital could be obtained to help in reconstruction and development, exports of goods and services must still be relied on to pay for most of the needed imports.

Norway's fundamental choice between early restoration of consumption standards and rapid reconstruction and renewed economic development had to be made with consideration given to two kinds of limiting factors — domestic and external. On the domestic side, powerful forces were certain to pull resources into production for consumption unless strong preventative techniques could be developed. Strong checks on consumption were bound to be difficult to establish and maintain within a peacetime democratic framework. On the external side, the foreign exchange needed for recovery and development would be tremendous at the same time that foreign-exchange earnings were bound to be far below normal.

Although Norway's problems at the end of the war were similar to those of many other European countries, two factors gave them a somewhat special character. The first was the combination of extreme dependence on foreign trade with the high degree of destruction of foreign-exchange earning power. Her problems in this area were similar to those of the United Kingdom in a somewhat heightened form. The second was the fact that the war had interrupted a process of rapid economic development, and Norway needed to resume development if the difficult natural conditions of the country were ever to be surmounted and rising living standards secured for the increasing population. The problems were not unique, but they were unusually intense.

2

Basic Decisions: 1945

Within a few months after the liberation in May 1945, the broad lines of Norwegian economic policy for the postwar recovery period had been determined. Some important steps were taken before the liberation, others just after the liberation. By the end of 1945, the basic decisions on financial and resource policy had been made; plans for carrying out the decisions were to be more fully developed in 1946.

During the occupation, the Norwegian government in exile had carried on in London. The government in power in 1939 was a Labor government which had been formed in 1935 with the support of the Farmers' Party. The Labor Party, although it had not received an absolute majority, had received the largest vote of any single party in each election from 1927 on. The government in exile had invited representatives of other political parties to join the government in order to ensure that important decisions made during the occupation had the widest possible political support.

The government in exile, preparing for the time of liberation, hoped to avoid chaotic conditions by having emergency legislation and decisions ready to carry out when the government could return to Norway. It was understood that all decisions and actions would be temporary and preliminary. The government planned to resign in favor of a coalition government, so that all parties would share in the immediate postliberation decisions. There would be an election as soon as feasible, to elect a new Storting (Parliament) and to determine the political character of the new government.

One of the most important decisions made before the liberation was that the full system of direct controls built up by the Germans during the occupation would have to be maintained in the first months after the liberation. Otherwise the monetary expansion and acute scarcities of essential goods would lead to violent price increases and to rationing by the purse rather than according to need.

After a new Storting was elected, it would reconsider the legislation on controls. In the meantime, the controls would be used to try to avoid inflation and maintain price and wage stability. A program of price and wage stabilization was worked out after discussions with representatives of the Norwegian Employers' Association, the largest association of employers, and of the National Federation of Trade Unions, which embraced most of the organized industrial workers.[1] These organizations were agreed that the wage-price structure of 1944 could not be maintained, and that some immediate adjustments in wage rates for industrial workers would be necessary since earnings had risen much less than the cost of living during the occupation. At the same time, the Associations did not wish to start a wage-price spiral. The idea was to make certain immediate adjustments in wage rates on the assumption that the cost of living would be kept stable. In September 1944, representatives of the National Federation of Trade Unions and of the Norwegian Employers' Association recommended that industrial wage increases be granted immediately after the liberation to compensate for the rise in the cost of living.

Another decision of considerable importance made before the liberation was the decision to maintain the prewar rate of exchange between the krone and sterling. This would be a temporary arrangement, pending consideration by the coalition government. The decision to maintain the prewar rate in spite of the huge monetary expansion was based on the assumption that price and wage stability would be achieved, at least for some time. A resolution was passed that the government should try to maintain the price level at the time of liberation, which meant that it would be necessary to sell imported goods at domestically controlled prices irrespective of the prices actually paid.

The coalition government which took over after the liberation in

[1] The members of the Norwegian Employers' Association actually employed only about 170,000 workers. Another 150,000 were employed by members of two or three independent employers' associations. The National Federation of Trade Unions before the war had about 350,000 members. After the war the membership increased sharply, and today there are about 550,000 members. There are about 1 million hired workers out of a total labor force of about 1.5 million.

May 1945 decided that elections could be held in October 1945, and
that in the meantime the government would be guided by a statement
of goals and principles for the recovery program agreed on by the
major political parties. This joint statement undoubtedly was strongly
influenced by Labor Party views, but it was an agreed program, aimed
especially at permitting the coalition government to proceed with
immediate reconstruction and recovery jobs.[2] The fact that the Labor
Party was the largest single party and that it also had the support of
both the Farmers' Party and the National Federation of Trade
Unions gave it a strong voice in the coalition government.

The agreed upon program included important statements of principles as well as specific recommendations. Emphasis was placed on full
employment, increased output, and a decent minimum standard of
living for all. The position of agriculture was considered a special
problem in connection with raising the standard of living and reducing inequalities. The program called for industry branch councils
to try to increase productivity, for more effective employment exchange offices and facilities for retraining, for avoidance of strikes
and labor conflict, and for facilities for mediation and arbitration.

A monetary policy which would bring stability and confidence and
a tax policy which would properly distribute burdens between
different income groups were advocated. It was suggested that special
tax reductions be given to families with children, and a number of
other specific tax problems were discussed. A series of objectives was
spelled out for each sector of the economy, with emphasis placed on
rapidly restoring prewar capacity in shipping, whaling, and fishing,
on rapid development of electric power and industrial facilities, and
on housing in the reconstruction period.

The statement of objectives and principles is significant because
it indicates that all parties were convinced that recovery, and even
development, must be given priority over rapid increases in consumption. If output were expanded as quickly as possible, a higher standard
of living for all might then be attained. The statement also suggests
support of the attempt to keep prices and wages stable for some time

---

[2] *Fellesprogrammet 1945. De politisk partienes samarbeids program for gjen-
reisiningen*, 1945. See also *Om gjennomföringen av fellesprogrammet, Stortingsmelding nummer 45, 1947*, for a comparison of the program with the results.

at least, and considerable support for measures aimed at a more equitable distribution of income.

One important specific recommendation was that direct controls over foreign-exchange transactions, raw materials and consumer goods allocations, and prices must be maintained until the new Parliament could consider the general problem. Another specific recommendation was that every effort should be made to obtain the cooperation and support of all private interests for carrying out the recovery program. In particular, the statement recommended the establishment of an over-all coordinating economic policy board to advise and consult with the government on broad policy problems. The board should be comprised of representatives from the private associations of workers, employers, farmers, bankers, shipowners, exporters, and other important groups.

In the election of October 1945, the Labor Party won an absolute majority. For at least four years Norway would have a government pledged to over-all economic planning and to using the controls necessary to carry out the plans.[3] The agreed upon program was undoubtedly important prior to the election, but in that period the Labor Party's own program also had considerable influence since the Party was the largest in the country and was the leader in the coalition government.

The Labor Party had formulated its own program, which was adopted shortly after the liberation by the independent National Federation of Trade Unions.[4] The official program statement was almost the same as that agreed on by the major political parties. The most significant point of difference in the Labor Party's program was its emphasis on an active and a purposeful policy of government to achieve the stated goals. Labor Party officials and economists made it clear that they believed in over-all economic planning for full employment, recovery, and development.

The statements of Labor Party leaders indicated that the Party was moderately to the left but was not revolutionary. Although many of the leaders had been radical socialists in the early days of the

[3] Four years later, the Labor Party won a much greater majority, but in 1953 it was slightly smaller, owing to a change in the electoral law.

[4] See the text of the program in *Vedlegg til Fri Fagbeveglse*, June 1945.

Party, there had been little or no apparent radical tinge among the leaders in the thirties and forties. The Labor Government in the thirties had been concerned primarily with unemployment; it had carried on a moderate policy and had not advocated nationalization or other socialist measures.[5] Possibly this was due in part to the fact that the most obvious targets for nationalization had been owned and operated by the government long before the Labor Party came to power. The railroads and all major public utilities had been government owned for almost a century, partly because difficult natural conditions had tended to discourage private capital. Power development had been carried out by the central government or the municipalities long before the war.[6] The Labor Party indicated that it did not consider socialism to be equivalent to government ownership, but that the owners of private enterprises must realize that they were entrusted with the management of capital and that such management had a profound effect on society. The emphasis was on the control and direction of private enterprise.

Labor Party economists and the officials responsible for economic policy emphasized four major objectives: (1) to maintain reasonably full employment, (2) to restore and develop productive capacity, (3) to keep prices and wages stable, and (4) to redistribute income in favor of certain low-paid workers.

Maintenance of full employment was considered an overriding necessity on political, social, and economic grounds. However, since the development and recovery program would place a strain on available resources of both manpower and goods, the problem was expected to be overfull employment or a scarcity of labor rather than unemployment. But to obtain maximum output and social welfare, the labor force should be fully utilized. Seasonal unemployment in building and construction in the winter months, especially in the northern part of the country, should be reduced. Priority should be given to construction and investment projects in areas where destroyed productive facilities left pockets of unemployment.

While the emphasis on restoring and developing productive capacity

[5] See Walter Galenson, *Labor in Norway* (Cambridge: Harvard University Press, 1949), for a much fuller discussion of the background.

[6] There were also long-established government monopolies for the import of wheat and spirits.

was partly the result of the heavy war damage, government officials also had in mind that Norway had been rapidly developing her resources and her industrial capacity before the war, and that development must continue in order to make possible a higher standard of living. A high level of investment would be necessary.

The plan to stabilize prices and wages at levels as close as possible to existing levels was designed to achieve a number of objectives. Cost-of-living stability would help avoid a wage-price spiral, keep strikes at a minimum, and restore confidence in the currency. More important, if prices and wages were kept stable while there was an inflationary boom in the rest of the world, it was believed that Norway would be in a position to avoid deflation and unemployment when world prices fell. A repetition of the thirties would be avoided.

The fourth objective was aimed at helping certain workers — women, unskilled workers, textile workers, farmers, foresters, and fishermen — whose incomes had been relatively low in the prewar period.[7] Wages in some of these sectors had risen sharply during the occupation, and the program would allow the workers to consolidate their improved position. It also would seek to raise the incomes of others.

Broader social goals, such as the achievement of a fair over-all distribution of income after taxes and provision for adequate housing, an improved diet, and extended health and social insurance, were also outlined. These goals affected policy decisions in a number of ways. Emphasis on a fair distribution of real income argued against rationing by the purse or the allocation of scarce supplies to consumers on the basis of ability to pay. It led to large benefits for children and to similar transfer payments. Most important, it led to price, subsidy, and indirect tax policies which resulted in a redistribution of real income greater than that of disposable money incomes.

As mentioned above, the chief difference between the Labor Party and the other political parties was probably in the emphasis placed on the need for comprehensive economic planning. The official economists were impressed with the usefulness of making aggregative estimates and of formulating over-all programs, and also with the

---

[7] Most of the farmers and fishermen were small, independent, self-employed workers, but most of the forestry workers were hired laborers. Considerable overlapping and seasonal shifts occurred among the three types of employment.

possibilities of influencing the use of resources by direct controls and other measures.

The attitude of the Party at that time toward economic planning has been described as follows:

> It would be essential that scarce resources be employed for such investments as would contribute most quickly to increased production. The government felt that it could not rely upon the market mechanism to attain this end, partly because the monetary system was dislocated, but also because the experience of the inter-war period had shown the imperfections of the principles of *laissez faire* in attaining full employment and the full utilization of available resources. Therefore, it should be the responsibility of the elected constitutional bodies, the Storting and the Cabinet, to take an active part in achieving full employment and the full utilization of resources through a planned economy, having powers to stimulate, control, and direct a mixed economy of private and public enterprise.[8]

Implicit in the Labor Party's emphasis on over-all economic planning was the idea that direct controls could play a useful part in the recovery program. Although all parties had agreed on the necessity of keeping the full gamut of direct controls in the immediate postliberation period in order to ensure the equitable distribution of scarce consumer goods and the allocation of resources to the most urgent reconstruction and recovery tasks, the Labor Party's program suggested that the Labor government would be in favor of maintaining controls for a considerable period of time.

The financial decisions, which in the end determined the duration of strict controls, were taken on independent grounds. The fact that the Labor Party was not opposed to direct controls, however, meant that these financial decisions were not made with the idea that the elimination of direct controls was a priority objective. Labor Party economists and leaders frankly considered that direct controls would be useful emergency measures to help regulate the use of resources for investment and consumption. Such controls were relied on to play a major role. It seems clear in retrospect that the financial decisions taken in fact placed an excessive burden on the controls.[9]

[8] Address by Minister of Commerce Erik Brofoss at the University of Oslo Summer School, July 1952 (mimeographed copy).
[9] There is a fuller discussion of this problem in Chapter 3.

In the period of the coalition government, the price- and wage-stabilization program was already being implemented. The government ratified the agreement reached in 1944 between the Norwegian Employers' Association and the National Federation of Trade Unions. Industrial wage rates were sharply increased, but the increases did not quite bring wages up to their prewar relation to the cost of living.[10] The price-control authorities announced that prices could not be raised to cover the higher wage rates except with their special approval.

In August 1945 the Federation of Trade Unions gave notice of cancellation of the existing industry wage contracts, which customarily ran for two years. Although the contracts officially covered only the 170,000 workers employed by members of the Norwegian Employers' Association, with which the principal wage negotiations were carried out, the agreements reached by the big associations tended to set the pattern for other industry contracts. Following cancellation of the industry wage contracts, the Trade Union Federation and the Employers' Association failed to agree on new contracts. Therefore, in accordance with an agreed postliberation arrangement, the case was referred to a special Wage Board established for the purpose, consisting of representatives of labor, employers, and the government.

At the time that the Federation of Trade Unions gave notice on the industry wage contracts, the farmers' organizations applied for increases in farm prices. Subsidies on domestic farm products, which had been instituted during the occupation, were continued and increased after the liberation. If farmers were to receive higher prices and at the same time the cost of living was to be kept stable, either the prices of other commodities would have to be lowered or subsidies to the farmers would have to be increased further.

Because of the difficulties arising from the wage demands and the demands for higher agricultural prices, the government reviewed its stabilization policy in August 1945. In this review, it consulted the Economic Coordination Board, the special economic policy board which had been established on the recommendation of the coalition government. This Board consisted of nineteen members — most of whom were elected representatives of the national associations of

---

[10] The increases granted were 30 öre an hour for men and 20 öre for women over the April 8, 1940, rates.

farmers, fishermen, trade unions, employers, workers, shipowners, cooperatives, and manufacturers — and also of representatives of three government agencies, a government chairman, and a government vice-chairman. The Board undoubtedly served principally as a sounding board for the government, but the idea was to be sure that the government's policy was understood, and agreed to, by the national associations, in order to obtain their cooperation.

The Economic Coordination Board reported early in September that it recommended continuation of the stabilization policy.[11] The principal purpose seemed to be to assure cost-of-living stability in order to keep at a minimum any wage increases that might be recommended by the special Wage Board. The Coordination Board recommended that the government reaffirm its stabilization policy, increase subsidies, if necessary up to the amount of the proceeds of the general sales tax, keep rents, interest, and dividends controlled at low rates, and levy a high tax on wartime increases in capital. Many of these recommendations were designed to assure the wage earners that incomes of all the other groups would be controlled.

A few days later, the Wage Board recommended another flat increase for industrial workers, which was intended to result in wages reaching the same level (in relation to the prewar level) which had already been reached by the cost-of-living index. The Board also accepted the idea of a cost-of-living escalator clause in future wage contracts. The demands of the farmers were met by increases in the prices of milk, meat, and bacon, which would be offset by increases in subsidies and thus not lead to increases in consumer prices.

In these few months the pattern to be followed for the next several years was established. Wage negotiations would center around changes in the cost-of-living index and farmers, foresters, and fishermen would negotiate with the government for price increases designed to maintain their relative earning position. Other incomes would be controlled. Subsidies would be increased. At each critical period the Economic Coordination Board would be consulted.

The coalition government's price-wage stabilization policy was clear: it necessitated continued price controls and increasing subsidies

---

[11] See *Om saerlige tiltak til trygging av landets ökonomi, Stortingsmelding nummer 43, August 18, 1947.*

to keep the cost of living stable. The immediate postwar industrial wage adjustments necessarily added to inflationary pressures even though they were limited to those amounts believed necessary to raise wages above the prewar level by the same percentage as the cost-of-living index.

Another recommendation of the Economic Coordination Board in September 1945 was that as soon as possible the coalition government should decide on the exchange rate. It had been understood that the government would reconsider the rate of 20 kroner per pound sterling, which had been maintained by the government in London before the liberation. A commission of experts appointed to study the question recommended 24 kroner per pound, a substantial devaluation compared to the prewar rate. The commission argued that this rate would facilitate exports and that high kroner import prices would help mop up excess purchasing power.

However, the Economic Coordination Board, when consulted by the government, recommended retention of the 20-kroner rate. This rate was decided upon in October 1945 principally to keep down the kroner import price level. Since import prices had a great effect on the cost-of-living index, lower import prices would make it easier to maintain cost-of-living stability. The government also believed that exporters could compete successfully at the 20-kroner rate if domestic costs did not rise sharply, and that the 24-kroner rate would result in excessive export profits and add to the pressure of domestic demand. In view of the difficulties in increasing the supply of the major export goods and services and in view of the apparently low elasticity of demand, the government believed that a lower currency value would increase domestic problems without adding significantly to export volume.

Another probable factor in the government's decision was the idea that devaluation of the krone would be interpreted as a sign of weakness and, perhaps, as an indication that the government did not believe it could stabilize prices and wages. The 20-kroner rate appeared more reasonable on the assumption that the price and wage stabilization program was to be successful. Both plans for cost-of-living stability and the 20-kroner rate reflected an underlying conviction that world prices would rise sharply for a while and then fall. But with the almost uninterrupted rise in world prices which actually occurred, even the 20-kroner rate was to lead to constant pressure on the domestic price level, and export profits were extremely high.

A full report on a plan for monetary reform, which had been prepared during the occupation by a group of officials and economists under the general direction of the Norges Bank, was presented to the government in July 1945. This plan assumed that more than half of the notes in circulation and about 40 per cent of the demand deposits in private banks would be blocked for some time.[12] It implied that total notes and demand deposits in the hands of the public were almost twice the amount that would be consistent in the short run with price and wage stabilization policy, which was an accepted assumption in the monetary reform program.

On September 5, 1945, a law to implement a revised version of this plan was passed by the Storting.[13] One important change in the situation had occurred since July when the plan had been presented to the government. In anticipation of the calling in of notes in circulation, the public had reduced its holdings of notes from 3 billion kroner to 1.4 billion by September 7, 1945, and increased its deposits accordingly.

The law provided for calling in all notes in circulation, issuing new notes immediately in amounts needed for current transactions, and blocking the remainder in the form of deposit accounts at the Norges Bank. It also provided that deposit accounts in private banks would be blocked temporarily, except for minimum working balances. The plan was to release, after a while, blocked deposits of a limited size, but to freeze the remaining deposits more permanently in special accounts at the Norges Bank. The blocked deposits might be released gradually as the financial situation became less critical or used to meet payments due on the planned postwar capital levy. Savings deposits in private banks would be subject to control but would not be blocked.

[12] Notes in circulation would be cut from about 3 billion to about 1.1 billion and demand deposits from 2.3 billion to about 500 million temporarily, but only about 800 or 900 million would probably be blocked over a considerable period. The rest would be released gradually and controlled in the same way that savings deposits were controlled.

[13] See *Om sanering av pengevesened, Stortingsmelding nummer 8, 1945–46,* for the law and the Norges Bank report.

This law was less strict than the Norges Bank plan. The law as passed resulted in the blocking of 351 million kroner on deposit at the Norges Bank as the counterpart of large note holdings. The note circulation was temporarily cut to less than 1 billion kroner. About 30 per cent of all demand deposits of more than 800 kroner was blocked on deposit at the Norges Bank, and another 30 per cent was to be used only with the approval of the Bank, which was also the case for a large percentage of savings deposits of more than 800 kroner. In accordance with these regulations, about 800 million kroner as the counterpart of deposits was blocked at the Norges Bank for a time. In November 1945, however, blocked deposits of 200 kroner or less were freed, and all temporary controls over savings deposits were eliminated. Also, special permission was granted to firms and individuals to use blocked deposits in certain cases. By the

Table 3. Money supply and private bank reserves, prewar and end of 1945
(billions of kroner unless otherwise indicated)

	Prewar[a]	End of 1945	Indices, end of 1945 (prewar = 100)
Money supply			
Notes in circulation outside private banks	0.4	1.4	350
Demand deposits in private banks	0.2	2.9	1450
Notes plus demand deposits	0.6	4.3	717
Savings deposits in private banks	2.8	4.7	168
Total deposits	3.0	7.6	253
Notes plus total deposits	3.4	9.0	265
Private bank reserves			
Joint stock banks			
Liquid reserves	0.054	3.2	5926
Ratio of reserves to demand deposits	31%	160%	516
Ratio of reserves to total deposits	5%	91%	1820
Savings banks			
Liquid reserves	0.031	1.8	5807
Ratio of reserves to demand deposits	111%	200%	181
Ratio of reserves to total deposits	1.6%	44%	2750

Source: Private bank data from *Maanedstatistikk over de Norske Aksje og Spare-banker*, and *Norges Privat Akajebanker og Sparebanker*. Notes in circulation from Norges Bank statements.

[a] End of 1938 data for money supply, end of 1939 data for private bank reserves and reserve ratios. Reserves and deposits were approximately unchanged from the end of 1938 to the end of 1939 except for an increase of 100 million kroner ni savings deposits.

end of 1945, total blocked deposits at the Norges Bank had fallen
from the temporary maximum of about 1,150 million kroner to about
500 million kroner.[14]

Except for the temporary blocking of large deposits and the small
amount of deposits more permanently blocked, the principal result
of the monetary reform seems to have been a shift from notes to savings deposits, partly in anticipation of the reform. The reform may
also have had some psychological effect. There is no clear explanation
of why the amounts blocked were smaller than originally contemplated in the Norges Bank plan, why a large part of the amount
blocked was rather quickly released, and why controls on savings
deposits were abolished.

The monetary reform did not mop up any substantial amount of
excess liquidity. At the end of 1945, notes and total deposits in the
hands of the public were almost three times the 1938 level (Table
3), the same as at the time of liberation. Demand deposits had risen
sharply during the occupation, apparently because banks had been
unwilling to accept large interest-earning savings deposits while their

Table 4. Loans of private banks, state banks, and credit institutions,
1939 and 1945 (millions of kroner)

	End of 1939	End of 1945
Private bank loans		
Mortgage	786	722
Short term	1846	942
Total	2632	1664
Other private lending institutions		
Municipal credit associations	181	213
Other	144	141
Total	325	354
State banks		
Municipalities bank	340	228
Other	771	548
Total	1111	776

Source: See Table 3 for source of data on private bank loans in 1939; data for
other private lending institutions and state banks from the *Statistisk Aarbok.* Data
for 1945, *Statistiske Meldinger* issues of 1954 and 1955.

[14] See *Stortingsmelding nummer 8, 1945–46.*

loans were drastically curtailed. Compared with prewar reserves, private bank reserves had risen to astronomic heights, and private bank loans were much lower than before the war[15] (Tables 3 and 4). The possibilities for further expansion of bank credit were enormous.

When the Labor government took office in November 1945, the price and wage stabilization policy had become an accepted fact, the monetary reform had not reduced the liquidity of the banks and the public to any substantial degree, and import prices were rising. The decision to maintain cost-of-living stability, combined with the decision to leave the private banks and the public in possession of huge liquid assets, made it almost inevitable that direct controls would be relied on heavily, and that inflationary pressures would persist for several years.

[15] There are no published figures on the distribution of bank reserves, but five or six of the largest banks probably had accumulated most of the increase.

3

Recovery Plans: Early 1946

When the new government began presenting its plans to the Storting early in 1946, its recovery program was already quite firmly established. The decisions taken in 1945 clearly indicated that the government felt inflationary pressures would persist for some time, and the program aimed at the gradual elimination of these pressures. As far as resource uses were concerned, emphasis would be placed on recovery and development rather than on rapid increases in consumption. The monetary, fiscal, and real resource programs fitted into an over-all plan for gradual return to prewar living standards and gradual elimination of detailed direct controls.

Some observers believe that Norway deliberately chose to have continued suppressed inflationary pressures in order to stimulate investment and maintain full employment.[1] There is little or no evidence, however, of positive interest in suppressed inflationary pressures. There was overwhelming enthusiasm for keeping prices and wages stable; and there was little enthusiasm on the part of the government for mopping up the excess liquidity. The result was suppressed inflationary pressures.

It may be argued, however, that the government believed that the inflationary pressures would not persist for long if the expected world depression occurred, and that, in this event, excess liquidity might help to delay and offset deflationary tendencies resulting from export difficulties. The fear of a postwar recession was widespread. Early in

[1] It has been suggested by one or two Norwegian economists in recent years that inflationary pressure was deliberately chosen as a means of creating enough jobs to take care of the large numbers of unemployed and the release of partially unemployed labor from agriculture, which, combined with a rapid growth of the labor force in the thirties, led to substantial unemployment even in the thirties. I believe this is an ex post rationalization. See also Mark Leiserson, "Wages in a Controlled Economy," doctoral thesis (Harvard University, 1955).

1946 government officials referred repeatedly to this possibility when discussing the existing inflationary pressures.[2]

Government economists were also inclined to argue that the amount of liquid assets in the country should not be taken as a positive indication that inflationary pressures would persist. The tremendous excess demand for goods was not only a reflection of the amount of liquid assets, but a reflection of demands that had been pent up during the war period and of real needs. When pent-up demands had been met and output increased, the large liquid assets might cease to affect spending habits. It was believed that the flow of current incomes and the taxes paid out of current incomes would be more important than the amount of liquid assets in determining the extent of the excess demand for goods and services.[3]

Probably the principal reason for the relatively slight interest in mopping up the excess liquidity was the fact that direct controls were expected to handle the situation for some time. Quantitative controls on both investment and consumption would determine the size of effective demand for goods and services, and price controls of all sorts would keep prices stable. Although a tight money policy and the wiping out of liquid assets might cut down demands, direct controls were believed to be necessary to ensure that the most important and essential demands were met first. Most government economists apparently were not seriously concerned about the possibility that the excess liquidity would interfere with the effectiveness of controls. Increases in output and the gradual meeting of pent-up demands for both consumer and producer goods were expected to result in a steady adjustment to the wartime monetary expansion. If inflationary pressures should continue, direct controls could simply be kept longer than they otherwise would have been. While the aim was to eliminate direct controls eventually, no urgent need was felt to eliminate them quickly.

Any drastic reduction of liquid assets in the hands of the public and

[2] See Finansminister Erik Brofoss, *Norges ökonomiske og finansielle stilling* (Arbeidernes Opplysningsforbund, 1946). In discussing what should be done with the capital levy, most of which would be paid in 1947, Minister Brofoss insisted that all would depend on the financial situation at that time.

[3] See Brofoss, *Norges ökonomiske og finansielle stilling;* Bjerve and Aukrust, *Hva krigen kostet Norge;* and also the discussion of this problem in Leiserson, "Wages in a Controlled Economy."

the banks would probably have interfered with the government's plans for a low interest rate. Too much ease was clearly preferred to too much tightness. In January 1946, the government reduced the discount rate, and also the rate on government obligations, from the wartime 3½ per cent to 2½ per cent. The principal argument advanced for the reduction was that the cost of investment should be kept down in such essential sectors as housing, plant construction, and power development — precisely the sectors in which the interest rate is an important element of cost and in which investment was most needed. The government did not believe that it would be desirable to use the interest rate to limit investment demand. Low-cost housing and power and construction would help to achieve the goal of price and wage stabilization. Also, a low interest rate had great political appeal at a time when rents, wages, and dividends were being strictly controlled.

To carry out a heavy investment program, business would need liquid assets and/or bank loans. If strict measures were taken in the early days of the government to freeze most of the liquid assets of the banks or of business firms, a rapid expansion of bank reserves and bank credit would be necessary later to finance the investment. Therefore, the better policy might be to allow the firms and the banks freedom in the use of their existing assets. Most of the liquid assets were believed to be in the hands of banks and business firms.

Another argument for monetary ease, in the minds of some officials, was that the Norges Bank might be unwilling or unable in the future to provide credit expansion on a sufficiently flexible basis. The Bank might not be as convinced as was the Labor Party of the need for full employment, and there was little or no tradition of an active and flexible central bank policy. Failure to mop up the existing excess liquidity of the banks would entail the danger of inflationary bank-credit expansion and it would be difficult to take strong measures to control the expansion. On the other hand, if the excess liquidity of the banks were wiped out, it might be difficult to agree on the rate at which credit should be expanded in the future.

Banks were required to hold reserves of cash, deposits with other banks, and government securities, but the requirements were based on considerations of "sound" business practice for the individual bank. Reserve requirements had not traditionally played any role in monetary policy. Legal reserves had generally been many times legal requirements; and liquid reserves, cash, and deposits at the Norges Bank also had generally been high.[4] Borrowing from the central bank was not common or generally accepted. The Norges Bank rate was effective in controlling private bank rates only because the banks had made a practice for many years of adjusting their rates to changes in the Norges Bank rate. The adoption of new reserve requirements making the banks really dependent on central bank policy would have been resented by the banking community. There was no tradition of, or facilities for, substantial open-market operations. Under these conditions, the possibilities did not seem too bright of gradually easing credit policy after tight reins over the banking situation had been established.

Certain government officials, however, were not convinced that inflationary pressures would not interfere with the recovery program. They recommended both drastic measures to freeze part of current incomes and the freezing of a substantial part of private bank reserves. Many government economists favored a much stiffer capital levy than was actually imposed. Although the government did not follow these recommendations, the fact that they were made suggests that inflationary pressure was by no means an agreed upon objective.

The considerations which led to the very mild monetary reform in 1945, and, in view of the price- and wage-stabilization program, to the persistence of substantial excess liquidity, seem clear. Whether the decisions made at this time were reasonable is another question. If inflationary pressures continued to be very strong it would place an undue burden on the control system and require maintenance of controls over too long a period. Also, the expectations on the future course of world prices and employment might well be mistaken. In retrospect it seems clear that a stricter monetary reform would

---

[4] The requirements applied to holdings of cash, of deposits with other banks, of government, municipal, and government guaranteed securities, and of certain other securities. Joint stock banks were required to hold reserves up to 20 per cent of demand deposit liabilities and 5 per cent of total liabilities. Savings banks were required to hold reserves up to 10 per cent of deposit liabilities. In the thirties, joint stock bank legal reserves had been 75 per cent of deposit liabilities or even higher, and at the time of liberation they were more than 150 per cent of deposit liabilities. In the thirties, savings banks held legal reserves of about 40–50 per cent of deposit liabilities, and at the time of liberation they were about 90 per cent.

substantially have reduced the difficulty of carrying out the stabilization program and of maintaining an effective control system.

By early 1946, official government statements consistently presented the view that inflationary pressures would be eliminated
gradually over a period of two or three years. Emphasis was placed on
the gradual decrease in liquidity which was bound to occur as the
over-all development plans were carried out. The intention was to
finance a tremendous investment program with the help of huge
import surpluses and substantial net government savings, both of
which would have important deflationary effects.[5] In particular, they
would result in a net reduction of reserves of private banks estimated
at about 4 or 5 billion kroner, or an amount equal to total private
bank reserves at the end of 1945. The reduction would be due to the
fact that import surpluses would have to be financed largely by the
use of government reserves or government borrowings from abroad.[6]
In either case, net sales of foreign exchange would lead to an equal
net reduction of private bank reserves. Government net savings in
excess of government investment expenditures would also lead to a
net reduction in private bank reserves.[7]

The government indicated its intention of using over-all national
budgeting to plan for resource uses in accordance with resource
availabilities. The aim was to prevent the big investment program
from adding to inflationary pressures. There would be direct controls
over investment, and strict controls over imports, construction, and
public and private consumption; and investment would be kept
within the limits of foreign and domestic financing capabilities.

[5] For a discussion by the finance department in February 1946 of the gradual
reduction of inflationary pressure through taxes and import surpluses, see *Om
utferdigelse av lov om engangskatt paa formuestigning, Odelstingsproposisjon
nummer 25, 1945–46*. See also Brofoss, *Norges ökonomiske og finansielle
stilling*.

[6] Over 2 billion kroner of sterling claims by shipowners had been taken
over by the government, but the gradual repayment of the equivalent local
currency debt to the shipowners would prevent any net reduction of private
bank reserves for the period as a whole.

[7] Considerable time and effort was wasted on discussions of how important or
meaningful it was actually to write off the bookkeeping occupation account debt.
Clearly, the fact that the funds were drained from the banks and the public
was the essential thing and there was no need of wiping out the debt. But
the Norges Bank and conservative circles wished to see the funds cancelled
out in this way, perhaps partly to ensure that they would not be spent later.

Assuming investment was kept within these limits, there would be no problem of cumulative net additions to the inflationary gap, and the gradual elimination of existing inflationary pressures would not be too difficult.

Implicit in the government's plans was the idea that expansion of private bank credit would in fact be restricted by the direct controls over consumption and investment, and that the credit expansion would presumably be limited to the amount of private and public savings. Net inflationary bank credit financing would be prevented.

As the recovery program developed, more and more emphasis was placed on the need for large public savings out of current income. The plans required public savings in excess of net public investment, or an over-all revenue surplus in order to raise the domestic savings rate above the prewar level and to help finance the huge planned private investment program. The popular idea that it would be wise to reduce the occupation debt to the Norges Bank helped the government to maintain a high level of public savings because it reduced the pressure for lower taxes or higher government expenditures.

In early 1946, the principal emphasis in fiscal matters was on a decrease in public expenditures in order to reduce public consumption of goods and services. For 1945–46, there would be a substantial deficit, which was to be met by further borrowing. Current tax rates were high and rising output and incomes would increase ordinary tax receipts from income and property taxes and from the 10 per cent sales tax. With rising tax receipts, a budget surplus should be possible after special postwar expenditures, including defense expenditures, were cut.

In the immediate postliberation period, the plans for a capital levy were given most attention. The committee under the general direction of the Norges Bank had proposed, as part of the monetary reform program, a levy on the wartime increase in capital. The Economic Coordination Board also had recommended a capital levy. A complete registration of liquid assets as of the date of the monetary reform was carried out, partly to help assess this levy.

According to the early plans of the Norges Bank, the capital levy was to be assessed as soon as possible, and the collection of the levy was expected to help reduce the liquidity of the banks and the public. Profiteers and Quislings should be heavily taxed, and the capital levy was considered a way of ensuring that part of the burden of postwar expenditures would be borne by those who had profited from the occupation. A third reason for the Norges Bank interest in the special capital levy was that the proceeds of the tax could be used to reduce the debt of the occupation authorities to the Norges Bank.

Actually there was delay in the passage of the capital levy law. In September 1945 the Storting voted that a law be prepared on the basis of the Norges Bank proposals. The Finance Department, however, withdrew the proposition, consulted a number of important national organizations, and appointed a special committee to consider the question. It finally presented a draft law on February 15, 1946, almost precisely along the lines recommended by this special committee, and the law was passed in July 1946. The law was much milder than the original Norges Bank draft. The first 5,000 kroner of capital increase was exempt and individuals were allowed an additional exemption of 1,000 kroner for each dependent. The earlier plan had not included any tax-free allowances. The tax rates also were lower than in the earlier plan except those on very large sums. The rates proposed in February 1946 ranged from 30 per cent to 95 per cent, in accordance with the size of the capital increase in excess of the tax-exempt amount.[8]

The report accompanying the law on the capital levy made it clear that the Finance Department did not believe that the tax would play any important role in reducing liquidity, if only because the work of assessing the tax would be long and actual payments on the tax would not begin for $1\frac{1}{2}$ to 2 years.[9] The tax was justified primarily on the grounds that those who had profited greatly during the occupation should be heavily taxed. The provision that the proceeds should be used to reduce the occupation account was eliminated from the law. It was believed that the financial situation

[8] See *Om engangskatt paa formuestigning, Stortingsproposisjon nummer 18, 1945–46,* and *Odelstingsproposisjon nummer 25, 1945–46* for full details. The actual percentages were 30 per cent on the first 10,000 kroner, 50 per cent on the next 20,000, 70 per cent on the next 40,000, and 95 per cent on anything above 70,000 — all amounts being above the tax-free amount.

[9] The first payments were in the 1947–48 fiscal year.

at the time when the tax was collected must be taken into account in any decision on use of the funds. The funds would be kept temporarily in a special account.

Plans were also made for a special war-damage tax, based on the value of property, to help finance government disbursements to cover war damage. This law was not presented to the Storting until November 1946 and was passed in June 1947. Payments began only in the 1947–48 fiscal year.[10]

Although price-wage, monetary, and fiscal problems required immediate attention after the liberation, the economists in the government were most concerned about an over-all program for resource availabilities and resource uses. The administration presented a report on basic resource problems as its first national budget, which budget was sent to the Storting in February 1946 as an appendix to the ordinary fiscal budget for 1945–46.[11]

The national budget emphasized that the central problem was that of choosing between rapid restoration of prewar consumption standards on the one hand and rapid recovery and development on the other. The budget did not present a definitive answer, but it was clear that the administration believed the proper course was to restrict consumption increases as much as possible and to carry on a heavy investment program.

The purpose of the first national budget was to indicate the order of magnitude of the recovery job and the effect of alternative economic policies on the recovery program. It placed before the public the basic facts of the alternatives to be considered but did not present a unique set of quantitative goals. The government indicated rather clearly, however, which of the alternative lines of policy it believed should be followed. The 1946 national budget was much more than an annual budget; it was a long-term plan.

The budget analyzed the basic alternatives in national accounts terms. It presented estimates of the Central Bureau of Statistics on national accounts data for the prewar and occupation periods, and

[10] The war-damage tax was equal to a ¾ per cent tax on total wealth or a 12½ to 25 per cent addition to the ordinary income tax, depending on which was the larger.

[11] *Nasjonalregnskapet og nasjonalbudsjettet, saerskilt vedlegg nummer 11 til statsbudsjettet, 1945–46.*

revised estimates of the cost of restoring prewar productive capacity. With these basic data and with certain assumptions on the outlook for the future, the budget analyzed alternative programs for resource uses from 1946 to 1950.

The budget, although emphasizing primarily the outlook for the next few years, discussed separately the outlook for 1946.[12] When the Finance Minister presented the budget to the Storting, furthermore, he discussed the year 1946 more fully. He reviewed the economic position of Norway at the beginning of the year, and discussed sector by sector the production outlook for 1946.[13] His address to the Storting covered many subjects later included in the annual budgets which were not treated in the budget appendix itself. It reviewed the financial policy of the government since the liberation and discussed the magnitude of the recovery problem.

The budget estimated resources available from domestic output from 1946 to 1950 on the assumption of full employment year after year and an increase in output of about 5 per cent a year. The increase over the four years 1946–50 was estimated at 20 per cent; and net national product in 1946 was estimated at 6.7 billion kroner, which was believed to be about 13 per cent below the 1939 level.[14]

Resources available from abroad from 1946 to 1950 were not estimated on the basis of available reserves or of possible credits but on the basis of certain alternatives; for example, what could be done if there were no import surplus, or what could be done if the average import surplus from 1946 to 1950 could be kept at the estimated 1-billion kroner level of 1946. A series of estimates was also made assuming an average import surplus of 800 million kroner, but total available resources on the basis of such an import surplus appeared to be too small to carry out the desired objective.

Independent estimates of investment needs based largely on war damage and on estimated amounts needed to restore productive

---

[12] It was rather technical and academic when compared with later national budgets. Twenty-one pages explained the basic concepts of national accounting; seven pages discussed the outlook for 1946 and possible plans for 1946–50 in rough aggregative terms.

[13] For the address by Minister of Finance Erik Brofoss, see *Norges ökonomiske og finansielle stilling.*

[14] Output in 1945 was estimated at about 20 per cent below 1939. The increase of 5 per cent a year was equal to the estimated average annual increase in the period 1935–39.

capacity were used as the starting point of one alternative program. It was calculated that it would cost about 2.6 billion 1939 kroner, or 4 billion kroner at early 1946 prices, to restore productive capital directly and to raise output to the 1939 level. In addition, net investment would be needed to restore war-damaged towns, to start meeting the severe housing shortage, and to restore consumer stocks. Essential investment in housing alone, to cover the estimated shortage of 100,000 family units, would cost 1.5–2 billion kroner. Also, investment must be carried out to expand and develop productive capacity beyond the prewar level. In all, more than 8 billion kroner of net investment at early 1946 prices would be necessary. If the recovery program was to be carried out in the period 1946–50, net investment would have to be 1.7 billion 1946 kroner a year. The budget estimated that this would mean net investment of double the prewar volume.

The budget also estimated independently the resources needed to raise private consumption to the prewar level. Such consumption in 1944 was estimated at 70 per cent, and in 1946 was expected to be at 90 per cent, of the 1939 level. The government considered it imperative that consumption be restored to the prewar level by 1951 at least. Total public use of goods and services, including state and local expenditures for both consumption and investment, was running at the rate of about 1.5 billion kroner, but special defense and postwar expenditures by the state would amount to about 600 million kroner. The administration hoped the public use of goods and services could be sharply reduced.

The budget calculated that even with an import surplus of 1 billion kroner, no resources would remain for private productive investment in 1946 if private consumption increased to the 1939 level and the public use of goods and services continued at 1.5 billion kroner. If private consumption in 1946 increased to only 90 per cent of the 1939 level, on the other hand, sufficient resources would be available, even without an import surplus, for a volume of investment equal to that in 1939. But at that rate of investment, it would take from eight to ten years to carry out the investment program.

If, however, the annual import surplus could be kept at the estimated 1946 level of 1 billion 1946 kroner, and public use of goods and services per year could be reduced to 1 billion 1946 kroner, the investment program could be carried out much more quickly and private consumption could also be raised gradually to the prewar level. On these assumptions, private net investment of about 8.5 billion 1946 kroner could take place in a five-year period, and at the same time private consumption could average 95 per cent of the 1939 level. This was the kind of program that the government believed the Storting should endorse.

If net national product should increase by 20 per cent from the then estimated 1946 level, at 1946 prices, the planned private net investment would be at a rate of 23 per cent of net national product. By 1951 private consumption would equal the 1939 level. Import surpluses of 1 billion kroner a year would be financing more than half of the annual net investment of 1.7 billion kroner.

The estimates involved in this analysis were rough, but they were intended only as illustrative figures. The level of output in 1946 in comparison with the prewar level was underestimated. The population increase after 1939 was not stressed, although it was clear that a volume of total consumption that equaled the prewar volume would not mean per capita consumption equal to the prewar level. Nothing was said about possible changes in the international terms of trade. Nevertheless, the budget set forth clearly the effects of alternative policy decisions on consumption and on the rate of recovery, and also set forth the type of program favored by the government. The basic policy decisions probably would not have been very different if they had been based on much fuller data.

The 1946 budget laid the groundwork for the main policy lines that have been followed in the years since then. To restore and develop productive capacity, a heavy investment program was needed, and private and public consumption of goods and services had to be restricted. The government had to adopt a deliberate policy of seeking to finance large import surpluses,[15] since only with such large surpluses could prewar productive facilities be restored, essential nonproductive investment be undertaken, and some investment be made with a view to developing resources and increasing output above the prewar level in the period from 1946 to 1950.

The character of the investment program to be followed was also

[15] Foreign exchange reserves could finance only about 2 billion kroner in import surpluses, so the government had to seek foreign capital. Gold and foreign exchange reserves amounted to 2.5 billion kroner.

clearly established in the first months after the liberation. Priority had to be given to the development of sectors that would earn foreign exchange. The two principal possibilities were to speed up hydroelectric power development and industries based on the use of cheap power and to restore and expand the merchant fleet. The most far-reaching feature of the program was the plan to increase electric power production greatly and to expand the electrochemical and electrometallurgical industries as fast as the power could be developed. The process of building the necessary dams and of tunneling through the mountains would be slow.[16] Restoration and expansion of the merchant fleet could proceed more quickly.

The government foresaw not only a general need for developing exports, but a special need for dollar foreign-exchange earnings. The slight prewar dollar surplus was a thing of the past. Norway would have to depend on the United States to replace Germany, and to some extent the United Kingdom, as a supplier of machinery, iron and steel, and ships. Grain, sugar, petroleum, and cotton would continue to come from the dollar area. Thus the government believed restoration and expansion of the merchant fleet was not only the most obvious way to increase total foreign-exchange earnings quickly, but also the best way to increase dollar earnings. Deliveries of new ships from abroad could begin in two or three years and would then provide immediate foreign-exchange earnings.

There were other reasons why merchant shipping received such a high priority, although restoration of the merchant fleet would take a tremendous proportion of the total resources available for investment. The shipowners had large sterling claims and also could obtain credits abroad to finance new ship purchase contracts.[17] Since the ships would be built abroad, Norwegian labor would not have to be diverted to the investment. The government decided to allow shipowners to place contracts to restore prewar tonnage and eventually to increase it.

Another obvious decision was to restore the whaling fleet as quickly as possible. The floating factories and catcher boats could be

---

[16] Also, orders were placed for turbines and generators, mostly abroad, and it soon turned out that deliveries were slow and could not be speeded up.

[17] The sterling claims of about 2 billion kroner were partly insurance claims on ships lost and partly wartime earnings.

built abroad, and many of the considerations that applied to shipping
also applied to whaling. However, the international limit on the
whale catch made it unreasonable to expand the whaling fleet.

The big iron ore mine had to be restored, but this would take years.
Also, a number of important manufacturing plants had to be
restored. The fishing fleet had to be brought back to prewar strength
and modernized. Investment in roads, saws, and cabins was needed
to help maintain the timber cut so that the pulp and paper industry
could run more nearly at capacity, but fishing and forestry output
could not be increased much above the prewar level. Considerable
investment in agricultural machinery, fertilizers, and silos would
increase output and efficiency and also release labor.

Although the nature of the investment program for recovery and
development was clearly established, the 1946 budget did not include
any over-all estimates of the precise amount of investment that would
be needed sector by sector either in 1946 or in the entire period
1946–50.[18] However, estimates by sectors were made of the cost of
investment needed to restore directly prewar productive capacity;
such investment accounted for almost half of the 8.5 billion 1946
kroner needed for total investment. In terms of 1939 kroner this
investment amounted to 2.6 billion kroner and was distributed as
follows: 900 million for replacement of the merchant fleet, 125
million for the fishing fleet, and 70 million for the whaling fleet;
over 700 million for restoring commercial and industrial stocks; 125
million for animal stocks; about 500 million for industrial buildings
and machinery; and 200 million for inland transport equipment.

The 1946 budget stressed the difficulties of carrying out the
full recovery program. It would be hard to restrict both private and
public consumption. Foreign credits might not be forthcoming.
Technical difficulties might retard needed investment in certain fields,
such as housing and shipping. Some irrational, nonpriority investment
was bound to occur.

To carry out most of the recovery program, reliance would be
placed on private enterprise; in fact, the program outlined was for
about 8 billion kroner of net private investment. There would also

---

[18] Later budgets and plans included goals sector by sector for both output and
use of resources for investment.

be important areas of public investment,[19] but the government's role would be to see that private investment and consumption decisions conformed to the over-all program. Presumably, direct controls would be relied on heavily. The program would have to be worked out in much greater detail. Future annual budgets would develop the basic program, establish annual goals, and develop in detail the techniques for controlling and directing the economy.

Thus by early 1946, less than a year after the liberation, the government had made the basic decisions on postwar economic policy. Recovery and development were to be stressed at the expense of rapid increases in private consumption. First priority would be given to investment to expand foreign exchange earnings. Foreign capital would be sought to finance more than half of the net investment program. The inflationary pressures inherited from the German occupation would not be allowed to work themselves off in a postwar inflation. The enormous liquidity of the banks and the public would not be wiped out. Import surpluses, high taxes, and increased output would be counted on to eliminate the inflationary pressures within a few years. Economic planning and direct controls to implement over-all economic plans would be all-important in the recovery program. Detailed direct controls would be abolished as soon as the principal recovery goals had been reached and inflationary pressures eliminated.

The particular policies and methods chosen were not peculiar to Norway. Most of the European countries were keeping direct controls for some period. Most of them realized the extent of the task to achieve recovery and had plans for meeting the problems. The United Kingdom had a program similar to Norway's with respect to eliminating inflationary pressures gradually over a considerable period of time. The outstanding feature of Norway's recovery program was that it represented a comprehensive plan of action. Furthermore, the plan was for an ambitious program of rapid recovery and development and for continued austerity. The United Kingdom also planned to restrict consumption increases, but it did not plan to devote such a tremendous proportion of resources to investment.

The influence of trained academic economists was noticeable in

[19] The data on the public use of goods and services in the budget were not divided into consumption and investment expenditures.

the Norwegian government's program. A number of economists trained by Ragnar Frisch at the University of Oslo were preparing the national budget and formulating administration policy. The program was something on the order of a laboratory experiment with over-all economic planning. Other European countries were pressing for rapid elimination of all controls and the return of the free price system and the profit motive to their traditional roles of allocating resources and output. Time alone would show the results of the Norwegian experiment.

4

The Stabilization Program: 1946–1949

The 1945 decisions and the 1946 resource plans provided the basic framework for the government's economic policy during the whole recovery period. The resource plans were further developed in the national budgets of 1947 and 1948; they were also revised and extended in the fall of 1948 under the stimulus of the Marshall Plan. But there was no significant departure from the policies outlined in 1946. The stabilization program was continued, in spite of unexpected difficulties, until the devaluation of the krone in 1949. After the devaluation, the program had to be modified.

In early 1946 the resource plans seemed ambitious, perhaps even unattainable. But in the next few years it was the stabilization program which constantly raised problems. The heavy investment program accounted for some of the pressure on prices and wages. Monetary and fiscal policies, designed to eliminate inflationary pressures gradually, were less effective than had been expected. The internal pressure for increases in wages and in farm prices was strong despite cost of living stability. But the most obvious and the greatest pressure was due to the steady rise in world prices.

From 1946 to 1949, rising import prices and successive wage and farm price demands led to increasing subsidies to keep the cost-of-living index stable. Price controls were quite effective for basic items, but there was a struggle to prevent wage payments in excess of the rates agreed upon in industry contracts. The pressure on wage rates was due in part to the fact that the investment program absorbed thousands of workers. By the end of 1946 unemployment was virtually nonexistent, as it has been ever since. During the 1946–49 period the government repeatedly reconsidered the stabilization policy. The Economic Coordination Board, which was consulted again and again, recommended each time that the stabilization policy be continued.

Until 1949 the government's overwhelming concern was to avoid a general cost-of-living wage adjustment and a vicious series of price-wage increases. The basic wage contracts before the war had provided for such adjustments; and the Employers' Association and the Federation of Trade Unions agreed early in 1946 that if the cost of living rose to 160.8 (1938 = 100) on certain critical dates there would be an increase in hourly rates by a certain number of öre for every increase of one point in the index.[1] The government was determined to keep the cost of living from reaching this "red line," since any increase under this basic agreement would be followed by similar wage increases for workers throughout the country. Some of the national industry wage contracts also had escalator clauses. The government did keep the index below the red line on the critical dates, and no cost-of-living adjustment was called for under the agreement from 1946 to 1949, but wage rates rose steadily during that period.

Although the Wage Board had approved two substantial increases in 1945, industry wage rates early in 1946 had not risen as much as had the cost of living above prewar levels. Consequently there was strong pressure for another flat increase. Some raises had been granted in 1945 under industry contracts; but since most of the contracts were due to expire in 1946, there were sure to be additional demands. The government tried to minimize any increases by assuring labor that it firmly intended to keep the cost of living stable; that controls over prices and nonwage incomes, and direct controls of all sorts, would be made more effective; and that subsidies would be used as necessary. Both the government and the trade union leaders stressed that money increases should be limited by productivity increases, and that wage policy had to be consistent with the government's over-all economic policy.[2]

[1] There are 100 öre per Norwegian krone. The amount of the adjustment was to be 1.5 öre per hour per index point. The critical dates were March 15 and September 15. Average hourly wage rates in mining and manufacturing in 1946 were about 2.5 kroner per hour. At the time of liberation the cost-of-living index was about 150 (1938 = 100).

[2] See *Odelstingsproposisjon nummer 25* of 1946; and Brofoss, *Norges ökonomiske og finansielle stilling.*

However, the pressure for a further general wage increase and for higher farm prices led the government in the spring of 1946 seriously to reconsider the stabilization policy for the first time. Rising import prices led to increasing subsidies on imports, and subsidies on domestic farm products were also increasing. The Economic Coordination Board in April 1946 unanimously recommended that the stabilization policy be continued. It was opposed, however, to further increases in subsidies to raise domestic incomes; and it recommended, more or less as an alternative, a system of family allowances. The government, after receiving the Board's recommendation, announced once more its intention of keeping the cost of living stable.

The Wage Board nevertheless approved in June 1946 another general adjustment of 15 öre per hour, or about 6 per cent, in industry wage rates. The increase was to be granted in three steps — the first in September 1946, the second in March 1947, and the third in September 1947 — the idea being that increases in productivity over this period would help to justify the step-by-step increases. This program by itself, however, would not mean that, when compared with prewar levels, industry wage rates at the end of 1946 would be higher than the cost of living.

This was the first of a series of important Wage Board decisions during the 1946-48 period. The government exerted an influence on the Wage Board through its representative; also, relations between the Labor Party and the Federation of Trade Unions were close. The government and the trade unions tended to reach agreements on the basic lines for wage policy. The wage adjustments recommended by the Wage Board tended to be greater than the government believed economically desirable, but represented the minimum increases the government could negotiate with the trade unions.

The June 1946 wage adjustment was accompanied by some adjustments in farm prices. Relatively low farm incomes and wages and the demand for labor in the cities were making it difficult to keep labor on the farms. Farm output was not increasing as fast as output in other sectors. Furthermore, the two powerful farmers' organizations and the Farmers' Party tended to support Labor Party programs.

Increases in the prices of domestically produced milk and bacon were granted on June 7, 1946. These increases were in both prices paid to producers and prices paid by consumers. To prevent the cost-of-living index from rising, prices of imported sugar and coffee were lowered and subsidies on these commodities were increased.

When these decisions were announced, the Prime Minister stated that the stabilization policy had been a success. There was stability and labor peace, inflation had been avoided, and reconstruction was progressing steadily. The policy could be continued successfully if all groups would cooperate. The demands of farmers, fishermen, and wage earners, though reasonable, must be restrained. Other incomes, especially interest, dividends, and salaries, would be controlled.[3] Children's allowances would be proposed.

The pressure for price and wage increases nevertheless continued; and in the summer of 1946 the Wage Board again approved a number of adjustments in industry wage contracts and rates were raised in all trades. Many of the increases granted were to previously low-paid workers, notably textile workers, women, and unskilled workers. The average increase, however, was 16 öre per hour, or about 6 per cent. Therefore, at the end of 1946 for the first time industry wage rates had risen more than the cost-of-living index above prewar levels.

New demands in the fall of 1946 for increases in farm prices were submitted to the Economic Coordination Board, which recommended that some increases should be granted to compensate for the wage increases in the summer of 1946, but that certain other prices should be reduced, to keep the cost of living stable. In accordance with the recommendation, prices of milk, meat, and domestically produced grain were raised, and prices of margarine and imported textiles were lowered. In January 1947, further price reductions were announced for margarine, sugar, and work clothes.

As a result of all these price changes, the cost-of-living index kept rising above the red line of 160.8 and then being pulled down again. In the fall of 1946 and the spring of 1947, the government stressed that wage increases were higher than justified by productivity increases and that the domestic cost level was rising. Not only were official wage increases driving up costs, but "black market" wages were being paid in 1946 and even more so in 1947, in the sense of wage rates in excess of those established in the industry agreements.

[3] See *Om saerlige tiltak til trygging av landets ökonomi, Stortingsmelding nummer 43, 1947.*

Although higher prices of domestic farm products and of imports were considered the most important causes of the cost of living increases, the rising wage level was also believed to be a factor.[4]

In the spring of 1947, import prices were still rising, there were further demands for increases in agricultural prices, and the cost of living was above the red line. Price stabilization subsidies had risen to almost four times the preliberation total. In order to avoid further increases in subsidies and to keep the cost of living stable, the government recommended in March 1947, and the Storting decided in June 1947, to reduce the general sales tax from 10 per cent to 6.25 per cent, except for agricultural commodities.[5] The sales tax is included in the calculation of the cost-of-living index. The receipts from the general 10 per cent sales tax had exceeded price subsidies in the early years, but with the cut in the rate receipts would fall below subsidies in the fiscal year, 1947–48.

The Monetary and Financial Council, a committee of financial experts from the government, the Norges Bank, and the University of Oslo which had been consulted frequently since the liberation, had recommended that the sales tax should not be reduced.[6] This committee considered it essential to keep up tax receipts and to take other measures to reduce inflationary pressures. Some prominent officials still regard the 1947 cut in the sales tax as a mistake. Presumably the alternative was further increases in subsidies, which might have helped to win support for stronger anti-inflationary measures.[7]

The government in the spring of 1947 again asked the Economic Coordination Board to reconsider the stabilization policy; and in July the Board again recommended that the policy be continued. The Board's report suggested that there were indications of falling prices and of recession in world markets; therefore, it was more important than ever to adhere to the stabilization policy and to prevent further increases in costs. Since the sales tax already had been

---

[4] See *Stortingsmelding nummer 43, 1947.*

[5] Also, luxuries subject to especially high excise taxes were not affected.

[6] This committee, unlike the Economic Coordination Board, was a committee chosen by the Cabinet. It was comprised of individual experts rather than representatives of organizations or institutions.

[7] Also, it would probably have been easier in later years to cut subsidies than to raise the sales tax again.

cut, there was less scope for using a reduction in the sales tax to lower domestic prices and keep incomes constant in Norway if world prices should fall. Considerable stress was also put on the restrictions on unilateral exchange-rate changes as a result of membership in the International Monetary Fund.

The Board's recommendations for holding the cost of living stable included more effective price controls, the lowering of profit margins and prices wherever possible, an attempt to eliminate "black market" wages, a provisional wage freeze until the end of the year (except for the increase to be made on September 1, 1947, as previously agreed), and a reduction to 6.25 per cent of the sales tax on agricultural commodities.

The government followed the recommendations of the Board. The sales tax on farm products was lowered in July. The government stressed that low wages in Norway meant low costs and high profits in the export industries. The subsidies were being offset more and more by increased taxes on exports. With falling world prices, these export taxes would be cut and subsidies on imports would fall. The government believed that Norway's stabilization policy would still prove valuable in avoiding deflation in a period of falling world prices. The cost-of-living index was expected to be below 160 on August 15, 1947, but the government would try to lower the index further. It would also try to reduce inflationary pressure arising from such internal factors as high investment, wage increases, high profits, and bank-credit expansion.

The cost of living fell to almost 157 in October 1947, partly because of the seasonal declines in vegetable prices, as well as the various price changes that had been made and the cut in the sales tax. The expected fall in world prices, however, did not materialize. While there were some price declines, Norwegian import prices did not fall significantly. By May 1948 the cost-of-living index was again above 160. Further price reductions and seasonal declines in vegetable prices lowered it to 157 by October 1948.

Most of the industry wage contracts which had been renewed for two years in 1946 expired in 1948. Although the Labor Party leaders had said in the fall of 1947 that the economic situation did not justify further general wage increases in 1948, the Federation of Trade Unions proposed increases of 10 öre per hour, or about 3 per cent of average hourly earnings in mining and manufacturing in 1948, for lower paid workers, setting up precise rates for men and women workers above which the increase would not be granted. This proposal was accepted and went into effect in April 1948.[8]

During 1948 and 1949 the government again reconsidered the stabilization policy. World prices remained high and no substantial decline seemed likely in the near future. Subsidies had risen to much higher levels than had been anticipated. It seemed clear that some upward adjustment of prices would be necessary eventually, but the automatic cost-of-living adjustment in the general wage agreement seemed to make any upward adjustment too dangerous. It appeared essential that this automatic adjustment feature be eliminated. In the spring of 1949, when several industry contracts expired, further wage increases were granted. Trade union and Labor Party leaders succeeded, however, in obtaining a revision of the general cost-of-living adjustment provision in mid-1949. The adjustment was made semi-automatic; the amount of the adjustment was to be negotiated rather than fixed, as in the past; the red line was raised to 165.6; and February 1950 was set as the first critical date.

For the period 1946–49 as a whole, the government was fairly successful in restraining wage increases for industrial workers. Wages rose steadily under the industry wage agreements, even though there was no general cost-of-living adjustment. Five or six per cent increases were negotiated each year. Special increases were granted in low-paid industries and to lower paid workers. There was also considerable upgrading as a result of full employment and labor scarcities. Piece rates were adjusted upward and there was a shift from time to piece rates; furthermore, the rates actually paid were higher than those established in industry contracts. The steady rise in wage rates strengthened the government's conviction that a cost-of-living adjustment should be avoided.

In 1948 and 1949, real hourly earnings in industry probably increased faster and were higher when compared with prewar levels than output per man hour, but the data for such a comparison are not available. Hourly earnings, deflated by the cost-of-living index,

---

[8] It went into effect in April for all workers under contracts expiring in 1948. Special negotiations determined the increases under contracts not expiring until 1949.

were as high, compared with prewar, as output per man in the
year 1949, whereas in 1946 and 1947 they had been somewhat
lower.[9] The deliberate policy of raising incomes of low-paid industrial
workers contributed to the rise in hourly earnings.

Hourly earnings in mining and manufacturing had not risen as
much as the average wage per employed worker in the country as a
whole. The increase above prewar levels in wage rates for farm and
forestry workers was substantial and there was a marked shift from
low-paid to high-paid jobs. Labor left employment on the farms, in
the forests, and as houseworkers for higher paid work in the cities.
The average wage per employed worker deflated by the cost-of-living
index was 21 per cent above prewar in 1946 and 44 per cent above
in 1949.[10] Gross national product per employed worker was 3 per
cent above prewar in 1946 and 19 per cent above in 1949.

The cost-of-living index had not risen as much as had wholesale
prices or prices of all consumer goods. The index was based on expenditures of a family of 3.6 units supported by one wage earner.
The total consumer price index probably is more suitable than the
cost-of-living index for deflating the money wages of the average
wage earner, who supported only one other person. The difference in
the results given by using the consumer price index is striking. The
average wage per employed worker, deflated by the consumer price
index, was 15 per cent above prewar level in 1946 and 24 per cent
above in 1949. Although the average real wage per worker in 1946
had been considerably higher than output per man when compared
with prewar levels, in 1949 it was only about 4 per cent higher than
output per man when compared with prewar levels. This suggests that
the government was fairly successful in restraining wage increases in
the economy as a whole from 1946 to 1949.

Subsidies were very high partly because import prices in 1946 were
two and a half times prewar prices, in 1947 almost three times, and
in 1948 and 1949 over three times prewar prices. Export prices from

---

[9] See Tables 28 and 58. In 1946 output per man for the economy as a whole
was almost 3 per cent above prewar, while real hourly earnings in mining and
manufacturing (deflated by the cost-of-living index) were at the prewar level.
In 1947 output per man rose more than 9 per cent and real hourly earnings
8 per cent above the prewar level. In both 1948 and 1949 real hourly earnings
rose about 5 per cent and output per man less than 3 per cent.

[10] See Table 58.

1947 to 1949 were about three times prewar prices.[11] Price stabilization subsidies, including subsidies on domestic farm products, amounted to almost 400 million kroner in 1946, or 13 per cent of total public revenues. Other subsidies amounted to about 200 million kroner. Although most of these other subsidies were for investment and war-damage compensation, they undoubtedly helped to prevent further price increases for farm products and fish. As subsidies rose, profits in the export industries rose, and export taxes helped to defray import subsidy costs. Price stabilization subsidies increased to over 600 million kroner in 1947, and to over 800 million kroner in 1948 and 1949. Other subsidies, notably to agriculture and fishing, rose to about 300 million kroner.[12]

Throughout the 1946–49 period, detailed price controls were practically universal. They could not be eliminated so long as cost-of-living stability was considered an overwhelming necessity. The government removed some commodities from detailed price controls and substituted general regulations permitting increases only to cover increases in costs. But the commodities involved were very unimportant. The government's major efforts were directed at controlling the prices of items weighing heavily in the cost-of-living index. The fact that larger increases were permitted in prices of other consumer goods is evidenced by the sharp rise in the total consumer price index compared with the cost-of-living index. It might appear that in order to mop up consumer purchasing power and to stimulate increases in output there had been a deliberate policy of permitting relatively sharp price increases for commodities not heavily weighted in the cost-of-living index, but there is little evidence for this, except for the tremendous excise taxes on luxuries.

The combination of large subsidies on all essential food and clothing items, of subsidized rates for electric power, and of rent controls at very low rates, with exceptionally high excise taxes on such "luxury" goods as cigarettes, whiskey, theatres, and restaurant meals, meant a much greater redistribution of real income than of money income compared with prewar years. In a sense, the stabilization policy, more than wage and direct tax policies, reduced inequalities in the real standard of living of various income groups. There was a

[11] See Table 11.
[12] See Table 51.

strong element of government influence over the composition of consumption. The government subsidized imported articles believed to be essential, and it taxed very highly articles, whether domestically produced or imported, which it did not consider essential or desirable in some sense.

The available income statistics seem to suggest that the price-control authorities followed a deliberate policy of keeping business incomes high, but there is no other evidence that this was the case. Because of export prices, determined on world markets, profits were very high (as they have been in all years since the war). Although the huge profits were taxed heavily, to prevent inflationary pressures, export profits after taxes remained high. In other sectors, most prices were not set at levels which would discourage output.

Even in the early period of serious scarcities, there were few, if any, important commodity black markets, probably because Norwegian people are highly disciplined and have a strong sense of social responsibility. For many basic items, the job of the price-control authorities was relatively simple in the sense that all supplies were imported, or there were only one or two large producers, or the price was negotiated with national organizations representing the producers. Farm, fish, and forest prices were negotiated each year with the producer organizations.

From 1946 to 1948 there was strict rationing of almost all basic foods and essential consumer goods. Although rations were increased quite consistently, the amounts made available did not approach prewar consumption levels. Strict controls on imports, allocations of producers' goods and raw materials, and construction licensing were also in force. Had this not been the case, the pressure on prices and wages would have been uncontrollable.

The government was concerned throughout this period about the effects of direct controls on productivity and on the allocation of resources. Some specific commodities, rigidly controlled in price because they entered the cost-of-living index, disappeared from the markets, and the consumer had to buy higher priced substitutes. Some producers seemed to be losing interest in lowering costs and improving efficiency. The government therefore proposed a law to give the price directorate sweeping powers to try to rationalize output policies in industries of low efficiency.

While government officials believed that direct controls were, on the whole, achieving the objective of ensuring that primarily essential goods were imported and essential reconstruction and development jobs were carried out first, they also believed that some scarce resources were going into nonessential consumer-goods industries and into unlicensed building and construction, especially into repair work. Their opinion was that persisting inflationary pressures were leading to such drains on scarce resources. For this reason the government emphasized its program of reducing inflationary pressures through high taxes, high public savings, and import surpluses.

The early 1946 plans had estimated that import surpluses and high taxes would reduce private bank reserves by 4–5 billion kroner by the end of 1950. The reduction had proceeded at about the expected rate; by the end of 1948 reserves had already fallen by 2.4 billion kroner.[13] Import surpluses financed by government reserves and credits accounted for about 1 billion of the decrease,[14] and government surpluses were substantial. Reserves also tended to decrease because of a 500 million kroner increase in notes in circulation outside the banks and the blocking of an additional 300 million kroner of deposits. But in spite of the big cut in reserves, the banks were not conscious of reserve pressure at the end of 1948.

The program for high taxes was designed primarily to provide public savings, not only to finance public investment, but to help finance the private investment program. Both state and municipal expenditures were high, owing to defense needs, to special postwar relief and reconstruction expenditures, and to subsidies. To achieve public savings, tax receipts had to increase more than current expenditures. As a percentage of net national product, tax receipts rose to almost twice the prewar percentage. Net revenues after subsidies and transfer payments, when compared with net national product, were more than 50 per cent above the prewar ratio.[15] Total public savings, state and municipal, rose from less than 100 million kroner in

---

[13] The net reduction by the end of 1950 turned out to be 4 billion kroner.

[14] The total deficit financed by these means amounted to 2.7 billion kroner, but about 1.5 billion came from shipowners' exchange balances and were offset by repayment to the shipowners.

[15] A consolidated account of state and municipal receipts and expenditures presents the best picture of over-all fiscal policy. In 1948, total tax revenues were 34 per cent of net national product at factor cost, compared with 18 per cent in 1938; and net available revenues, after subsidies and transfer payments, were raised to 19 per cent of net national product, compared with 13 per cent in 1938. See Tables 51 and 52.

1946 to 789 million in 1948; after 1946 they substantially exceeded public investment.[16] Public savings accounted for about 40 per cent of total domestic savings in 1947 and 1948. Clearly, the program for substantial public savings was successful.[17]

The steady increase in tax receipts partly reflected the continued upward adjustments of wages and prices, but special postwar direct and indirect taxes were also important. The maintenance of substantial public savings year after year was not easy. Demands for additional government expenditures were strong and persistent. Even before the Marshall Plan was fully under way, there were substantial kroner receipts, in addition to current tax revenues, accruing to the government as a result of foreign grants and credits. Although political pressure to spend these funds was inevitable, the receipts were kept idle in government accounts at the Norges Bank and later used, for the most part, to reduce the occupation debt to the Norges Bank.

Other factors help to explain the building up of large revenue surpluses. Year after year, actual revenues substantially exceeded the budget estimates. The high taxes were defended as a means of reducing inflationary pressures, not merely as a way to cover expenditures. The strict limits placed on public consumption and also on public investment were not explained in terms of lack of funds but in terms of scarcity of real resources. In addition, there were many funds for special purposes kept outside the regular accounts, and the surpluses reflected in part the operations of these funds. The ordinary budget presentations did not show as large surpluses as were actually realized.

Direct tax receipts rose sharply, compared with prewar amounts. The capital levy and war-damage tax payments did not begin until 1947 and became substantial only in 1948. However, some funds from the capital levy were blocked at the time of assessment.[18] Fines and

---

[16] In the same years, public net investment rose from about 260 million kroner to over 500 million kroner. There was a net over-all deficit of less than 200 million kroner in 1946, but net over-all revenue surpluses, after financing state and municipal investments, of about 200 million in 1947 and about 300 million in 1948. See Table 51.

[17] See Table 50.

[18] The war-damage tax was almost fully paid up by 1948; but payments on the capital levy continued at almost the same rate through 1950, and were still substantial in 1952. During 1946 the amount of blocked deposits rose from 500

confiscations of Nazi and Quisling property were large in 1946 and 1947. Income tax receipts increased partly because of increases in rates and, more important, because most income recipients were in much higher tax brackets than before the war.[19]

The increase in indirect tax receipts over prewar levels was even greater than that of direct tax receipts. This reflected the general sales tax, which had not existed before the war, and numerous high excise taxes on luxuries, such as alcohol and tobacco. In addition, as export profits rose, special excise taxes on exports were levied.[20]

The opposition parties constantly criticized the continued complete reliance on detailed direct controls and argued that monetary and fiscal policies were not sufficiently restrictive. There was no basic change in the easy money policy, the 2½ per cent interest rate being maintained. No measures were taken to freeze private bank reserves or to control the rate of expansion of private bank credit, aside from the measures leading to a reduction in bank reserves, described above. Loans outstanding of private banks, of other credit institutions, and of the principal state banks at the end of 1945 had been at about two thirds the prewar level. It was obvious that loans would expand with the recovery of output, with most domestic prices and wages being one and one half to two times the prewar level, and with import prices from two to three times prewar levels. In spite of a one-third

---

million kroner to 941 million kroner. There is very little precise information on the blocking of deposits and on the method of determining the amounts released. Apparently, substantial deposits were blocked under a special provision that the amounts would be tax free provided they were not spent until the government considered that their expenditure for investment purposes would not be too inflationary. The long-term program prepared in the fall of 1948 contains a general survey of the various blocking operations from 1946 to 1948.

[19] Since income taxes are levied by both municipalities and the state, any simple description of personal or business income taxes is virtually impossible. Municipalities collect about half the direct taxes, including social insurance premiums. They also make half the transfer payments to the private sector, including social security payments. Including the capital levy and war-damage tax, direct taxes amounted to 20 per cent of private factor income plus grants in 1948, compared with 11 per cent in 1938 (see Table 53). The ratio was almost as high in 1946 and 1947. The special postwar taxes reached a peak of 700 million kroner, or 28 per cent of total direct taxes, in 1948.

[20] Indirect tax receipts were 46 per cent in 1946 and 47 per cent in 1947 of total tax receipts, compared with 42 per cent in 1938. They fell to about 40 per cent in 1948, when receipts from the special postwar taxes reached a peak and the general sales tax had been cut to 6.25 per cent (see Table 51).

increase in loans outstanding in 1946, the absolute prewar level was not reached until early 1947. In 1947 loans outstanding again increased by almost one third, and in 1948 by almost one quarter. At the end of 1948, however, the absolute amount of loans outstanding was only about one and one half times the 1939 level.[21]

Although there was considerable concern on the part of the government, no positive steps were taken to control bank-credit expansion. In 1947 the government indicated that the private banks should cooperate and restrict their lending activities.[22] In 1947 and 1948 loans of state banks and of private credit institutions other than private banks actually increased at a faster rate than private bank loans.[23] While the government apparently believed that a considerable expansion of bank credit was necessary during these years, it was concerned that bank credit should not help to finance projects which the government considered should have low priority. But direct controls over construction and controls over machinery imports were believed to be quite effective in restricting investment in such projects.

The slowing down in the rate of expansion of private bank loans in 1948, though no doubt partly attributable to the decline in private bank reserves, reflected also the increasing indebtedness of private business to the banks. Much of the expansion in bank loans was to finance ordinary commercial transactions at higher prices and to finance imports at rapidly rising prices. In general, the larger companies did not rely on bank credit for plant expansion since profits were high, dividend payments were limited, and idle funds were accumulating.

The stabilization policy was continued from 1946 to 1949 in spite of all the difficulties encountered. In retrospect it is tempting to suggest that it should have been abandoned early in the postwar period. But the escalator clause in the general wage agreement made a decision to abandon the stabilization policy seem almost impossible at the time, and the future course of world prices was not at all clear. Until the Marshall Plan got under way, there was reason to expect that the postwar world prosperity would come to an end. Falling

[21] See Tables 4 and 14.

[22] *Stortingsmelding nummer 43, August 15, 1947.*

[23] The state banks had been founded at various times before the war for special purposes. The state bank loans were mostly mortgages or loans to municipalities.

world prices would have lessened the subsidy burden and the huge export profits. The insistence on cost-of-living stability as the goal was probably reasonable at the time.

As far as the rate of money wage increases is concerned, the government clearly had a difficult job. Some levelling out of wage differentials was a basic objective, but at the same time the maintenance of worker incentives was necessary if output increases were to be achieved. The trade unions and farmers were the leading groups in the Labor Party. On the whole, the government's record in restraining wage increases and in eventually obtaining a revision of the general cost-of-living escalator clause is a good one.

The longer range plans for high taxes, high public savings, and a gradual reduction of liquid assets in the hands of the banks and the public were being carried out. The expansion of private bank credit, however, was greater than was consistent with the basic objective of noninflationary financing of the investment program.

5

Development of Annual National Budgets: 1946-1948

A detailed national budget for resources and their use had been mentioned in the Labor Party's original postwar program statement and was stressed by the Prime Minister and other Cabinet members soon after the election. The government then told the Storting that it believed that its main task was to assume responsibility for the reconstruction, and that it intended to act according to a comprehensive plan to ensure that projects were undertaken in the proper order and that productive capacity was used efficiently. It would appraise the importance of various projects from the point of view of the community, prepare a national budget for the future use of labor, equipment, and materials, and take such action as was necessary to ensure that the budget was carried out.

The 1946 analysis of the total resources that might be available from 1946 to 1950 and of the way in which they should be used provided the framework for the annual national budgets in the period 1946–48. The 1946 budget was more of a long-term plan than an annual budget. Both long-term plans and annual budgets would be necessary instruments of economic planning. Plans covering a period of years, when fully developed, would establish long-range targets and be more important for planning purposes than the annual budgets. The 1946 plan, however, only outlined the order of magnitude of the problem and the solution advocated by the administration. The annual budgets of 1947 and 1948 followed the general policy lines of high investment, large import surpluses financed with loans, and restricted private and public consumption.

The 1947 budget discussed the role of annual budgets as distinct from long-term plans. Annual budgets would necessarily consider output increases and import surpluses more as estimates than as goals. The estimates would reflect the outlook for foreign loans and the available productive capacity when the budgets were prepared. There would be targets for the planned use of resources for investment and consumption; in this sense the annual budgets would be programs, not mere estimates. And the budgets would outline the necessary policy instruments to keep within the planned resource uses. Long-term plans, however, could establish targets for output and import surpluses as well as targets for resource uses. The government indicated that it intended to frame a fuller long-term program as soon as possible. In this program, output, balance of payments, investment, and consumption goals would be determined for each sector of the economy. Annual budgets would then be prepared in the light of the new program.[1]

The 1947 budget, though much more of a program for the coming year than the 1946 budget, was said to be in some respects a compromise.[2] It was not a forecast or an estimate of uncoordinated plans of individuals, but neither was it a full program budget. The fiscal budget had been prepared before the national budget, and the government's plans, reflected in the fiscal budget, had to be accepted in working out the national budget, which was not finished until February. It was pointed out that government expenditure and tax policies in the future should be determined on the basis of the outlook and program for the coming year. The government's economic policy as a whole should be decided in the light of the program for available resources and their uses. The 1948 budget would be more of a program budget and would spell out more fully the measures needed to achieve the goals.

From 1947 to 1952 the national budgets were set forth in great detail and were prepared in much the same fashion. In each sector, specific goals were established for investment, employment, output, exports, imports, and the use of materials. The budgets emphasized that the detailed goals must be based on certain assumptions, were often minimum rather than maximum goals, and were often largely determined for the coming year by decisions taken in previous years.

---

[1] The new long-term program did not appear until the fall of 1948, after the inauguration of the Marshall Plan.

[2] The budget, prepared by the Ministry of Finance, was presented to the Storting in February 1947 after the fiscal budget for 1947–48. *Om Nasjonalbudsjettet, 1947, Stortingsmelding nummer 10, 1947.*

But the detailed goals were part of a general program rather than mere estimates or forecasts.

The task of coordination, and the development of guiding principles, was handled in one small office, the National Budget Office.[3] The Central Bureau of Statistics was responsible for compiling data for past years and prepared an economic survey of the previous year. The agriculture, fisheries, industries, and other departments responsible for particular sectors of the economy, and the offices in charge of price and labor policies, prepared preliminary budgets for their sectors on the basis of guiding principles issued early in the summer by the National Budget Office, with the approval of the Economic Committee of the Cabinet, composed of the Prime Minister, the Foreign Minister, and the Ministers of Finance, Trade, Industry, and Labor.

Preliminary budgets for the various sectors were due in the early fall. Each Ministry responsible for preparing these subbudgets worked closely with the business association in the particular field covered, for example, the association of exporters, shipowners, or farmers. The Ministry obtained information from them on plans and expectations with respect to investment, output, and prices.

A technical committee of experts from the various government departments, under the chairmanship of the National Budget Office, reviewed the sector budgets and eliminated the major inconsistencies.[4] The fact that the budget was so detailed meant that the job of eliminating inconsistencies was a big one. The precise plans or estimates for the use of materials had to be consistent with the estimates for production, import, and export of these materials. Estimates of consumption by commodity also had to be consistent with the production, import, and export of the commodity. Estimates of employment of each type of labor had to fit with the estimated available supplies

[3] The National Budget Office was in the Finance Ministry in 1946 and 1947. It moved to the Department of Commerce before the preparation of the 1948 budget; at that time the former Minister of Finance, Erik Brofoss, became Minister of Commerce. In 1953 the office moved back to the Finance Ministry.

[4] The Committee originally included representatives from government departments and from the Central Bureau of Statistics. The Economic Coordination Board was also represented as long as it existed. Today the Norges Bank is represented.

of such labor. And the sector budgets at times had to be adjusted to remove inconsistencies with the basic guiding principles.

When the inconsistencies had been eliminated, the National Budget Office presented a draft of the entire budget to the Economic Committee of the Cabinet. This Committee reviewed the budget in the last few weeks of the calendar year and formulated proposed Cabinet decisions on the major politico-economic measures necessary to implement the budget. The budget was then presented to the entire Cabinet for review before being sent to the Storting at the beginning of the calendar year.

The method of preparing the national budget, especially the important role played by the Economic Committee of the Cabinet and finally by the entire Cabinet, indicates that it was not just an economic report to be read by experts. It was the principal vehicle for the development of administration recommendations to the Cabinet, and the basis of major economic policy discussions in the Cabinet. The budget was also the focal point for policy discussions in the Storting, the principal target of the opposition parties, and the subject of continuous debate in the newspapers. Members of the Cabinet, the Storting, and the press learned to discuss Norway's problems in terms of national budget concepts.

The budget document changed considerably in form and emphasis year by year, but it still retained essentially the same basic content. In 1946, only rough aggregates were considered and more emphasis was placed on the period from 1946 to 1950 than on the year 1946 itself. The principal emphasis, aside from spelling out alternatives for over-all resource uses, was on explaining the meaning of national accounts.[5] Most of the discussion was amazingly technical and academic for a document presenting basic policy alternatives to the Storting for consideration. A considerable amount of detailed work had been done on estimates for 1946, and some of these were presented orally by the Minister of Finance.

In 1947, the principal emphasis, aside from the actual budget estimates, was on a long discussion of the possible measures available to the government for achieving its goals. Every type of direct control

[5] The document started off with a statement that the system used was developed by Professor Ragnar Frisch.

was discussed and the possible functioning of each type of control was explained. Import controls, quantitative controls, price and wage controls, were given great weight. But the budget also explained how subsidies of various kinds, tax policies, government loans or guarantees, and a host of other measures could be used to achieve the objectives that were set forth in detail.

The 1947 budget also stressed that the control machinery must be made more effective. Larger staffs were needed. The people must be persuaded away from the belief, prevalent in the occupation period, that it was smart to evade government regulations. Great care must be taken to ensure that specific controls over prices and output did not interfere with increasing productivity and efficiency.

The emphasis on controls followed from the fact that investment and consumption demand were far in excess of resource availabilities. The 1947 budget stressed that there were three basic scarcities — labor, building materials, and foreign exchange — and that the controls must be effective enough to ensure that these scarce factors of production were used to carry out only the most important investment projects and to provide the most essential consumer goods. The budget included a mass of detailed statistics and estimates. In addition to estimates of national accounts, it included detailed estimates for the various sectors.

The 1948 budget was more readable and less academic than those for the two preceding years.[6] The policy emphasis early in 1948 was on the steadily worsening balance of payments position. This problem colored most of the decisions in the various budgets for investment, consumption, and output. While the great mass of statistical data was similar to that in the 1947 budget, it was presented less conspicuously.

Up to and including 1949 there was relatively little discussion in the national budgets of such problems as price and wage stabilization, and monetary and fiscal policies. Special reports on these problems were made to the Storting, but the budgets did not treat them fully or analyze their influence on the implementation of resource plans. The basic data on financial claims and savings were not being developed as rapidly as data on output. The first budget to give

[6] *Nasjonalbudsjettet 1948, Stortingsmelding nummer 1, 1948.*

prominence to these problems was that for 1950, when the stabilization policy was clearly in the foreground.

The practice of publishing interim reports on the budget was begun in 1948. The Cabinet received quarterly progress reports, and the Finance Committee of the Storting requested that at least one interim report a year be published — a practice that has been followed since 1948.[7] Often the report is published in the fall and summarizes the results achieved in the first half year. These reports have become more and more useful as quarterly data on the economy have been improved.

Until 1952, the budgets focused more and more on a discussion of basic policy issues, but there was little change in the methods of programming and estimating. Detailed estimates and programs were made and reconciled. When steps seemed necessary to make certain that a program was carried out, such steps were recommended. The character of the budget document changed in form and presentation, but not in substance. The detailed sector budgets and subbudgets were published for a few years and then completely dropped.

Since 1952 there has been a fairly substantial change in the basic character of the budget. As detailed controls were abolished for more and more imports and for a larger proportion of total domestic output, there was a shift away from very detailed targets for consumption and investment. Sector estimates are made, but in less detail, and are more in the nature of estimates than targets. Efforts to rely on over-all monetary and fiscal policies have fundamentally altered the character of the budget in some respects.

As the basic statistical data on the Norwegian economy have been developed, the budgets have become more realistic and useful. The national accounts work begun in the Central Bureau of Statistics during the occupation has been expanded. The Bureau has had a program of improving, year by year, the collection of basic current data and also of compiling data for past years. Each successive national budget has been able to consider in detail some problem that previously had been treated superficially because of lack of basic data.

[7] The 1948 interim report was *Gjennomföringen av nasjonalbudsjettet 1948, Stortingsmelding nummer 50, 1948.*

The emphasis placed on development of the statistical basis for national budgeting helped to make the government plans realistic. Nevertheless, the completely revised data on national accounts, finally published in 1952 but available in part to government officials for some time earlier, suggest that the government's data in the early years were quite incomplete and to some extent misleading.[8] During the years 1946 to 1948 there was a tendency, especially on the part of the opposition parties, to compare the budget estimates or targets and the results year by year and to emphasize the divergencies. The government in these early budgets explained, according to the data then available, how results had differed from the previous year's estimates or targets and the reasons for the differences.

There were numerous statistical problems in comparing plans and results. One was the price problem. Estimates of total available resources and resource uses were based on certain assumptions concerning prices; the results were in terms of actual prices. In the early annual budgets, the price assumptions were not made clear, apparently in part as a deliberate matter of policy. Estimates were generally made either according to prices prevailing in the late fall, when the budget estimates were being developed, or according to more definite price expectations for a particular good or service. Another type of statistical problem resulted from a gradual redefinition of concepts and the development of more adequate data even before the publication in 1952 of the revised estimates of national accounts.[9]

[8] Annual budgets and longer term plans, formulated in terms of the data available before 1952, should not be compared with results, based on the revised data, without careful consideration being given to the real meaning of the comparisons.

The revised data were based on detailed new production statistics and on detailed information on the flow of goods from one sector to another. The new kroner totals are much higher than all previous estimates for all the basic aggregates, except public use of goods and services, a sector in which very comprehensive data had always been used.

The translation of budget targets, or long-term plan goals, into expected rates of change eliminates some of the statistical problems, and in fact presents the targets and goals as they were actually developed by government economists. Unfortunately, it is difficult, if not impossible in most cases, to derive expected rates of change from the material published in the earlier national budgets.

[9] In 1948 and 1949, for example, a change in the definition of investment resulted in important changes in the magnitudes.

More important than the statistical problems is the fact that annual comparisons of estimates and results must take into account the nature of the budget estimates. The productive equipment in existence at the beginning of a year and the heavy machinery on order tend to determine the level of output and foreign-exchange earnings in that year.[10] Of course, there are possibilities for adjustment, but they are limited. The foreign exchange that will be available from the use of reserves, aid, and credits is also pretty well known for a year in advance. Therefore, the figures for total available resources for the coming year tend more to be estimates than goals. The most important targets concern the use of the estimated total of available resources. As available resources change, however, in comparison with the estimates, the changes must be taken into account and reflected in revised targets.[11] For example, plans to restrict consumption increases need not be carried out if resources are available to meet investment goals and also permit greater consumption increases.

Possibly in part because the most important targets in the annual budgets were those for resource uses, there was a tendency to underestimate total available resources. The budgets generally made conservative estimates of output and fairly pessimistic assumptions on the terms of trade. This seems to have been deliberate. Low estimates of total available resources may have helped to win political support for continued strict controls over nonproductive investment and for policies aimed at a slow rate of increase in private and public consumption. Furthermore, it is easier to make rational adjustments to an unexpectedly high total of available resources than to an unexpectedly low total.

The limitations on the planning significance of the annual budgets explain the emphasis placed on the longer term plans. In a program covering a period of years, it is possible to work out real goals for output and for import surpluses. Loans can be negotiated, machinery can be ordered, factories can be built. Productive equipment can be substantially expanded over a period of years. Targets for investment

[10] Import programs, of course, have to be geared to output plans, and output will not increase at a maximum rate unless full employment is maintained.
[11] This is obvious in the case of unexpected increases in the output of particular commodities which the government is attempting to increase.

and consumption, of course, will reflect the goals for output and for import surpluses.

In the following chapter, actual developments from 1946 to 1948 are considered essentially in terms of the plan presented in 1946 for the period from 1946 to 1950. The specific targets and goals in the annual budgets are also explained. In most cases, they were consistent with, and simply a development of, the 1946 plan. The budget each year, however, tended to reflect too much the precise situation at the beginning of each year. It is more reasonable to expect results to conform to plans covering a period of years than to plans covering one year only, since temporary divergences may be ironed out. On the other hand, any plan must be based on certain assumptions and revised in the light of changes. Any comparison of results and plans for a period of four or five years must take such factors into account.

By the fall of 1948, the government had a comprehensive program for the period 1949 to 1952, which was submitted to the Organization for European Economic Cooperation. It was based on the assumption of aid under the Marshall Plan and superseded the original 1946 plan for the remainder of the period originally covered by that plan. After 1948, the annual budgets were of course drawn up on the basis of the new long-term program. The actual results from 1949 to 1952 are discussed in this study primarily in terms of the new long-term program rather than of the annual budgets.

The fact that it seems more reasonable to compare results over a series of years with long-term plans made for the whole period, than to concentrate on year-by-year comparisons of annual budgets and results, does not in any sense mean that the annual budgets were not important. Without the annual budgeting process, the long-term plans would be mere pieces of paper. The annual budgets were the means by which the long-term plans were developed, implemented, revised, and carried out.

To go one step further, the long-term plans and annual budgets as documents, are less important than the constant analysis and daily and weekly decisions necessary to adjust the plans to current developments. Policy problems did not always arise at the beginning of the calendar year. Government officials were constantly watching developments, and changes in specific conditions required revisions of policy decisions. In the course of a year, new projects were presented and either approved or rejected, import and export licensing was adjusted to changes in availabilities and prices; rations were increased when supplies became greater than had been expected. These day-by-day decisions, however, tended to be made in the framework of the long-term plans and annual budgets, and to be reflected in the next annual budget.

6

Results Achieved: 1946-1948

The ambitious plans made in 1946 for a high level of investment, restricted increases in consumption, rapidly expanding output, and large import surpluses were approximately realized during the period from 1946 to 1948. As indicated by the comparison of plans and results presented in this chapter, there were certain significant differences between actual developments and plans. On the whole, however, it appears that the basic objectives of the plan were being achieved.

The ultimate aim of the 1946 plan was to increase output, particularly in export sectors, in order to support the growing population at prewar living standards. The increase was to be achieved by a heavy investment program, more than half of which would have to be financed by import surpluses. In order to release resources for investment, increases in consumption would have to be restricted severely. The planned increases in output, and the planned investment program necessary to achieve these increases, constituted the real goals of the 1946 program. Large import surpluses and restricted increases in consumption were means of achieving these goals.

It is abundantly clear that output increased much more rapidly from 1946 to 1948 than had been expected. Data available at the end of 1946 indicated that output had risen that year to about 95 per cent of the 1939 level,[1] which was far greater than expectations at the beginning of the year. In the 1947 budget, the emphasis shifted from restoration of prewar productive capacity to the need for raising output above the prewar level in order to support the growing population. Investment was needed not only to restore productive capacity but also to expand capacity.

The plan for the period 1946–50, which was formulated early in

[1] Since there are no final revised estimates for output in 1945, the exact increase in 1946 cannot be stated.

1946, aimed at an annual average increase of 5 per cent in output. The latest estimates that are now available indicate that net national product rose by 14 per cent in 1947 and by 4 per cent in 1948. Unemployment in 1946 was already negligible, i.e., less than 1 per cent. On the average, output increased faster than planned, and in both years the increases in output were much greater than had been estimated in the annual budgets.[2] In 1948, however, the inauguration of the Marshall Plan changed the basis for estimates of output.

The latest estimates now available show that output in the period from 1946 to 1948 not only increased much more rapidly than had been expected, but also was much higher compared with prewar output and much larger absolutely than was realized at the time. The latest estimates of 1946 output, at 1946 prices, are about 40 per cent higher than those made from 1946 to 1948. The new estimates for the postwar years are not only much higher than the old estimates at postwar prices; when measured in constant prewar prices, they are also considerably higher than the old estimates compared with the prewar levels. Present estimates indicate that output in 1946 was not 4 or 5 per cent below output in 1939, as had been estimated at the end of 1946, but was 4 per cent higher than in 1939.[3]

Clearly, then, the 1946 plan and the 1947 and 1948 budgets were based on an incorrect picture of the situation at that time, and when compared with prewar years. The essence of the 1946 plan, however, was not in the measurement of the absolute level of output or of output compared with prewar output. The plan was essentially to achieve certain increases in output above the 1945 level. Specific output goals in terms of tonnage, kilowatt hours, and cubic meters were stated, and the annual budgets referred to output goals by sectors in these terms. Even in 1946, excellent data were available on the major commodities, such as production of ores and metals, the timber cut,

[2] The 1947 budget estimated about a 6–7 per cent increase in net national product, and the very pessimistic 1948 budget, an increase of less than a ½ per cent. The 1947 budget assumed that a 6–7 per cent increase in output would raise output in 1947 to 3 per cent above the 1939 level.

[3] The 1946 plan was worked out early in 1946 in the belief that 1946 output would be about 13 per cent below the 1939 volume. At current prices net national product was estimated at 6.7 billion kroner for 1946. The new data show net national product in 1946 of 9.3 billion kroner, with the volume 4 per cent above 1939 and 9 per cent above 1938. Output was grossly underestimated early in 1946, particularly compared to prewar output.

the fish catch, the tonnage of the merchant fleet, pulp and paper output, and electric power production; and these data show that by 1948 the increase in output of these goods and services was greater than had been expected in 1945 and in the 1946 plan. The fact that the output of certain goods and services was underestimated was not of crucial importance.[4]

The fact that output was rising more than expected up to and including 1948 did not assure a continuation of rapid output increases. In late 1947 and early 1948, inability to finance import surpluses of the planned magnitude seemed likely to interfere seriously with the program. The sterling claims of shipowners had been drawn down heavily in the early postwar years. Also, large credits had been negotiated, both government and private. Private credits had been received to finance new shipbuilding contracts in the United Kingdom and Sweden. The government had obtained large dollar credits from both the United States and Canada, notably from the Export-Import Bank of Washington.

According to estimates available late in 1946, the import surplus in 1946 was 750 million kroner,[5] and the 1947 budget aimed at financing a current deficit of 900 million kroner. But in that year there was an exchange crisis and a sharp curtailment of import licensing. Foreign-exchange reserves and credits were running out. Rising import prices, especially for ships, were exhausting foreign-exchange resources much more quickly than might have been expected in 1946. Furthermore, toward the end of 1947 the terms of trade, which had been at about the prewar level, began to deteriorate sharply, largely because freight rates were not keeping pace with import prices. At the end of the year, the deficit was estimated at 1,400 million kroner.

The 1948 budget indicated that the current deficit must be cut to about 600 million kroner. In real terms, a much greater volume of exports of goods and services would be needed to finance a given volume of imports because of the sharp deterioration in the terms of trade. In the course of 1948, however, especially after the initiation of the Marshall Plan, the outlook improved. Partly because the Marshall Plan led to such a change in outlook, the government published

---

[4] See the fuller discussion of this problem later in this chapter.

[5] Imports had not increased as rapidly as planned in 1946. Deliveries were slow. The transfer of imports to private hands also caused delays.

in September the first interim report on the budget, covering the first half year.[6] Although some $20 million of aid had been received late in the second quarter, actual imports had not been affected to any extent. But the fact that aid was being negotiated for 1948–49 and that exports were running higher encouraged the government to grant import licenses more freely. As a result, imports in 1948 were expected to be about 10 per cent higher in value than had been estimated in the budget.[7]

The latest available data show that import surpluses from 1946 to 1948 did not contribute as much in real terms as had been planned in 1946. This was due mainly to rising import prices which reduced the buying power of reserves and credits. The adverse shift in the terms of trade added to the problem by reducing the real buying power of current exports. Import surpluses at current prices, according to the latest estimates, averaged 900 million kroner per year from 1946 to 1948, which was close to the 1-billion kroner average of the 1946 plan; but at 1946 prices, the surpluses did not approach the goal of 1 billion kroner a year.[8] At 1946 prices the average import surplus for 1946 and 1947 was 600 million kroner, and in 1948 there was an export surplus of 200 million kroner.

The new data indicate that total available resources from 1946 to 1948 were higher than expected when the 1946 plan was prepared. The underestimation of the level of output and of the rate of increase in output more than offset the overoptimism on the resources to be provided by import surpluses. It is not surprising, therefore, that the latest estimates indicate both that the volume of investment carried out during these years was somewhat greater than planned, and that private consumption was higher compared with prewar years and increased more rapidly than planned.

Estimates available at the end of 1946 had indicated that the volume of investment in 1946 fell short of the goal, and the 1947 budget therefore had planned an increase of more than 50 per cent, so that the average for the two years would equal the 1946 goal. This increase was achieved in 1947, but prospects for 1948 indicated that a 25

---

[6] *Stortingsmelding nummer 50, 1948.*

[7] Since import prices were rising, the increase in volume would be less than 10 per cent.

[8] The import surplus at current prices was over 600 million kroner in 1946, over 1200 million kroner in 1947, and over 700 million kroner in 1948.

per cent cut would be essential even if there was almost no increase
in consumption. This cut did not prove to be necessary, however, because of the improved foreign-exchange outlook, and investment in
1948 remained at roughly the 1947 level.[9] Whether the cut in investment could have been met if no change had occurred is difficult to
say.[10]

The net investment goal of the 1946 program was 1.7 billion
kroner at 1946 prices, which was believed to mean investment equal
to twice the prewar volume, and a net investment rate of about 23
per cent. The estimates of investment available before 1952 indicate
that for the three years 1946–48 net investment had only averaged
about 1.3 billion kroner at 1946 prices, and for the two years 1947–48,
1.4 billion. The latest revised data indicate average net investment
from 1946 to 1948 of 1.8 billion kroner at 1946 prices, a volume of
investment about 84 per cent above prewar, and a net investment rate
of about 23 per cent. Investment in 1946 was much lower than in
the two later years, largely owing to delays in obtaining imports. The
average for 1947 and 1948 was more than double the prewar figure.[11]

The latest revised investment estimates are much higher than
estimates available either when the 1946 plan was drawn up or during
the years 1946–48. The differences between the revised estimates and
earlier data are due in part to better information on the physical
volume of investment and in part to changes in the methods of estimating the costs of a given volume of investment. According to the
old data, investment was below the target; according to the new data,
it was above. The old data are more nearly comparable to the planning figures. But it is also significant that the government succeeded
in raising investment to almost double the prewar volume and in
devoting about 23 per cent of the total output to net investment.

[9] Indications were that total net investment of only 1.3 billion kroner had
been realized in 1946. The 1947 budget called for investment of 2 billion in
order to reach the planned average of 1.7 billion kroner a year. The increase was
almost entirely in volume rather than in prices. The tendency from 1947 on
was to describe the goal as 1.7 billion kroner of public and private net investment. Public expenditures were divided into consumption and investment. In
the 1948 budget it was estimated that net investment had reached 2.1 billion
kroner in 1947 and that only 1.5 billion could be financed in 1948.

[10] See Tables 16 and 18 for investment according to the latest revised data
and for a comparison of investment results with annual budgets.

[11] The average is 206 on the base 1938 = 100; see Table 16.

Furthermore, the volume of investment in the priority sectors of shipping, whaling, electric power, and industries based on cheap power tended to be equal to or in excess of planned levels.

The 1946 plan as developed from 1946 to 1948 was not only to achieve a given volume of investment, but also to concentrate investment in the priority sectors. Investment demand was excessive, even in 1947. Both public authorities and private business wanted to carry out much more investment than could be financed. In 1947 the government was forced to cut proposed investment by at least 20 per cent because of scarcities of labor, materials, and foreign exchange; and direct controls were used to limit investment in nonpriority sectors.[12]

Ever since 1947, excessive investment demand has been considered a serious problem. The job of controlling the volume of investment has been difficult because of the huge pressure for both private and public investment. On the other hand, the ambitious plans for a large private investment program would have been completely impossible if private investment demand had not been sufficient. In a sense, maintenance of conditions necessary for promoting private investment was a *sine qua non* for the Norwegian recovery program. Very little was said about policies to encourage private investment in 1946; the assumption was that investment demand would be excessive, which proved to be the case.

The reasons for the high level of private investment demand are worth exploring; for the most part they operated throughout the recovery period. One important factor was the strength of the underlying investment opportunities, such as substantial undeveloped power resources and opportunities for expanding industries based on cheap power. Furthermore, a vast range of secondary manufacturing industries had never been established in Norway; some of these could produce efficiently for Norway's relatively small domestic market. But these underlying investment opportunities were not a sufficient condition for the postwar level of private investment demand. Wartime destruction also may explain some of the postwar investment

---

[12] The budget indicated that scarcities of labor, materials, and foreign exchange had made it necessary to reduce gross investment plans of private business and public authorities from 4 billion kroner to about 3.2 billion, of which 2.3 billion was private gross investment.

demand, although war losses were large in many European countries and did not lead to comparable investment pressure. Because of the underlying investment opportunities in Norway, however, the war may have provided more stimulus for investment there than in other countries.

Undoubtedly the most important factors underlying the strong private investment demand were the government's economic policies. The stabilization policy and continued inflationary pressure led to high profits in both export and domestic sectors.[13] Despite the high taxes on business incomes, there were considerable profits after taxes, and the policy on dividend limitation helped to channel these funds into investment. The low interest rate stimulated investment, particularly in housing and construction; and easy credit financed plans which otherwise might have fallen by the wayside.

High profits in export sectors obviously followed from the stabilization policy. In domestic sectors, the inflationary pressure and the scarcity of basic imported consumer goods led to substantial increases in demand. The price-control authorities were aiming at profit margins at the April 1940 levels, but profits continued high for a number of reasons. In some cases, the government wanted to stimulate output and deliberately raised prices and profits. For many domestically produced goods and services, constant prices meant much larger profits because of the full use of capacity. In other cases higher prices were permitted, or prices were hard to control. The higher prices of non-basic items helped to mop up purchasing power.

High profits meant high taxes. This tended to increase investment expenditures which could be considered deductible costs. Since all repair and maintenance expenditures were deductible, they tended to increase.[14] Rising import prices for equipment and machinery were not as much of a deterrent as they might have been because of a law dating back to the first World War which permitted special initial

[13] From 1946–48, commodity export prices were between 46 and 72 per cent higher than domestic wholesale prices, and they were 30 to 41 per cent higher than the average wage paid per man year; all these comparisons are based on indices with the 1938 average equalling 100 (see Table 11). Since forest and fish products were both exported largely after manufacture and processing, the average wage does not exaggerate the low domestic cost level even though wages in mining and manufacturing rose much less than in forestry and fishing.

[14] Repair and maintenance expenditures on houses were not deductible.

depreciation allowances when extraordinary prices were paid for equipment; for this purpose, all postwar prices were interpreted as "extraordinary." Certain major projects for plant expansion in export sectors benefited from special laws passed to give them generous depreciation allowances.

Subsidies on imported grain, feedingstuffs, and agricultural machinery, and on the building of silos, as well as consumer subsidies on milk and bread, helped to maintain farm incomes and stimulated investment in agriculture. The high price set for domestic grain was probably most important. Investment subsidies were granted to foresters and fishermen. The government also gave direct assistance in a number of other ways. It guaranteed certain loans and made direct loans to some firms. New agreements with foreign-owned companies made conditions attractive for expansion of capacity in Norway. In every case, the price set for the final product was important.

The Labor government's policies apparently did not cause businessmen and business firms to worry about investment to expand capacity. The fact that there was almost no nationalization was important. In addition, government officials helped to promote confidence; despite controls and high taxes, they convinced many firms that the aim was to encouarge private business to invest and expand output. Loans, guarantees, or import licenses that would encourage investment in an export- or import-saving sector were, on the whole, favored by the government.

Although nationalization of existing privately owned enterprises was not an important feature of the Labor Party program, it was considered suitable and desirable to have the government own and operate certain large industrial plants. The government took over from the Germans a few major enterprises, such as the Aardal aluminum plant, and set them up as independent government corporations. It also took over German-owned shares in the huge Norsk Hydro electrochemical plant. Plans for a government-owned steel mill were made in the early postliberation days. The government believed that it was impossible for private enterprise to raise at reasonable rates the capital for such huge undertakings; and it probably believed also that it could control investment and employment more easily with some major public enterprises.

The high investment demand in shipping was more a reflection of world economic conditions. Most of the ships were built abroad at costs unrelated to economic conditions in Norway. The normal routes of most Norwegian ships never touch Norway; operating expenditures are determined largely by cost levels abroad, and receipts reflect freight rates which are internationally determined. Norwegian internal policies, therefore, had less to do with profits in shipping than in other export sectors; nevertheless, depreciation and tax policies were important, and wages were in line with Norwegian wage levels.

The existence of a demand for investment that was much greater than could be permitted necessitated rigid controls. Import controls and controls over building and construction were both used — first, to keep total investment within the limits of available resources, and second, to ensure that the distribution of investment corresponded to the government's plans. The existence of tremendous excess demand made the first job more difficult than it might have been, but it made the second job somewhat more easy. High profits in export sectors and high investment demand helped to channel investment into priority sectors. High profits in domestic sectors ensured adequate demand in sectors that the government believed should have priority; in others, the investment demand had to be severely restricted.

Import controls were a quite effective means of controlling investment in new productive facilities, since Norway depended on imports for most of its heavy machinery and industrial equipment, all construction steel and equipment, trucks, tractors, large merchant ships, and whaling factories.[15] Domestic output included some power machinery, some electrical equipment, wire, and a few rolled-steel products; also some ship repairs and ship construction were carried on within the country.[16] There were, in addition, workshops where tools, nails, and spare parts were made and machinery was repaired. Some investment in new productive facilities could therefore be carried out without imported machinery and equipment. The government did not try to regulate the sale of machinery and equipment produced in Norway or of second-hand machines and equipment. Small enter-

[15] Immediately after the war, catcher boats for whaling also had to be imported.

[16] In the early years after the war, ships of 10,000 tons were the largest built in Norway. In recent years a few 30,000-ton vessels have been built.

prises invested in old machinery and some new equipment to produce such consumer goods as ashtrays, wrought-iron decorations, procelain and enamelware, and automobile spare parts. Most of the investment in these "ashtray" industries occurred from 1946 to 1948.

The controls over building involved both a licensing process and the allocation of important building materials. Since timber, cement, and bricks were available locally, and only construction steel was imported, the control over building was not as fully effective as the control over investment in machinery and equipment. But no large building, factory, apartment house, theater, or hotel could evade the controls, particularly in a country where there are few large towns.[17]

In view of the severe housing shortage and the generally high investment demand, it is not surprising that the controls were evaded in small ways; garages and additions to houses were constructed in the city, small cabins were built in the woods, silos and woodsheds were built on the farms. Repair and maintenance work on buildings was hard to control. While these small evasions led to the use of some timber and cement, the labor involved did not mean an equal reduction in alternative employment and much of the timber would otherwise not have been cut and sent to market. Most of these small buildings were built by the owners or farmers, or with spare-time help which otherwise would have been idle.

Under an act of July 1947, the government had power to control any construction project requiring three or more laborers. This made it possible to control all construction and helped somewhat with the problem of repair and maintenance of buildings. Equipment controls sufficed to control most private construction work, as distinct from private building activity. About three fourths of total construction, however, was state or municipal work on railroads, roads, dams, and power plants.

The problem of state and municipal building and construction was political. The pressure on Storting representatives for public works was intense. Many isolated communities demanded road connections with the interior and also electric power. The North wanted better communications with the South, partly for defense reasons. The destroyed towns pressed for quick rebuilding. The increasing population and more comprehensive medical and social insurance strained

[17] Only two towns today have a population of 100,000 or over.

the school and hospital systems. The roads and railroads required continued repair and maintenance because of damage from snow, ice, and avalanches.

The system of direct controls, though not completely effective, did result in a distribution of investment broadly corresponding to the government's plans. The 1947 and 1948 budgets specified detailed investment goals by sectors. The 1946 plan had only a few rough estimates. On the whole, the distribution of fixed investment corresponded fairly well to the 1947 and 1948 plans. The distribution of total investment between stocks and fixed investment did not, however.

The 1946 plan had estimated that restocking needs would absorb about 16 per cent of total net investment from 1946 to 1950;[18] but the 1947 budget estimated negligible investment in stocks, and the 1948 budget, slight disinvestment. According to the latest estimates, investment in stocks from 1946 to 1948 averaged about 22 per cent of total net investment.[19] Direct controls over imports, materials, production, and consumption did not succeed in preventing large accumulations of stocks during these years. The planning process was not thrown off as much as it might have been, however, because total output and total resource availabilities were so much higher than actually realized at the time that most of the planned fixed investment in 1947 and 1948 could be carried out in spite of the heavy accumulation of stocks. Net fixed investment in 1946, according to the latest estimates, was about 10 per cent above the prewar volume; in 1947 and 1948, it averaged 74 per cent above that in prewar years, which was fairly close to the volume increase that had been estimated in the 1946 plan.

The percentage distribution of planned net fixed investment by sectors for 1947 and 1948 (Table 5) shows the tremendous importance of shipping in the program. In 1947 shipping was planned at 26 per cent of net investment; and in 1948, with increasing emphasis on the need for quickly adding to foreign-exchange earnings, it was

[18] About 800–900 million kroner at 1939 prices, which would mean about 1.3 billion kroner at 1946 prices, was the 1946 estimate of the cost of investment in stocks.
[19] The average was 500 million kroner a year at current prices, and 400 million kroner a year at 1946 prices.

Table 5. Net fixed investment: percentage distribution by
sectors, as estimated in 1947 and 1948 budgets

	1947 budget	1948 budget
Agriculture	3.8	5.0
Forestry	0.3	0.8
Fishing	1.6	3.2
Whaling	4.4	2.2
Mining and manufacturing	15.2	14.8
Electric power	7.1	8.3
Shipping	25.8	36.3
Inland transport and communications	14.1	10.7
Housing	24.4	14.1
Miscellaneous	3.2	4.5
Total[a]	100.0	100.0

Source: Calculated directly from the data in the 1947 and 1948 national budgets.
For Norwegian titles and document numbers, see references in Chapter 5. Data
are for civilian investment (excluding stocks).

[a] Details may not add up to 100 per cent because of rounding.

planned at 36 per cent. Investment in whaling, fishing, and forestry
was relatively small, as was investment in electric power development.[20] Investment in mining and manufacturing, also directed at
expanding exports, was planned at about 15 per cent of total net
investment.

The two areas which would not directly increase output, and yet
for which planned net investment was relatively high, were housing
and inland transport. The destruction in western and northern Norway
necessitated a rapid rate of construction. The investment planned in
inland transport reflected not only the need to repair war damage,
but also the need for new construction, which would be expensive.[21]
The 1948 budget, however, called for a sharp cut from the 1947
budget in housing and inland transport investment, in order to concentrate more in export sectors.

Sector-by-sector comparisons of actual results with the 1947 and
1948 budget plans for investment are plagued by differences between
the data on which the plans were based and the revised data available
since 1952. The plans for carrying out given real projects were pre-

[20] Power development is slow and expensive in Norway, requiring long tunnels
through mountains in inaccessible mountain areas along the fjords.

[21] In a country like Norway, roads and railroads are extremely expensive to
build and, of course, to maintain.

sented as value estimates based on existing data. The revised data,
in some cases, reflect changes in measurement only, for example, in
classification or in depreciation estimates; in other cases, the changes
are based on revised estimates of the actual physical investment that
took place. The two sets of estimates for gross investment are more
comparable than the net investment estimates. For all types of investment, however, the revised data are higher than the earlier estimates.[22]

When all the statistical difficulties are considered, the revised data
indicate that the percentage distribution of gross fixed investment in
1947 and 1948 corresponded fairly well with the budget plans[23]
(Table 6). One factor to be borne in mind is that in 1948 the institu-
tion of the Marshall Plan permitted a rather sharp revision of the
plans that had been set forth in the original 1948 budget. In terms
of real resources, investment in housing and miscellaneous buildings,
partly in repairs and maintenance, was considerably greater than was
planned or realized at the time. To a large extent, the unplanned, or
unrealized, investment was carried out with domestic materials and
by the use of labor which did not reduce the labor supply to other
sectors.

[22] The classification of investment by sectors is slightly different in the revised
data; for example, the revised data put all transport equipment under the sector
using it, whereas previously it had been classified under transport.

The revised data show that both total gross and total net investment are 22
per cent higher than the 1948 estimates. The differences, therefore, are not only
in depreciation estimates. Furthermore, the revised data show higher investment
in almost every sector. Also, gross investment in each type of fixed asset —
buildings, construction, and equipment — are from 21 to 23 per cent higher in
the revised data.

The revised data indicate relatively higher gross investment in power, housing,
shipping, and miscellaneous business and public buildings. Only in housing and
miscellaneous building is net investment also relatively much higher according to
the revised data. Investment in inland transport is relatively smaller because
previous data based on public expenditures were quite complete.

The gross investment estimates are higher mostly because repair and
maintenance, both on buildings and equipment, were apparently underestimated.

[23] Comparison of the percentage distribution of value estimates at current
prices is at best a rough indication of how plans worked out. Changes in
relative prices and costs lead to shifts in such percentages even when the real
programs are stable. Small changes in plans during the year in an unimportant
sector may double or cut in half the percentage of total investment planned
to be devoted to this sector. Percentages of actual realized investment in all
sectors are affected by any large deviation from plans in any single sector.

Table 6. Planned and actual percentage distribution of gross fixed investment
by sectors, 1946–1948

	1946	1947		1948	
	Actual	Budget	Actual	Budget	Actual
Agriculture.................	7.7	4.7	6.0	8.7	6.7
Forestry...................	0.4	0.6	0.4	0.6	0.5
Fishing....................	2.1	1.4	2.1	2.7	2.1
Whaling...................	1.4	3.4	3.2	3.3	2.9
Mining and manufacturing...	15.1	15.9	17.0	17.8	19.4
Electric power production....	5.1	5.5	5.2	5.2	6.1
Shipping..................	22.5	23.0	24.3	25.3	23.7
Other transport and communi-cations..................	17.0	21.1	14.3	16.8	13.5
Housing...................	18.4	20.6	17.7	15.0	15.5
Miscellaneous..............	10.3	3.7	9.7	4.6	9.4
Total[a].................	100.0	100.0	100.0	100.0	100.0

Source: Actual data from *National Accounts, 1930–39 and 1946–51* (Central
Bureau of Statistics, 1952). Budget data calculated from the actual budgets. See
references to exact titles and document numbers in Chapter 5. Data cover civilian
investment (excluding stocks).

[a] Details may not add up to 100 per cent because of rounding.

Norwegian economists and government officials were greatly concerned then, and they still emphasize, the misallocation of resources
involved in the unplanned investment. Clearly, more effective controls
could have diverted even more labor and materials to priority building
and investment. On the whole, however, it appears that the unplanned
investment was not too wasteful of men or materials. To be sure,
there was some unplanned investment in the "ashtray" industries,
but most of the unplanned investment in miscellaneous building and
repair work was essential and reasonable, though postponable.

The fact that planned investment was the heart of the recovery
program, and also the fact that the planned volume and distribution
of investment were both approximately achieved after 1946, are
essential background information against which to review the plans
(and results) concerning the use of resources for private consumption.
The 1946 plan called for severely restricted consumption increases
in order to release resources for investment. The restriction of increases in consumption was definitely a means to an end, but not an
end in itself.

The 1946 plan assumed that private consumption could increase
by only 10 per cent in the entire period from 1946 to 1951; the latest

revised data indicate that private consumption rose by 10 per cent in 1947 alone, and by a further 2 per cent in 1948,[24] which was considerably more than had been planned (Table 22). However, the increases in consumption apparently were not seriously interfering with the over-all recovery program, for available resources were increasing more rapidly than had been expected and the investment program was being carried out according to plans.

The actual increases in consumption must be analyzed commodity by commodity to determine whether consumption increases hindered a much higher rate of investment. The purpose of restricting consumption was to release for investment such scarce resources as foreign exchange (which was the most important factor), skilled labor, construction labor, and building materials. If the restrictions on consumption had been greater, would these scarce resources have been released for investment?[25]

During the years from 1946 to 1948, the government believed that consumption was increasing too rapidly and that the level of investment was tending to fall below plans. It seemed clear that the prewar consumption level was being restored well ahead of schedule; data available at the time indicated that prior to 1951, per capita consumption would equal the prewar level.[26] There was no indication, however, of the true extent of the improvement in total consumption compared with prewar. According to the latest data now available, total private consumption in 1946 was 9 per cent above the prewar level, and in 1948, 22 per cent above. Per capita consumption was slightly above prewar in 1946, and 12 per cent above in 1948.

But the comparison with prewar years, though significant, confuses the picture. For a specified list of commodities, including almost all basic items of food and clothing as well as beverages and tobacco,

[24] The 1946 plan assumed that total consumption in 1946 was about 90 per cent of prewar; the revised data indicate that it actually was 9 per cent above prewar. See Tables 22 and 24.

[25] Presumably, even if consumption had been kept down, the government would not have sought to reduce import surpluses so long as investment was believed to be somewhat below the planned level and financing was available.

[26] Private consumption, according to data then available, had risen faster than planned; in 1946, total private consumption was about 93 per cent, and per capita consumption was estimated at 89 per cent, of the 1939 level. The 1947 budget called for a further increase in consumption in 1947, to the 1939 level. But the rapid rise in population from prewar years indicated that per capita consumption in 1947 would be 95 per cent of prewar.

the government had complete data even in 1947 and 1948. On the basis of these data, the government believed that the amount of these commodities consumed in 1946 was about 5 per cent below the prewar average; recent calculations, in contrast, indicate that the amount was 9 per cent above prewar. Consumption of these specified items in 1948 was calculated as a little above prewar; it is now estimated to have been 16 per cent above.[27] The problem appears to be one of index number calculation rather than underestimation at the time of prewar consumption of these goods.

Table 7. Value and volume of private consumption in 1948: total and commodity distribution, comparison of revised and unrevised data

	Value of consumption 1948 prices		Volume of consumption 1938 = 100
	Unrevised data	Revised data	Revised data
	(millions of kroner)		
Specified basic items			
Food...................	2182	2344	114
Beverages..............	597	563	143
Tobacco................	337	341	147
Textiles................	813	863[b]	106
Footwear..............	169	150[c]	102
Total................	4098	4261	116
All other.................	3128[a]	4358	131
Total, uncorrected...........	n.a.	8619	123
Correction................	n.a.	223[d]	
Corrected total..............	7226	8396	122

Source: Revised data from *National Accounts, 1930–39 and 1946–51*. Old data from *Nasjonalbudsjettet 1950, Stortingsmelding nummer 1, 1950*.

[a] A rough total estimate. For purposes of comparison, a 264 million estimate for soap, radio, and imported fuels is included in the "all other" sector. The correction was not given separately.

[b] Excludes sewing and sewing repairs.

[c] Excludes rubber footwear and shoe repairs.

[d] Correction for stocks, consumption of Norwegians abroad and of foreigners in Norway, and one or two other minor items.

Food accounted for half the total of these specified items in 1948, and total food consumption is now estimated to have been 14 per cent above prewar in 1948 and per capita food consumption almost 4 per cent above prewar (Table 24). Again there seems to be an index

[27] See Table 7. The increase would be more like 10 per cent if 1948 rather than 1938 weights were used. Population was 10 per cent higher than in 1938.

number problem, however, since the government, and the average Norwegian, knew at the time that per capita consumption of flour, bread, cheese, margarine, sugar, coffee, meat, bacon, eggs, fruit, and chocolate were all below prewar. Consumption of potatoes, vegetables, fish, milk, and butter were above prewar. The food standard of living was well below prewar if account is taken of lack of free choice. Per capita consumption of textiles and footwear were below prewar in spite of the severely depleted consumer stocks. The volume of tobacco consumed per person had increased sharply, however. In general, the quality of consumer goods was below prewar and the composition of consumption was not in accordance with consumer wants.

Not only was consumption of basic items high when compared with the prewar average, but the rate of increase was high. The increase in the consumption of foods was based on domestic output. Imported feedstuffs and tractors led to unexpectedly large increases in output. Total food consumption rose from 3 per cent above prewar in 1946 to 14 per cent above in 1948. Consumption of imported foods such as chocolate, sugar, rice, coffee, and tea was severely restricted. Rations of chocolate, coffee, and sugar were increased slightly, however, from 1946 to 1948. Most beverages were domestically produced with materials produced at home. Tobacco and rubber and textile materials were imported. The volume of tobacco consumption actually fell slightly from 1946 to 1948 but was very high compared to prewar. Clothing and footwear consumption rose rapidly from 90 per cent of prewar to 107 per cent. On the whole, however, the increased consumption of basic food and clothing items from 1946 to 1948 did not seriously interfere with the diversion of scarce foreign-exchange resources to investment.[28]

It would seem reasonable to expect government controls over consumption to have been effective in Norway. The country depended on imports for most of its grain and feedstuffs, for all sugar, coffee, rubber, and most textile materials, for tobacco, drugs, gasoline, and many durable consumer goods, such as automobiles, and, until recently, for refrigerators and washing machines. Import controls on machinery and equipment could presumably regulate investment in domestic consumer-goods industries. Some important consumer goods were produced domestically, for example, bicycles, kitchen ranges,

[28] See Table 24 for volume of consumption indices.

pots and pans, glassware, china, pottery, electrical equipment, furniture, firewood, soap, radios, beer, and aquavit. And of course most services were produced at home.

But as revised data show, consumption of items other than food, beverages, tobacco, and clothing increased rapidly in the early postwar years in spite of government efforts to restrain consumption. The government apparently believed at the time that total consumption of goods and services other than the "specified" items was about at the prewar level in 1947 and 1948. The revised data indicate the 1948 volume of consumption of such goods and services was 31 per cent above the 1938 level (Table 8). Most of the increase was in

Table 8. Value and volume of private consumption in 1948: revised data for goods and services not specified in unrevised data

	Value (millions of kroner)	Volume[a] 1938 = 100
TOTAL...............................	4358	131
Goods		
Fuel, excluding electricity...............	241	93
Durable household goods................	593	132
Nondurable household goods............	163	217
Rubber footwear.......................	41	88
Drugs................................	61	n.a.
Cosmetics............................	73	99
Cars, bicycles.........................	62	13
Books and magazines..................	203	156
Radios, music, toys, etc................	224	199
Other................................	184	127
	1845	128
Services		
Rents................................	476	105
Domestic.............................	162	62
Other................................	1876	164
	2514	132

Source: *National Accounts, 1930–39 and 1946–51.*
[a] Based on 1938 price weights.

domestically produced goods and services, however, and the real resources involved were much less than would appear at first sight.

As far as goods, as distinct from services, are concerned, investment controls prevented any substantial expansion of plant capacity, and controls over raw-material imports were extremely effective. The largest increases were chiefly in domestically produced goods, i.e., household goods, books and magazines, radios, music, toys, and certain other small items (Table 8); these did not require any substantial plant capacity or depend to any extent on imported raw materials. Also, there was some use of scarce labor and second-hand equipment in the so-called "ashtray" industries, small shops producing miscellaneous household items of wood, paper, plastics, glass, porcelain, wrought iron, and pewter. Probably the use of scarce resources in the production of these items was not serious, however, or in proportion to their value.[29]

As far as consumer services are concerned, the increased volume of consumption in most cases involved some increase in employment but very little use of other resources.[30] The increase in the volume of consumption was high compared with the addition to the numbers employed. Total employment in the sectors producing services, other than housework, in 1948 was 36 per cent, and the volume of consumption 64 per cent above the 1938 average (Table 9). And the mass of the workers were in such sectors as electric power and transport, producing services primarily for industry and commerce.[31] In the sectors producing only consumer services, the volume of consumption in most cases increased about twice as fast as employment. Investment in hotels, restaurants, and cinemas as well as investment

[29] Production statistics at the time did not cover shops employing less than 5 persons. Output estimates in the national accounts for these small shops were too small. These goods amounted to 1,845 million kroner, or 22 per cent of consumption, in 1948. They were relatively high priced and not subsidized as were many of the basic food and textile items. Their prices were not held down so closely to costs, and were much harder to control. In 1938, these same goods amounted to only 19 per cent of total consumption.

[30] The numbers in domestic service had decreased from 128 thousand in 1938 to 91 thousand in 1948. See above discussion on investment on rents and the housing problem.

[31] Transport and communications services were from about 60 to 80 per cent for business and government, education 92 per cent for the government in 1948. From 1938 to 1948 the sale of electricity to consumers increased less than the sale to business but at a faster rate. On balance it seems unlikely that increased sale of services to consumers could have accounted for more than half of the total increase in employment, which would mean an 18 per cent increase in employment compared with a 64 per cent increase in the volume of consumption.

Table 9. Revised data for value and volume of consumption of miscellaneous services in 1938 and 1948 and employment in related producing sector

| Services | 1948 consumption | | Employment in related producing sector | | |
	Value (millions of kroner)	Volume[a] 1938 = 100	1938	1948 (thousands)	Index, 1948 1938 = 100
Electricity.............	170	390	6.9	9.4	136
Public transport	374	202	44.8	61.7	138
Hotels, restaurants, and boarding houses......	189	127	23.0	26.2	114
Post, telephone, and telegraph...........	52	167	15.1	24.1	159
Banking and insurance..	266	132	11.6	16.0	138
Schools...............	32	85 ⎤			
Entertainment.........	70	166 ⎟			
Beauty services........	57	187 ⎬	10.4	14.1	136
Medical care..........	257	114 ⎟			
Other personal services..	108	123 ⎦			
Sewing and repairs.....	150	n.a.			
Shoe repairs..........	83	141			
Maintenance of cars and bicycles.............	69	143			
Total............	1876	164	111.8	151.5	136

Source: *National Accounts, 1930–39 and 1946–51.*
[a] Calculated with 1938 price weights.

in transport and power facilities was strictly limited and effectively controlled.[32]

The increase over the prewar level in the volume of services consumed represented to a large extent increased output resulting from better or fuller use of existing facilities, such as railroads, hotels, and cinemas. In these areas, the increases in the volume of consumption were most out of line with the increases in employment. Except for the public transport sector, these service industries use relatively small amounts of materials. Little was lost, therefore, from failing to realize the extent of the increase in the volume of consumption of these services.

[32] There was little, if any, investment in the postwar period for the purpose of increasing consumer services. Schools, theaters, and hospitals were built only in cases of extreme need, usually only to replace destroyed facilities. A few new hotels were built for tourist traffic. Power development was generally geared to industrial needs. Investment in transportation was limited to essential transport facilities.

The extensive increases in private consumption of domestically produced goods and services appear to have been in sectors employing relatively little of the scarce real resources. Private consumption of food rose sharply in 1946 and 1947, partly because imported feed-stuffs and tractors produced unexpectedly large increases in agricultural output. Consumers, unable to obtain basic commodities, spent an unusual share of their incomes on cinemas, train trips, restaurants, and some domestically produced articles, such as pottery and wrought-iron work. The pattern of consumption was abnormal and clearly not in accordance with consumer needs and wants. But the spill-over expenditures from controlled basic items to less-controlled goods and services helped to reduce inflationary pressures. While there was clearly some misallocation of resources, it was not enough to interfere seriously with the basic investment and recovery program.

A comparison of the actual developments from 1946 to 1948 with the 1946 plan for resource availabilities and uses suggests that, in spite of difficulties which seemed serious at the time, the principal goals were achieved.[33] Output increased faster than had been estimated, but investment was at about the expected level after 1946. Import surpluses did not contribute as much to financing investment as had been planned; but even so, the investment program was substantially carried out and private consumption rose much more rapidly than had been considered possible. Data now available show that output increased much faster than had been expected, and was so much higher than was realized at the time, that it much more than offset the effects of import surpluses that were lower than estimated.

In late 1947 and early 1948 it seemed clear that the recovery program had been proceeding quite successfully. Investment was not quite up to plans, but a high proportion of resources was being devoted to investment. Investment was leading to speedy reconstruction of the merchant, whaling, and fishing fleets, and to rapid development of electric power. Consumption was being restricted, at least consumption of imported goods or goods with a high import content, and the level of consumption was still believed to be close to the prewar level in spite of rather rapid increases. The combination of inflationary pressures and direct controls probably seemed a more

[33] For full statistical tables covering the period 1946 to 1952, see Chapters 8 to 12.

desirable state of affairs to Norwegian government officials in 1948 than it had in 1946 even though they were having difficulties in carrying out the domestic stabilization policy. The really serious problem seemed to be the inability to raise sufficient foreign loans to meet balance-of-payments deficits of the size contemplated in the plan. Rising import prices reduced the real purchasing power of reserves and credits, and an adverse shift in the terms of trade reduced the real purchasing power of current exports of goods and services.

7

The 1948 Four-Year Plan

The inauguration of the Marshall Plan in 1948 meant that the chief bottleneck which Norway seemed to be encountering in continuing to carry out its 1946 plan would be solved. It is not surprising, therefore, that the government decided it could proceed with a program along the lines of its original plan. The proportion of total output devoted to investment would have to continue to be high. The need to develop productive capacity was greater than had been realized in 1946. The steadily growing population could be supported at prewar living standards, according to government estimates, only if productive capacity in export sectors could be increased enough to offset the deterioration in the international terms of trade which had occurred since 1946. Private consumption still had to be restricted to release scarce resources for investment.

The administration had promised the Storting as early as 1947 that it would work out a fuller long-term plan to provide a framework for future annual budgets. The countries cooperating in the Marshall Plan, furthermore, agreed that each country, assuming aid would be made available, would prepare a program for reaching balance-of-payments equilibrium at a reasonable standard of living by 1952–53. The work which the administration had been initiating for its own planning purposes was quickly completed and fitted into the agreed upon pattern.

The government accepted quite literally the advice to prepare a program for viability at a decent standard of living, assuming that sufficient aid would be available to carry out such a program. Norway expected from 80 million to 100 million dollars of aid in the fiscal year 1948–49 and believed it would receive a larger amount of aid during the following year, after it had exhausted its dollar loans. At the outset, the government had not wanted to ask for any Marshall aid, and later it had said that it would need only a small amount for a year or so. But as the terms of trade became more unfavorable and foreign credits more difficult to obtain, the government became convinced that the country needed a substantial amount of aid.

The experience with long-range planning and annual budgets from 1946 to 1948 meant that the new long-term program could be more complete than the 1946 plan. The data available were much fuller than those available in 1946. It must be remembered, however, that the revised national accounts estimates that were published in 1952 had not even begun to be usable at this time. The 1948 plan was based on a picture of the Norwegian economy and of how it had progressed from 1946 to 1948 which was not completely accurate. The current levels of output, investment, and especially of consumption were seriously underestimated, both absolutely and in comparison with prewar levels.

In September 1948, the Minister of Commerce outlined the rationale of the new long-term program.[1] The starting point was an estimate of the foreign-exchange earnings needed to restore 1938 per capita consumption. The population in 1948 was already about 10 per cent above the prewar level and it was expected that by 1952 it would be 14 per cent above. The increase in population alone would necessitate a higher volume of imports. The extra imports needed would cost 400 million kroner at 1948 prices. In addition, the terms of trade had deteriorated by 12 per cent from 1938 to 1948. Since, at the 1948 terms of trade, it would take an additional 500 million kroner in export earnings to buy the 1938 volume of imports, it was essential that the program aim at increasing exports of goods and services enough to earn in 1952 about 1 billion kroner more than in 1938, at 1948 prices.

The government had considered each sector of the economy and possible ways in which net foreign-exchange earnings might be increased. It had decided that the primary emphasis would be on expanding exports of goods and services, but that in some cases Norwegian dependence on imports could be reduced. The additional net foreign-exchange earnings of 1 billion kroner could be achieved if net investment of 9–10 billion kroner at 1948 prices could be carried out

[1] Address, delivered by Minister Erik Brofoss on September 30, 1948, at Oslo Chamber of Commerce.

from 1949 to 1952, i.e., net investment of about 2¼ billion kroner per year.

The aim was to raise domestic savings from the then estimated 10 per cent of net national product in 1948 to 12 per cent.[2] Imports of capital of 1.1 billion 1948 kroner a year (or 220 million dollars at the current exchange rate) would also be required. Half of the planned investment program would have to be financed by import surpluses. An inflow of capital of about 150 million kroner a year even after 1952–53 would be necessary for continued economic development.

In the fall of 1948 the Norwegian government submitted to the Organization for European Economic Cooperation its "long-term program" (for the years 1949–52), which was worked out precisely along these lines.[3] It presented a plan for increases in investment and output, sector by sector, which in 1952 would yield the needed 1 billion kroner in foreign-exchange earnings. The program outlined gross civilian investment goals, sector by sector, which would cost 4.2 billion 1948 kroner per year.[4] Civilian net investment would be 2.1 billion. This investment program was expected to make possible a 15–20 per cent increase in total output by 1952–53, and a 25–30 per cent increase in the volume of exports. It was estimated that per capita consumption, believed to be below prewar in 1948, would reach the prewar level by the end of 1952.

Although the program was in terms of the volume of investment needed to achieve given increases in output and exports, it can be translated into assumed investment rates. Gross national product in 1948 was about 11.6 billion kroner, according to estimates available at the time, and net national product was 9.5 billion. If gross and net national product both rose 15 per cent by 1952, the average gross investment rate over the period 1949–52 would be 33 per cent, and the net investment rate 23 per cent. Domestic savings and the import surplus would each be about 12 per cent of net national product.

The essential similarity with the 1946 plan is abundantly clear.

[2] The domestic savings rate was then estimated to have averaged about 8 per cent from 1935–39.

[3] The program was published in English in the *Interim Report on the European Recovery Program*, vol. II (Paris: Organization for European Economic Cooperation, December 30, 1948).

[4] This is the total for civilian gross investment, both public and private.

Although the starting point in 1948 differed from that of the 1946 plan, there was a basic continuity of goals and means. The investment rates contemplated were approximately those of the 1946 plan. The hoped for absolute volume of investment was less than that in the 1946 plan, but above the then estimated 1948 level.[5] Huge import surpluses would be relied on again to finance half of the net investment program.

Per capita consumption at least equal to that of prewar years was the goal for 1952–53. Under the 1946 plan, the goal for 1951 had been total consumption equal to that of prewar years, or per capita consumption below the prewar level. The increasing awareness of the population increase led to stress being placed on per capita consumption goals rather than on total consumption. But the program was about as strict as the 1946 plan. The assumed increase over a period of four years was about 10–15 per cent; the 1946 plan had called for a 10 per cent increase in an equal period of time. More emphasis was placed on the need for increasing the consumption of basic food and clothing in order to eliminate rationing. In general, it was emphasized that inflationary pressure in the consumer goods sphere must be eliminated.

The discussion of the public use of goods and services was based on a sharp distinction between public consumption, including defense consumption of goods and services, and public investment. Public consumption had to be held at the 1948 level. The attitude toward public investment depended on the type of investment.

This program was bold and ambitious. To continue for several years more the existing program for restricting private consumption would be difficult. The planned investment rates were almost unprecedented. The average annual aid assumed was much greater than the amount expected in 1948–49. If the plan had not been essentially the same as the one that had been prepared in 1946, it might have appeared that it was designed to make a case for increased aid.

The continuity with the 1946 plan was striking also in respect to the stabilization program and monetary and fiscal policy. It was stated that the price-stabilization policy not only had avoided a wage-

[5] Net civilian investment of 2.1 billion kroner at 1948 prices was less than private net investment of 1.7 billion at 1946 prices, as contemplated in the 1946 plan.

price spiral but also had created a buffer for Norway against a fall
in world prices. If world prices should fall, the internal price and
wage structure could be maintained and subsidies reduced. The government explained its program for the gradual elimination of inflationary pressure, the gradual reduction of private bank reserves, and a
reduction of the occupation debt. The desire was to eliminate detailed
direct controls gradually. The low interest rate policy and the program for high public savings would be continued.

The balance-of-payments implications of the program were not
spelled out in terms of year-by-year commodity and service forecasts.
The plan seemed to be to have huge current deficits for four years,
and then reduce the annual current deficit to about 150 million
kroner, or 30 million dollars. Sharp cuts in imports would be possible
by 1952–53, and the planned increase in exports would tend to be
concentrated in the later years. The implication was that there would
not be a steady and sharp reduction in the current deficit year by
year from 1949 to 1952, since the assumed average deficit was about
at the level being planned for the calendar year 1949.

The assumption of more or less constant current deficits proved to
be out of line with the tapered aid philosophy which grew up in the
course of administering Marshall Plan aid. At the time the program
was prepared, no such philosophy had been stated. Some countries
probably assumed that aid appropriations would tend to decrease as
the years went by, and that the wise course was to plan on obtaining
as much aid and imports as possible in the early years. In some
countries this led to rather sharp increases in consumer imports in an
effort to improve worker morale and to eliminate direct controls
quickly. It also led to pushing forward certain big investment projects.

Although interpretations of the motives and underlying philosophies
of governments are risky, it appears that the Norwegian government's
approach was quite the opposite. Its basic idea was that aid should
not be used to raise consumption levels. The administration believed
that investment was the key to increases in output and in the
standard of living. Direct controls were not believed to be seriously
interfering with the recovery program. It was agreed that they had
to be eliminated eventually, but quick action was not essential. The
investment rate was already about as high as Norway could manage.
There was overfull employment and a lack of skilled labor and

construction materials. Current deficits were already large for such a small country. All of these considerations suggested that Norway should use aid merely to continue along the lines of her original plans. Sudden increases in consumption and investment were not feasible or reasonable.

It is unlikely that more aid would have been allocated to Norway in the early years of the Marshall Plan even if the government had embarked quickly on a program of elimination of trade controls, substantial consumer goods imports, and more rapid elimination of internal direct controls. The result of such a program would have been increased consumption, probably at the expense of investment and of a more rapid rate of development.

The planned distribution of investment for the years 1949 to 1952 was worked out largely on the basis of the original 1946 program and the experience gained in carrying out that program. The percentage distribution of investment differed somewhat from that in the 1947 and 1948 national budgets, partly because of the actual progress which had been made in meeting certain targets[6] (Table 10). By the

Table 10. Comparison of percentage distribution of gross fixed investment by sectors in the 1948 program and in the 1947 and 1948 budgets

Sector	1947 budget	1948 budget	Fall of 1948 program
Agriculture	4.7	8.7	6.8
Forestry	0.6	0.6	0.6
Fishing	1.4	2.7	3.6
Whaling	3.4	3.3	1.5
Mining and manufacturing	15.9	17.8	22.8
Electric power	5.5	5.2	5.1
Shipping	23.0	25.3	22.8
Other transport	21.1	16.8	16.6
Housing	20.6	15.0	13.9
Miscellaneous	3.7	4.6	6.4
Total[a]	100.0	100.0	100.0

Source: Data for civilian investment (excluding stocks) from original documents (cited in footnotes in Chapters 5 and 7).

[a] Details may not add to 100 per cent because of rounding.

[6] Comparison is made with the budgets, rather than with actual investment in 1947 and 1948, because the purpose is to show how the plans differed. Furthermore, the distribution of actual investment, according to the revised data since 1952, cannot be readily compared with plans that were based on the data available at the time.

fall of 1948, the whaling fleet had been pretty much restored. Transport and housing investment had been high in the immediate reconstruction period.

Electric power development and merchant shipping continued to be the two pillars on which the structure was based. Although by the end of 1948 the fleet would be restored to its prewar size, the plan was to raise it 20 per cent above the prewar level. The ability of the merchant fleet to earn both sterling and dollars led to the emphasis on merchant shipping. Also, relatively lower freight rates reduced net earnings per ton compared to 1946 and 1947. In spite of the planned rapid expansion of the fleet, investment in shipping would not quite reach 25 per cent of total gross investment, as assumed in the pessimistic 1948 budget, but would be about at the 1947 budget figure of 23 per cent. The annual increase in tonnage would be less than in 1948.

The program indicated that the proportion of total investment alloted to power development would be about the same as in the 1947 and 1948 budgets, but that investment in industries based on cheap power would be given a greater relative weight. The rate of power development was as fast as the government believed technically feasible. The investment in mining and manufacturing (expected to be about 15 per cent higher in volume than in 1948) would be concentrated in the electrochemical and electrometallurgical industries.

It was stated that expansion of the pulp and paper industry would not be reasonable because the timber cut, at the full annual rate of growth, could not supply sufficient raw material to operate existing pulp and paper mills at anywhere near capacity. Therefore, investment must be aimed at increasing productivity and modernization, but not at expansion. More investment in forestry was needed merely to maintain the cut. The program also called for relatively more investment in fishing, with emphasis on larger power-driven boats and more modern equipment, rather than on expanding the fleet. An expansion of fish processing plants was advocated.

In industries producing for the domestic market, investment would be allowed for modernization and rationalization of existing capacity, but not for expansion, except in rare cases. In the textile industry, however, some expansion had already been planned, despite opposition from certain policy makers. The introduction of modern methods in agriculture would make possible an expansion of output for the domestic market, which would reduce imports. The pressure for more self-sufficiency in basic foods is explained in part by the experience during the years of occupation and also during the first World War; but the political strength of the farmers was also important.

The increase in the 1948 program in the proportion of investment in the miscellaneous sector reflected political pressure for schools, hospitals, cinemas, town halls, roads, and railroads. Although the housing shortage in 1948 was no less acute than in 1946, since total construction had not kept up with new family formation since the war, the 1948 plan did not call for an increase in investment in housing. Housing construction would continue at the 1948 level.

The program prepared in late 1948 clearly reflected the government's experience with planning since 1946. The government was convinced that it could continue to achieve steady increases in output. The stabilization policy and inflationary pressures were resulting in full employment. Direct controls appeared to be obtaining approximately the results aimed at in terms of over-all investment and consumption, and also approximately the planned distribution of investment by sectors and of consumption by commodities. Inflationary pressures were beginning to decrease.

One point stressed was the importance of the actual terms of trade during the period covered by the plan. The assumption on which the plan was based was that the terms of trade would be, on the average, at the 1948 level, which was considerably less favorable than the 1938 level (Table 35). The effect of the adverse shift in the terms of trade on the volume of imports from 1946 to 1948 was all too clear.

It is tempting to wonder how the 1948 plan might have been altered if the national accounts estimates at that time had been the same as the revised estimates which appeared in 1952. The government's concern about misallocation of resources because of excessive investment in small buildings and repairs and increased consumption of domestically produced goods and services might have been much greater. The government might have planned on using even stricter controls over both consumption and investment. It might even have tried to keep consumption stable, cutting consumption of some domestically produced items.

The full data now available probably would, on balance, have confirmed the government's attitude that more of the same sort of planning would be good. The complete facts on output from 1946 to 1948, as well as on the absolute amount of investment being carried out, would have been encouraging. The nature of the 1948 plan would probably have been essentially the same.

Like most plans for the future, the 1948 plan assumed no violent changes in the world economic and political situation. Within a year, this assumption was out of date. The changes in the world situation were much greater than those from 1946 to 1948. Devaluation and the Korean war led to serious difficulties and problems for the Norwegian economy. The stabilization program was more obviously affected than the resource plans.

8

The Stabilization Program: 1949-1952

The difficulties encountered from 1946 to 1948 in carrying out the stabilization program had arisen primarily from rising world prices. Internal pressures for wage increases and higher farm prices had added to the problem. The principal difficulty encountered in the period from 1949 to 1952 was devaluation, which necessitated a serious revision of the program. Sharply rising world prices after the outbreak of the Korean war aggravated the situation. On the other hand, a gradual reduction of internal inflationary pressures from 1949 to 1952 helped to make the situation manageable. There was a moderate upward price adjustment, and a new stabilization line seemed to be reached in 1952.

The devaluation of the pound in September 1949 was a blow to the Norwegian stabilization policy. The government believed it had no alternative but to devalue its currency in the same proportion.[1] Such a large share of Norway's foreign transactions were in sterling that it was feared failure to follow the pound would cause trouble for exporters and shipowners. Norwegian export prices had fallen slightly in 1949, and profits were apparently lower in 1949 than they had been in 1948. Although exporters of goods and services had been making substantial profits since the war, maintenance of the value of the krone in the face of the 30 per cent devaluation of the pound and the probable devaluation of many other European currencies by about the same percentage could clearly wipe out substantial profit margins. Devaluation by a smaller percentage than the pound might have been reasonable, but the government was probably more impressed than it had been in 1945 with the difficulty of stabilizing internal prices and wages. Domestic prices and wages were likely to

[1] The krone rate was changed from 4.97 kroner to 7.14 kroner per dollar.

rise even if the krone was not devalued. But it was probably hoped that stable or falling world prices would mean that one of the factors leading to pressure on domestic prices would be less of a problem than it had been.

In view of the world price rises that occurred as a result of the Korean war and led to huge export profits, it may be argued in retrospect that Norway would have been better off if she had not devalued in 1949.[2] The pressure on the internal price-wage structure from rising krone import prices would have been much less serious. Presumably, it would have been possible to keep the Norwegian cost structure sufficiently low to avoid serious interference with exports. But at the time of devaluation of the krone, of course, the Korean war had not begun, and there were signs of deterioration in the world economic situation which, it was believed, might bring the fall in world prices that the Norwegian government had been expecting since the end of World War II. If a substantial fall in world prices had occurred, failure to follow the pound would have turned out to be a mistake.

Norway expected no advantage from devaluation in the form of an expansion of the volume of exports. Norway's export industries, including shipping, were operating at full capacity and selling as much as they could produce at prices that were still profitable in 1949. Devaluation could not be allowed to cut imports from the dollar area and from other countries which did not devalue because imports were limited to essential commodities. The higher cost of imported materials and machinery would raise the cost of investment. Rising prices of imported food, feedstuffs, and textiles could not be allowed to lead to higher domestic prices even if the result would be a cut in consumption.

In view of the fact that world prices showed no tendency to decline after 1949, it may be that devaluation had a salutary effect in forcing some revision of the subsidy policy and some upward adjustment in domestic prices and wages. The tendency for European prices in general to rise after 1949 was due to the devaluations as well as to the Korean war. The upward adjustment did not alter substantially the degree to which Norwegian prices and wages were out of line

---

[2] Governor of the Norges Bank, Erik Brofoss, apparently took this position in an address in Zurich in January 1956.

with export and import prices. But it did result in a series of changes which helped to reduce internal inflationary pressures.

In December 1949, after consulting the Economic Coordination Board, the government decided that price stabilization subsidies could not be raised sufficiently to offset the effect of devaluation on krone import prices and keep the cost of living stable. The government announced that, since the rise in world prices was not likely to be reversed and subsidies had been intended as temporary measures, permanent import price subsidies of large magnitude could not be considered a reasonable economic policy and that subsidies should be reduced.[3]

The cost-of-living index at the time of devaluation, was 159. A cut in subsidies was bound to lead to a rise in the index. Although the agreement of mid-1949 concerning the cost-of-living adjustment was an improvement over the previous agreement, there were still bound to be wage increases. The red line under the new agreement was 165.6, the first critical date was February 15, 1950, and the amount of the adjustment was to be negotiated.[4]

Increases in wage rates under industry contracts and increases in earnings resulted from such factors as upgrading and shifts to piecework schedules had resulted in a 5 per cent increase in hourly earnings of adult men in industry in the spring and summer of 1949. The delayed effect of these wage increases together with the cut in subsidies were bound to push the index above the new red line.

The government tried, through stricter price controls and temporarily high subsidy expenditures, to postpone the rise in the cost of living and the inevitable wage adjustment. In November 1949 a general price freeze, at predevaluation prices, was declared. No increase could be made without approval of the price directorate. Subsidies rose sharply, until early in 1950 the annual rate of subsidy

[3] During 1949, price stabilization subsidies amounted to 800 million kroner. The government estimated 1.1 billion in all would be necessary if subsidies were increased sufficiently to offset the effects of devaluation. The plan was to cut subsidies to 600 million kroner in 1950–51, compared with about 800 million in 1949–50, and to continue reducing subsidies to perhaps only 200 million kroner by 1952.

[4] If the negotiations did not lead to agreement, the contracts could be terminated with a month's notice. There had been some expectation of price falls and the agreement had provided for decreases as well as for increases in wages.

expenditure reached 1,050 million kroner. As a result of these measures the cost-of-living index was held at 159 through the first critical date in February 1950, but it was evident that it would rise to a level well above the red line as soon as subsidies were reduced. Furthermore, there were sure to be some wage increases in the spring of 1950 under certain industry contracts, although most of them had been renewed in 1949 and did not expire until 1951.

The government took the initiative in March 1950 and called for new wage negotiations in accordance with a recommendation of the Economic Coordination Board.[5] The new agreement that was then reached left the red line at 165.6, but shifted the first critical date to September 15, 1950. This six-month delay was considered an important victory for the government. The provision for the cost-of-living adjustment was made even less automatic than that in the mid-1949 agreement; any adjustment had to be negotiated. The government also won the point that any adjustment made must be based on changes in the cost of living resulting from the change in subsidy policy rather than on all changes in the cost-of-living index for whatever reason.[6]

The government announced the details of the revised subsidy policy and the resulting price increases in April 1950. Again an effort was made to postpone the effect of the cut in subsidies on prices. The cost of living was expected to rise about 5 per cent and to exceed the red line when the price increases became fully effective. In an attempt to postpone price increases, the government directed that stocks in hand had to be sold at the old prices. In general, also, no producer was permitted to raise his prices as a result of higher import prices if he could make a reasonable profit at the old prices. Price controls were tightened, and some price increases were delayed completely until summer.

The early 1950 plans for aiming at a new stabilization line and cutting subsidies were upset by the Korean war and the sharp increases in import prices which followed. These rapid increases meant

[5] The government and the trade union leaders undoubtedly cooperated closely on this occasion.

[6] It was agreed that a new cost-of-living index based on the postwar distribution of consumer expenditures, which had been compiled by the Central Bureau of Statistics, would help to determine the amount of the wage adjustment, though not the red line.

that a further upward domestic price adjustment would be necessary and that subsidies would have to continue at a high level in spite of such an adjustment. During 1950 hourly earnings rose as a result of the increases granted under certain industry contracts and other factors, even though the general cost-of-living adjustment was postponed until late in the year. These wage increases added to the pressure on prices.

The new red line was exceeded by more than 13 index points on September 15, 1950, when the cost-of-living index reached 179.5. The ensuing negotiations led to a series of agreements, announced at the end of October, which were reasonably satisfactory to the government. First, a cost-of-living adjustment equal to an increase of about 6 per cent in wages was granted; second, negotiations on all individual industry contracts, most of which would expire in 1951, were postponed until 1952; and third, a new agreement was reached providing for one automatic cost-of-living adjustment in March 1951 and for negotiation of any future adjustments.

The cost-of-living adjustment of about 6 per cent was much less than might have been necessary under the pre-1949 agreement, with the old red line of 160.8 and the fixed adjustment per index point. The index had risen from 159 at the time of devaluation to over 179, an increase of almost 13 per cent. Even with the new red line as a base, the increase was over 10 per cent. The adjustment was described as two-thirds compensation for the rise in the cost of living since devaluation.[7]

The postponement of the industry wage contracts expiring in 1951 was a strong point in the series of agreements. The arrangement for an automatic cost-of-living adjustment in March 1951 was less fortunate. The idea of even one automatic adjustment was, in a sense, a retrogression. The over-all wage increases in October and the effects of the Korean war seemed certain to lead to price increases in 1951, and the trade unions insisted on being covered. The size of the automatic adjustment was also a relatively weak point. The

[7] The increase was 18 öre per hour for adult men in industry, about a 6 per cent increase on the average. This was estimated to provide two-thirds compensation for an index family of 3.6 units. Later estimates suggest that the increase provided 80 per cent compensation for the index family and more than full compensation for the average worker supporting only one other person. See *Ökonomi,* (Nummer 12, January 1951) "Omkring lönnsopjöret hösten 1950."

adjustment would be higher proportionally than that granted in October.[8] Furthermore, the adjustment would be made any month after March 1951 if the cost of living had not reached the new red line on March 15. Six months after the one automatic adjustment, negotiations would take place on a further adjustment if the new cost-of-living index had risen 5 points.

Another aspect of the agreement was less favorable than it might have been. The government was convinced that the building up of its defense program because of the Korean war would require a substantial diversion of scarce resources. It believed that consumption increases had to be more carefully restrained. As part of its over-all financial program, the government had decided even before October to raise the general sales tax again to 10 per cent.[9] The increase in the sales tax would lead to a further rise in the cost-of-living index. The suggestion was made at the time that the unions be persuaded to accept the principle that the increase in the cost of living owing to the rise in the sales tax should not be included in the March 1951 adjustment. No agreement to this effect was reached, however. The government apparently decided that it would be better to delay the sales tax increase until after the March adjustment, perhaps with the idea that future negotiated adjustments would be less complete.

Under the October 1950 agreement, two wage adjustments took place in 1951. The automatic clause led to a 5 per cent wage increase on the basis of the March 1951 cost-of-living index.[10] In April the sales tax was raised to 10 per cent. By September 1951, the rise in the cost-of-living index was sufficient to require new negotiations.[11] The trade union and employers associations could not agree on the adjustment to be granted. The state mediator could not persuade the trade unions to accept less than full compensation, and the employers refused to grant such substantial increases. A strike was set for December.

[8] The adjustment would be 2.6 öre per index point if the new index (1949 = 100) rose 5 points by March 15, 1951. In September, the new index was 108.3. An increase of 3 öre was believed to provide full compensation for an index family.

[9] It had been cut to 6.25 per cent in 1947.

[10] The index had risen 7 points by March 15. The automatic increase of 17 öre amounted to about 5 per cent for adult men in industry.

[11] The index had risen 11 points since March; negotiations were required if the index rose 5 points.

In order to avoid the strike, the Storting passed a law creating a special wage board to decide on the adjustment. The board's negotiations were difficult and protracted; no agreement was reached until December. The increase granted, retroactive to October 15, provided about a two-thirds compensation.[12] More important, the system of automatic, or semi-automatic, wage adjustments was abolished. The new general agreement and the new individual industry agreements would not contain such clauses.

In the midst of all these price, tax, and wage adjustments during 1951, the government had not considered it feasible to aim at a new stabilization line. At the end of 1951, the outlook for 1952 seemed better; but in the course of 1952, the prospects began to appear less favorable.[13] Most of the industry wage contracts expired in the spring; and in May 1952 they were renegotiated with 4 or 5 per cent increases in contract wage rates. In July, price controls were lifted on certain important domestic farm products and some increases in prices occurred. Then in September 1952 there was a sharp rise in prices which was due partly to the removal of sugar and coffee subsidies.[14] Rising import prices had kept total price subsidies up in spite of the April 1950 revisions. The government was determined to reduce the subsidies. The rise in sugar and coffee prices was a shock to the trade unions, which had been expecting stable prices. But toward the end of 1952 some price reductions were achieved, partly by a reduction of the import duties on sugar and coffee and partly by reintroducing a 10-öre subsidy on milk. At the end of the year, prices seemed to be stabilizing.[15]

The cost-of-living wage increases granted during the period of upward adjustment from 1950 to 1952 were restrained. They were

[12] The increase was 21 öre, or 2 öre per index point.

[13] The Economic Coordination Board believed it was too early to aim at a new stabilization line in July 1951 but believed the situation was more hopeful at the end of the year.

[14] In spite of the early 1950 revisions in the subsidy policy, price stabilization subsidies had amounted to 770 million kroner in 1950, compared with 886 million in 1949. In 1951 they were again 776 million kroner, and in 1952 814 million kroner.

[15] During 1952, detailed price regulations were abolished for a series of items, including fruits, conserves, candy, herring, leather and hides, shoes, and meat and meat products. Furthermore, considerable relief was granted in the price regulations on textiles and ready-made clothing.

excessive in the sense that they tended to more than compensate the average worker for cost-of-living increases and therefore added to inflationary pressures. But the government succeeded in keeping the wage increases within manageable limits and in avoiding a violent wage-price spiral. The trade unions did not press for wage demands far out of line with the government's over-all economic policy. The wage-price spiral would probably have gone farther and faster if the Labor Government and the trade unions had not worked in close harmony. Union demands would probably have been less restrained under another government.[16]

The principal cause of the upward adjustment was clearly rising krone import prices; the inflation was primarily an imported cost inflation. But continued internal inflationary forces added to the pressure for higher wage rates. There was a substantial upward movement in wages as a result of upgrading, changes to piece rates, and "black-market" wage rates in the sense of payments above those in the wage agreements. Inflationary pressures were becoming less serious throughout the period, partly because price increases in advance of wage adjustments led to a squeeze on real wages. Real wage rates were approximately constant from 1950 to 1952, in contrast to the period from 1946 to 1948 when they had risen sharply.[17]

The upward adjustment of prices and wages from 1950 to 1952 did not reverse the relation between domestic prices and wages and krone export prices. Export prices continued to be much higher compared to domestic prices and wages than they had been before the war (Tables 11 and 12). The government taxed away a considerable part of the export profits, but profits were high, especially in 1951, and continued to play a role both in helping to concentrate investment demand in export sectors and in adding to inflationary pressures.

In spite of devaluation, the Korean war, and the price-wage adjustments, the government did not abandon the easy money policy. The official discount rate and also the government long-term bond rate remained at 2½ per cent. The effective rate on long-term governments climbed to 2.7 per cent by the end of 1950 and 3 per cent by

---

[16] See Leiserson, "Wages in a Controlled Economy," for a full account of the administrative and political aspects of wage policy during this period.

[17] See Tables 58 and 59.

Table 11. Various indices of prices and wages, 1946 to 1952 (1938 = 100)

	1946	1947	1948	1949	1950	1951	1952
Prices							
Cost of living..............	155	159	160	159	167	193	211
Consumer prices............	163	175	180	185	199	224	238
Wholesale prices............	169	175	181	184	209	258	276
Import prices							
Goods and services........	242	293	324	315	351	419	431
Goods...................	240	283	308	302	339	415	428
Ships...................	227	298	362	394	410	441	493
Export prices							
Goods and services........	275	295	300	288	313	441	433
Goods...................	247	282	312	305	316	436	436
Wages							
Hourly earnings in mining and manufacturing............	155	171	180	189	200	229	255
Total wages paid per man year —hired workers...........	188	206	221	229	244	272	308

Source: Indices of the Central Bureau of Statistics. The cost-of-living and wholesale-price indices are published regularly in *Statistiske Meldinger*. The indices of consumer prices, export and import prices, and wages paid per man year are from *National Accounts, 1930–1939 and 1946–1951* and *National Accounts, 1938 and 1948–1953*. A few figures are from *Economic Survey, 1955*, and for 1952 from *National Accounts, 1949–1955*. The index of hourly earnings in mining and manufacturing is from *Economic Survey, 1952*, supplemented by data on a new basis for the last few months of 1952 taken from current sources.

Table 12. Ratio of commodity export prices to wholesale prices and to wages, 1946–1952 (1938 = 100)

	Ratio to domestic wholesale prices	Ratio to average wages per man year
1946..........................	146	131
1947..........................	161	137
1948..........................	172	141
1949..........................	166	133
1950..........................	151	130
1951..........................	169	160
1952..........................	152[a]	136[a]

Source: See Table 11.

[a] Index of export prices for all goods and services, which moves closely with commodity index, was used to obtain this ratio.

the end of 1951. The increase in the effective rate reflected the opinion of private banks and the public that the government would be forced to raise the discount rate.[18] This opinion led to and was

[18] The Central Bank publicly favored an increase.

reinforced by the difficulties of the state banks in selling government guaranteed securities to the private banks at the official rate. The state banks depended on selling their securities to the private banks to finance their loans. The government several times reiterated its intention of maintaining the 2½ per cent rate, but the private banks seemed determined to force an increase.

Easy money also persisted until 1950 in the sense that the liquidity of the private banks, though steadily reduced, permitted a continued rapid expansion of private bank loans. Private bank reserves declined each year from 1946 to 1950; the total decline by the end of 1950 was almost precisely as planned in 1946 [19] (Table 13). A little more

Table 13. Private bank reserves and deposit liabilities, 1945 and 1950
(billions of kroner unless otherwise indicated)

	End of 1945	End of 1950
Joint stock banks		
Liquid reserves...........................	3.2	0.8
Demand deposits..........................	2.0	1.7
Savings deposits..........................	1.5	2.2
Ratio of reserves to demand deposits.........	160%	47%
Ratio of reserves to total deposits............	91%	21%
Savings banks		
Liquid reserves...........................	1.8	0.3
Demand deposits..........................	0.9	0.7
Savings deposits..........................	3.2	4.0
Ratio of reserves to demand deposits.........	200%	43%
Ratio of reserves to total deposits............	44%	6%

Source: See Tables 3 and 4.

than half the net decline was due to net sales of foreign exchange from government reserves, government credits, and aid.[20] The principal factors accounting for the remainder of the decrease were net increases in notes in circulation outside the banks and the state's accumulation of idle funds through receipts in excess of total expenditures.

By 1950 the ratios of reserves to deposits of most joint stock banks were at or below the prewar levels even though, on the

[19] From 1946 to 1948 reserves had decreased by about 2.4 billion; in 1949 and 1950 by about 1.5 billion.

[20] The net sales were 4.4 billion, but about 2 billion were offset by repayment of the shipowners' claims. The shipowners had turned over sterling claims to the government in 1945, to be gradually used for payments on ship contracts.

average, the joint stock banks still had a slightly higher ratio.[21] Some small joint stock banks had reserves close to the legal minimum, while the few large banks apparently had substantial liquid reserves. For savings banks, the ratios of reserves to deposits at the end of 1950 were, on the average, below prewar ratios. Many of the private banks were beginning to be concerned about their reserve position.

The steady reduction in private bank reserves did not prevent a rapid expansion of private bank loans; and the other private lending institutions and the state banks also expanded their loans. The rate of expansion, however, slowed down year by year (Table 14),

Table 14. Loans outstanding of private banks, other private lending institutions, and state banks, end of year, 1946–1952

	Private banks		Other private lending institutions	State banks	Total	
	Mortgage	Short term			Amount	Increase over previous year
	(millions of kroner)					(per cent)
1945	722	942	354	776	2794	
1946	914	1604	416	787	3721	33
1947	1152	2282	540	849	4823	30
1948	1391	2853	639	1027	5910	23
1949	1685	3162	730	1457	7034	19
1950	1924	3761	808	1881	8374	19
1951	2072	4386	875	2291	9624	15
1952	2235	4814	975	2750	10774	12

Source: *Statistiske Meldinger*, 1954 and 1955.

partly because of falling reserves, partly because of the increase in private debt, and, after 1950, partly because of high profits. Until 1950 the government took little or no action to restrict credit expansion.

As early as 1947 the government had spoken of asking the private banks to cooperate in restricting their lending activities. Although some officials urged new reserve legislation in 1948 and 1949, the monetary authorities seemed opposed and seemed to favor raising the interest rate instead. In 1950 a committee of experts under Governor Jahn of the Norges Bank recommended giving the Norges Bank power to set reserve requirements, but this recommendation was not

[21] Compare Table 13 and Table 3.

adopted. Possibly the reason was that, by this time, only the few big banks had large excess reserves, and the difficulties in selling state bank securities seemed to argue against imposing new reserve requirements.

The Finance Minister and the governor of the Norges Bank held meetings with the bankers during 1950 in an attempt to restrict bank loans and to ensure that they did not finance nonessential projects. The meetings continued in 1951, and qualitative directions were issued to the banks attaching priorities to certain types of loans.[22] There is no evidence that the measures taken to restrict bank loans had much effect.

The government deliberately aimed at no further reduction in private bank reserves in 1951 and 1952, partly because of the financing difficulties of the state banks and partly, in 1952, because of some fear of deflation. Bank reserves rose slightly in 1951 and were about constant in 1952. The government financed the state banks by direct loans;[23] and loans by the state banks expanded rapidly, particularly for housing. The private banks continued to be unwilling to buy the state bank securities. Finally, in June 1952 the private banks agreed to take a small amount of 10-year state bank securities at 2½ per cent. This issue marked the beginning of the end of a strict official 2½ per cent rate for long-term loans.

In May 1952 draft legislation giving the government authority to impose higher reserve requirements was presented to the Storting.[24] While the bill was before the Storting, the government told the banks it did not intend to raise reserve requirements under existing condi-

[22] The need to cut civilian investment to finance the defense effort and the approaching end of ECA (Marshall Plan) aid led to greater efforts to control investment.

[23] In 1951 reserves rose 300 million: 500 million of blocked deposits were released and 500 million was lent to the state banks; together these transactions more than offset the net 400 million decrease in reserves, owing to government receipts in excess of total expenditures and to the effect of some net government sales of foreign exchange. In 1952 government receipts exceeded expenditures by 250 million and the state lent 300 million to the state banks. Private bank reserve ratios tended to be stable or rose slightly in 1951. Deposits rose because of the release of blocked deposits. In 1952 savings deposits rose sharply and the savings banks reserve ratio fell.

[24] Under this draft law, the government could require that a bank's deposits at the Norges Bank be up to 25 per cent of deposit liabilities, and could vary the requirements with the size of the bank.

tions; and every effort was made to encourage the banks to buy state bank securities. The law was passed in July, with government assurance that it did not believe at the time that the situation would require use of the law. The government undoubtedly hoped that the banks would expand their purchases of state bank securities.

In spite of the rapid increase of bank loans, total notes and total deposits in the hands of the public did not expand at an excessive rate, compared with output, from 1947 to 1950; but in 1951 and 1952, the expansion was more rapid than output. A substantial part of the increase, however, was due to the release of blocked deposits and to increases in savings deposits.[25] The fact that the total money supply, including savings deposits, and total bank loans outstanding were at or below the prewar ratio to gross national product in 1952 (Table 15) suggests a gradual return toward more normal relationships.

Table 15. Money supply, bank loans outstanding, and gross national product at current prices, selected years, 1938–1952

	End of 1938	End of 1945	End of 1948	End of 1952
	(billions of kroner)			
Money supply				
Notes..........................	0.4	1.4	2.1	2.7
Demand deposits.................	0.2	2.9	2.7	2.9
Savings deposits.................	2.8	4.7	5.5	6.9
Total.......................	3.4	9.0	10.3	12.5
Bank loans outstanding				
Private........................	2.6[a]	1.7	4.2	7.0
Other.........................	1.4[a]	1.1	1.7	3.8
Total.......................	4.0[a]	2.8	5.9	10.8
Gross national product[b].............	5.9	11.0[c]	14.1	22.8
	(per cent)			
Per cent of gross national product				
Money supply...................	58	82	73	55
Bank loans outstanding..........	68	25	42	47

Source: See Tables 3 and 4.
[a] End of 1939.
[b] Annual totals.
[c] Total for 1946.

[25] The annual rates of expansion of notes and deposits were: 1946, 0; 1947, 9 per cent; 1948, 4 per cent; 1949, 3 per cent; 1950, 1 per cent; 1951, 7 per cent; 1952, 7 per cent.

The inclusion of savings deposits in the money supply is appropriate because large interest-earning savings deposits held by business firms played an important role in the prewar period. During the occupation, when bank loans and bank earnings had been very low, the banks had been unwilling to accept such deposits and as a result there had been a tremendous and disproportionate growth in demand deposits (Table 15). After the liberation savings deposits began to grow and demand deposits remained virtually stable. Nevertheless the huge growth in demand deposits during the occupation, and the maintenance of this volume of demand deposits after the liberation, indicate that these demand deposits were playing a role in the postwar period that was played by savings deposits in the prewar period. Money supply comparisons with prewar that excluded savings deposits would give a false impression of the situation.

Government officials were concerned by the expansion of private bank credit year after year. The government was not only trying to reduce investment, particularly investment in nonpriority sectors, but also trying to have private investment financed by savings. From 1946 to 1950, the increase in private bank loans outstanding amounted to a little more than half of private net investment. With high profits and increased self-financing by business, the increases in private bank loans outstanding amounted to about 30 per cent in 1951, and 20 per cent in 1952, of private net investment. State bank loans were financing an even higher proportion of net investment in these years.

From 1949 to 1952, the government's fiscal policy proceeded very much in accordance with plans in spite of the Korean war and the cost inflation of 1950–52. Public savings rose from about 800 million kroner in 1949 to 1.4 billion in 1952. Public savings continued to exceed public investment.[26]

On the whole, the program of gradually eliminating inflationary pressures seemed to be progressing satisfactorily in spite of devaluation and the Korean war. Private bank reserves were at reasonable levels again, and the total money supply was close to its prewar relation to gross national product. Heavy taxes were producing large

---

[26] In 1949 and 1950, the over-all revenue surpluses, after financing net investment, ran 200 to 300 million kroner. In 1951 and 1952 they were about 600 million and 500 million kroner. See Table 51.

public savings, more than sufficient to cover public net investment. Rationing of consumer goods had been abolished. Price controls were beginning to be eliminated. The easy-money policy had not been abandoned.

The fact that prices were rising sharply in 1951 and continued to rise in 1952 cannot be taken as an indication either of a gradual reduction of inflationary pressures arising from internal factors or of an increase in such pressures. Many prices were still controlled. And the principal cause of the upward price and wage adjustments was the devaluation and the rise in world prices, combined with the ensuing cut in subsidies. The lag of cost-of-living wage increases behind price increases and the resulting stability of real wage rates from 1950 to 1952 were quite certainly helping to reduce internal inflationary pressures.

The stabilization program was clearly not maintained in the sense of cost-of-living stability from 1949 to 1952. But the goals of the stabilization program were retained. The upward adjustment of prices and wages, though substantial, was kept within manageable limits. Also, the level of prices and wages within Norway was kept well below the level of export and import prices. Price subsidies were still huge, however. The course of events clearly had not been precisely that expected in 1948. It may be that the shock of devaluation had, in fact, led to much more of a reduction in inflationary pressures than would have been achieved without it.

9

Investment and Consumption: 1949–1952

The 1948 long-term program continued the basic policy lines of the 1946 plan. The proportion of total output to be devoted to investment was almost identical, and private consumption was to be restricted in order to release resources for investment. But when compared with the 1946 plan, the program involved changes in the distribution of planned investment and in the composition of private consumption.

Even if total consumption could not be increased rapidly, the government aimed at a substantial improvement in the supplies of essential consumer goods. The Norwegian people had had three years of peacetime direct controls and of scarcity of certain basic items of food and clothing. While the austerity policy would be continued as long as necessary, it was recognized that the sooner prewar living standards could be restored the better, with account taken of quality, freedom of choice, and similar factors. The Norwegian public could not be expected to accept postponement of such conditions much longer. Furthermore, consumer price controls and rationing should be eliminated as soon as supplies of essential consumer goods would permit an equitable distribution without such detailed direct controls. The abolition of consumer price controls and rationing could be carried out only if consumer incomes and spending could be kept in line with total available consumer goods and services. Inflationary pressure in the consumer sector would have to be eliminated.

There was considered to be little or no possibility, however, of abolishing inflationary pressure in the investment sector. Demand would continue to exceed the amount of investment that Norway could finance. Foreign exchange, building materials, and skilled labor would still be scarce resources. Direct controls would be used to ensure that these resources were channeled into the most important investment sectors as well as to control the total volume of investment. The principal concern of government officials responsible for economic policy in the next four years was the constant struggle to decrease the volume of investment. Investment tended to exceed the amount that Norway could finance without adding to inflationary pressures.

Investment demand was excessive, but the high level of private investment demand was, at the same time, an indication of the success of Norway's postwar economic policies. Large profits, especially in export sectors, resulted partly from the stabilization program. Large profits, combined with an easy money policy, encouraged private investment, which amounted to four fifths of total investment. A high level of private investment demand was a necessary condition for carrying out the recovery program.

Excessive investment demand made it difficult to control total investment, but it made the task of controlling the composition of investment easier than it might have been, without much greater public investment. While import controls continued to be effective, controls on building and construction continued to be evaded, to some extent.[1] Both types of control were somewhat eased under external and internal pressures.

By the end of 1952, import controls on investment goods had been relaxed, owing to pressures exerted by the Organization for European Economic Cooperation. In order to cooperate with the European trade liberalization program, Norway first freed certain imports of consumer goods, so that controls over machinery imports might be retained as long as possible. It was difficult to free general classes of imports of equipment without adding to investment in nonpriority sectors, but machinery imports were freed gradually. In 1951, agricultural machines and electrical equipment were placed on the free list, and in 1952 machine tools and machines for the textile and footwear industries, to help them compete with free imports of the finished products.[2] The relaxation of import controls led to somewhat greater

---

[1] The Central Bureau of Statistics estimated that, in 1951, 25 per cent of total gross investment was in direct imports of investment goods, and another 10–15 per cent was in imports of steel and other materials for construction, or for the production of investment goods.

[2] Furthermore, by 1952 the textile market had shown considerable weakness in Norway, as in the rest of the world, and the danger of excessive investment seemed to be less.

investment than would otherwise have been permitted, at least in certain sectors.

The political pressure for more housing, and for more municipal building in general, led to a certain easing of restrictions on building In 1949, the Storting decided that cement should no longer be rationed; in 1950, however, it seemed clear that much unlicensed construction had been taking place, and therefore cement rationing was restored. In 1951 and 1952, the Storting again made special rules on house building for those who had their own timber. At the same time, the housing program was greatly expanded. The net result of these various political decisions was to make controls over building and construction less effective than they had been. The economic policy makers found it difficult to persuade members of parliament, who knew funds were available if only from aid counterpart, that real resources did not permit greater expansion of public construction. It was even harder to control the municipalities whose tax receipts were rising sharply.

In spite of the weakening of direct controls, the over-all level of investment was quite successfully held down from 1949 to 1952. Although government officials were not satisfied with the effectiveness of their control system, especially with the lack of complete control over building and construction, the record is surprisingly good. Investment was remarkably stable from 1949 to 1952 (Table 16). Total

Table 16. Indices of volume of gross and net investment, including and excluding stocks, and of private and public consumption, 1946–1952 (1938 = 100[a])

	1946	1947	1948	1949	1950	1951	1952
Gross investment..............	119	151	150	153	147	166	166
Stocks.....................	551	576	535	382	71	563	139
Excluding stocks............	104	136	136	145	149	151	167
Net investment................	145	212	200	198	173	209	181
Excluding stocks.............	108	179	169	181	182	178	182
Private consumption...........	109	120	122	130	135	135	142
Public consumption...........	186	178	167	176	182	195	208

Source: Central Bureau of Statistics. Indices for 1946 and 1947 are from *National Accounts, 1930–1939 and 1946–1951;* for 1948–51, from *National Accounts, 1938 and 1948–1953;* and for 1952, from mimeographed document *National Accounts, 1949–1955,* except for unpublished estimates for net investment, which may not be strictly comparable. More recent data for 1952 in *Economic Survey, 1956,* are not comparable with data for earlier years and, therefore, are not used in this study except in Chapter 13. They show substantially higher net investment and somewhat higher gross investment at 1952 prices, and very slightly higher private consumption.

[a] At constant 1938 prices.

net investment was below the 1948 level, which had been 6 per cent below 1947 each year except 1951, when it almost reached the 1947 peak.[3] Net fixed investment throughout the four years was steady at about the 1947 volume.[4] Gross investment tended to be higher compared with 1947 and 1948 levels, especially in 1951 and 1952.

The national budgets in 1949 and 1950 called for more restriction of gross fixed investment than actually occurred.[5] A revision of the 1948 long-term program, prepared in late 1949, also called for a cut in investment.[6] During 1949 and 1950 the government tended to be pessimistic and to assume that the 1948 plan could not be fully carried out; the record now shows, however, that resource availabilities actually tended to exceed expectations. Investment cuts were not quite in line with the annual budgets, but investment was held down sufficiently to keep the balance-of-payments deficits in 1949 and 1950 within Norway's financing abilities despite sharp increases in consumption. Marshall Plan aid turned out to be much higher than expected in 1950. The budget for 1951 called for a slight cut in gross fixed investment, and the 1952 budget planned for no increase.[7] In fact, there was a slight increase in 1951 and a substantial increase in 1952.[8] But there were no balance-of-payments problems in those two years.[9] On the whole, the actual investment carried out was consistent with financing capabilities.

No special measures were taken in 1949 to restrict investment,

[3] Investment in stocks had been heavy in both 1947 and 1948, and was high again in 1951. See Table 16.

[4] Gross investment in 1949 and 1950 remained approximately at the 1948 level, though excluding stocks it was 6–10 per cent higher. In 1951 and 1952, gross investment was about 10 per cent above the 1948 level on either basis. See Table 16.

[5] See *Nasjonalbudsjettet 1949, Stortingsmelding nummer 1, 1949,* and *Nasjonalbudsjettet 1950, Stortingsmelding nummer 1, 1950.* But investment in stocks, which had been extremely high from 1946 to 1948, fell substantially in 1949, and very sharply in 1950. The magnitude of investment in stocks in 1948 was not realized at the time. See Table 18.

[6] See the memorandum submitted to the Organization for European Economic Cooperation, in December 1949, published in English by that organization in Paris in April 1950 under the title, *General Memorandum on the 1950–51 and 1951–52 Programmes, Norway.*

[7] See *Nasjonalbudsjettet 1951, Stortingsmelding nummer 1, 1951,* and *Nasjonalbudsjettet 1952, Stortingsmelding nummer 1, 1952.*

[8] See Table 18.

[9] See Tables 37 and 49.

although the budget called for investment slightly lower than the 1948 plan. Increasing concern about inflationary dangers after devaluation, and later the effects of the Korean war, led to some special measures to reduce investment demand in 1950 and 1951. The administration laid down rules to be followed in cutting state-financed construction and it also required a reduction of municipal building.[10] Government officials tried to control private and state bank loans. The government changed its tax regulations to reduce private investment demand. The right to special initial depreciation allowances on equipment purchased at "extraordinary" prices was suspended in 1950 for projects to be instituted in 1951 and 1952.[11] All firms were permitted to make certain limited tax-free appropriations to funds for subsequent purchases of equipment, provided these funds were blocked until the government was willing to release them. The arrangement, in essence, postponed tax payments, and it was hoped that it would postpone machinery purchases.[12] All firms wishing to claim depreciation on capital equipment in 1950 had to deposit 10 per cent of the depreciation claimed in a special account, which could be released only by the government. Also, permission to deduct all repair and maintenance expenses on buildings, other than houses, for income tax purposes was eliminated.[13]

The value of fixed investment in 1949 and 1950, at 1948 prices, was higher than called for in the 1948 plan according to the data then available.[14] The latest revised data indicate that actual investment

[10] The law on projects requiring three or more laborers was referred to when direct instructions were issued, in the later years, requiring reductions in municipal construction activities.

[11] This did not apply if the investment was already under way or the machinery already ordered. Special allowances were granted in certain cases.

[12] When the blocked funds were actually spent, the new equipment purchased was to be written off by an amount equivalent to the funds used which had been blocked, and this write off would not be deductible for tax purposes.

[13] Firms were allowed to deduct only very small percentages (1–1½ per cent) except in special cases. This deduction could be claimed whether or not the repairs and maintenance were carried out. The hope was to reduce actual repairs and maintenance. At the end of 1950, it was roughly estimated that 40 per cent of those employed in the building trades in Oslo were doing repair and maintenance work. Data on employment and building activities in the country as a whole suggested that repair and maintenance activities were generally high.

[14] Gross civilian investment, including stocks, actually averaged about 5 per cent above the 1948 level as planned. Excluding stocks, the average was 10 per

was 20 to 25 per cent higher than believed at the time (Tables 17 and 18). This largely reflects the fact that investment in small

Table 17. Comparison of 1948 plan and actual gross and net investment according to revised and unrevised data at 1948 prices, 1948–1952[a] (billions of kroner)

	1948	1949	1950	1951	1952
GROSS INVESTMENT					
1948 plan — including stocks...........		————Average 4.2————			
Results					
Revised data....................	5.1	5.2	5.0	5.7	
Unrevised data..................	4.0	4.4			
1948 plan — excluding stocks...........		————Average 4.1————			
Results					
Revised data....................	4.6	4.9	5.1	5.1	
Unrevised data..................	3.8	4.2	4.1		
NET INVESTMENT					
1948 plan — including stocks...........		————Average 2.1————			
Results					
Revised data....................	2.8	2.7	2.4	2.9	
Unrevised data..................	2.1	2.4			
1948 plan — excluding stocks...........		————Average 2.0————			
Results					
Revised data....................	2.3	2.4	2.5	2.4	
Unrevised data..................	1.9	2.1	2.1		

Source: See Table 16 for source of revised data. Unrevised data are from the national budgets for 1949 and 1950. Basic data corrected to 1948 prices by using the price indices in *National Accounts, 1938 and 1948–53*.
[a] Data cover civilian investment only.

buildings and in repairs and maintenance was much greater than realized. The planned investment was carried out by and large and there was additional unplanned investment as well.

cent above 1948, compared with the planned 8 per cent. (See Tables 16, 17, and 18.) The figures of 4.2 billion and 2.1 billion kroner for planned investment including stocks in Table 7 are based on revised calculations made a few weeks after the 1948 plan; these showed 17.6 billion kroner, including 840 million defense investment, as the total goal for gross investment, and 8.6 billion for net. The 1948 plan gave 16.8 billion gross and 9 billion net. But estimates of investment in electric power and in mining and manufacturing were changed a few weeks later. The change was mostly in the basis of calculating depreciation.

Increases in agriculture and forestry stocks are included with other stocks for both the plans and the unrevised data for 1949 and 1950, to make the data comparable with the revised data on this point. Net defense investment in the 1948 plan was estimated by the author at half of gross defense investment.

Table 18. Planned changes in the volume of gross fixed investment, 1948–1952, and actual results according to revised data

	Plan	Results
Fall of 1948 plan for 1949 to 1952.....	8% above 1948[a]	10% above 1948
Fall of 1949 plan for 1950 to 1952.....	4% above 1948[b]	12% above 1948
1949 budget.........................	Slightly below 1948	7% above 1948
1950 budget.........................	20% below 1949[c]	3% above 1949
1951 budget.........................	Slightly below 1950	1% above 1950
1952 budget.........................	1951 level	11% above 1951

Source: See Table 16 for source of data on results. For data on actual plans see *Interim Report on the European Recovery Program*, vol. II, *General Memorandum on the 1950–51 and 1951–52 Programmes, Norway;* and *Stortingsmelding nummer 1*, 1949 through 1952.

[a] Based on comparison of early 1949 estimates of actual investment in 1948 and the fall of 1948 plan.

[b] Based on comparison of revised and original plans.

[c] Total decrease, including stocks. Rough estimate.

Gross and net investment rates, at current prices, were about as planned. The gross investment rate averaged 35 per cent in the 1949–52 period, and the net investment rate averaged 21 per cent. The 1948 plan called for investment rates of 33 per cent and 23 per cent, respectively. The fact that just about the expected proportion of total output was devoted to investment is a significant indication of the success of the 1948 plan.

The distribution of investment by sectors corresponded fairly well with the government's program. But the investment in stocks, though well below the early postwar years, except in 1951, was higher than expected.[15] In 1949, the rumored devaluations and expectations of rising prices tended to lead to investment in stocks; in 1951, defense stockpiling and expected price increases were both important. Government efforts to restrict investment during 1949 and to hold investment constant in 1951 were hindered by the inability to prevent stock accumulations.

The original 1948 plan for fixed investment by sectors was substantially carried out. It was revised slightly in the fall of 1949, and more fully in the 1950 and 1951 national budgets. The revisions were made because it seemed necessary to cut total investment, and the aim was to reduce investment which would not be directly productive. The actual composition of investment carried out corresponded more closely with the original 1948 plan than with the

[15] The plan assumed investment in stocks of about 100 million kroner a year at 1948 prices; except in 1950, the actual investment was from 3 to 6 times the amount planned (Table 17).

revisions.[16] This was partly because in 1951, after the budget was prepared, and in the 1952 budget, the pendulum swung again toward greater emphasis on housing and public buildings (Tables 19 and 20).

Table 19. Planned gross fixed investment by sectors, long-term plans and annual budgets, 1948–1952 (percentage distribution)

	Fall of 1948 plan	Fall of 1949 plan	Budgets		
			1950	1951	1952
Agriculture...............	6.8	6.8	7.0	6.6	8.6
Forestry..................	0.6	1.0	0.6	0.6	0.6
Fishing...................	3.6	3.5	2.5	2.7	2.0
Whaling..................	1.5	1.6	1.8	2.1	1.9
Mining and manufacturing..	22.8	21.2	25.2	20.4	18.1
Electric power............	5.1	5.3	5.4	6.0	7.7
Shipping.................	22.8	23.8	24.8	26.5	20.2
Other transport...........	16.6	17.2	17.2	19.7	14.1
Housing..................	13.9	14.3	13.7	11.8	15.9
Miscellaneous.............	6.4	5.4	1.9	3.6	11.0
Total[a].................	100.0	100.0	100.0	100.0	100.0

Source: See Table 18.

[a] Details may not add up to 100 per cent because of rounding.

Table 20. Actual percentage distribution of gross fixed investment by sectors at current prices, 1949–1952, compared with distribution planned in 1948

	Fall of 1948 plan[a]	1949	1950	1951	1952	Average, 1949–52
Agriculture..............	6.8	6.3	6.0	6.4	6.2	6.2
Forestry................	0.6	0.5	0.5	0.6	0.7	0.6
Fishing.................	3.6	2.1	2.0	2.4	2.0	2.1
Whaling................	1.5	1.6	1.5	1.9	1.1	1.5
Mining and manufacturing	22.8	19.2	19.2	18.2	19.0	18.9
Electric power..........	5.1	6.4	7.1	7.1	7.2	7.0
Shipping...............	22.8	24.7	22.6	19.9	19.2	21.6
Other transport.........	16.6	12.7	12.8	13.2	13.2	13.0
Housing................	13.9	17.0	17.4	18.4	19.7	18.1
Miscellaneous...........	6.4	9.6	10.9	12.0	11.6	11.0
Total[b]...............	100.0	100.0	100.0	100.0	100.0	100.0

Source: See Table 18.

[a] In the revised program, fall of 1949, investment in forestry was raised to 1 per cent, shipping to 23.8 per cent, other transport to 17.2 per cent, and housing to 14.3 per cent. Investment in mining and manufacturing was cut to 21.2 per cent and miscellaneous to 5.4 per cent. See Table 19.

[b] Details may not add up to 100 per cent because of rounding.

[16] See Chapter 6 for a discussion of the problems in comparing results according to the revised data with plans based on the unrevised data.

A rough attempt to compare the volume of fixed investment by sectors with the 1948 plan indicates that the 1948 goals were met in shipping, and exceeded in electric power, the two key areas. In manufacturing, the results seem to be far below the 1948 program and correspond more to the cut in the 1949 revision. These calculations are quite uncertain, however.[17] Investment in forestry, fishing, and whaling appear to have lagged behind plans. Investment in inland transport and miscellaneous buildings was kept below the ambitious 1948 planned levels, but investment in housing rose sharply (Table 21). Investment in the so-called "ash tray" industries was no longer much of a problem.

Table 21. Indices of actual volume of gross fixed investment by sectors, 1949–1952, compared with increases planned in 1948 and 1949 (1948 = 100)

	Fall of 1948 plan for 1949–52	Actual 1949	Fall of 1949 plan for 1950–52	Actual average 1950–51
Agriculture	109	103	102	110
Forestry	144	125	123	112
Fishing	155	108	141	120
Whaling	83	54	83	58
Mining and manufacturing	115	100	100	99
Electric power	94	109	92	124
Housing	102	121	98	138
Shipping	93	111	90	91
Other transport and communication	107	103	103	96
Miscellaneous	140	112	109	119

Source: Data on planned investment at 1948 prices from sources cited for Table 18. The plans at 1948 prices were translated into volume goals by comparing them with estimates available in 1948 and 1949 for investment in 1948. The plans are compared with volume indices based on revised actual data for the years 1949 to 1951 at constant 1938 prices from *National Accounts, 1938 and 1948–53*.

Probably the best way to determine the success of the investment plans is to translate investment goals into physical goals, for example, shipping tonnage or housing units. In most sectors these physical goals were output goals. The goals were met in most of the important sectors[18] and in some they were exceeded, indicating greater success than had been expected for the most part. In the building sector,

---

[17] The change to the revised data undoubtedly affects the volume increases. Also, even the revised data are not completely comparable before and after 1948. See introduction to *National Accounts, 1938 and 1948–53*.

[18] For a discussion of output compared with plans, see Chapter 10.

however, where the government tried to restrict investment, the fact that the plans were substantially exceeded was a sign of failure rather than of success.

The excess of actual investment in housing over the amount originally planned resulted partly from the relaxation of controls and partly from a political decision to expand the housing program in 1951. The building of small cabins, extra rooms, garages, and small farm buildings, as well as maintenance and repair work, continued to represent the most significant evasion of the control system. In large part, however, this investment did not utilize resources which could have been diverted to other uses.[19] Foreign exchange, building materials, and skilled labor were the three scarce factors, the use of which the government was trying to control. Foreign exchange was not being used for materials for these small buildings. The materials and labor involved were provided mostly by the owners, or by spare-time help on the farms.

On the whole, both the volume and composition of investment were fairly successfully controlled. At the time, the fact that controls were not completely effective was taken very seriously; it was emphasized that only priority investment should take place. But it now appears that not only the priority projects but also some less urgent small-building and repair jobs were carried out. The extent of the misallocation of resources seems relatively unimportant, since most of the resources going into the small-building jobs could not have been mobilized for more essential projects and the basic development program was being carried out. The evasions were not sufficiently important to upset the planning and control mechanism. The general effectiveness of the investment controls was due in part to the great reliance on imports for heavy machinery and equipment and the ease of controlling any large building project.

The 1948 program for consumption was also carried out, on the whole. The plan envisaged a return to at least prewar per capita consumption by 1952–53, or about a 10–15 per cent increase in total consumption over the 1948 level. The actual increase in this period was 16 per cent (Table 22). The planned change in the composition of consumption, especially the increases in the supply of basic food and clothing items, was also carried out.

[19] See the discussion in Chapter 6.

Table 22. Actual changes in the volume of private consumption compared with
annual budgets and 1948 plan, 1946–1952

	Plan[a]	Actual percentage increase	Volume indices Total (1938 = 100)	Per capita
1946	....		109	103
1947	not much increase.................	10	120	111
1948	about the same....................	2	122	112
1949	an increase.......................	7	130	118
1950	some increase.....................	4	135	122
1951	small increase at best.............	0	135	121
1952	3 per cent increase................	5	142	125
1948	Plan for 1949–52 10–15 per cent.....	16		

Source: See Table 18.

[a] Plans are based on annual budgets except for the 1949–52 figure, which is
from the 1948 plan. The plans are described in terms of the relation between
consumption in the budget year and consumption in the previous year. The actual
percentage increase is also compared with the previous year.

With the exception of 1951, the actual increases in consumption
each year exceeded the targets set forth in the annual budgets (Table
22). The budgets proved to be too pessimistic in regard to total
resource availabilities, which meant that both consumption and
investment were higher than planned. In 1950 and 1951, total output
increased considerably faster than expected; in 1949, a little faster. In
1949 and 1950, the increases in domestic output of consumer goods
exceeded expectations; in 1950 imports of freed goods were high.
When each annual budget was prepared, the amount of aid under
the Marshall Plan that would be available during the year was uncertain; through 1951, it turned out to be higher than expected.
After two years of substantial increases in consumption, almost no
increase was planned in 1951 and none occurred. This reflected the
progress which had been made in cutting down inflationary pressure
in the consumer sector.[20]

The program to eliminate inflationary pressure in the consumer
goods sphere required not only substantial increases in total consumption and a change in the pattern of consumption, but price-wage,
monetary, and fiscal policies which would keep personal disposable
incomes in line with available consumer goods and services. In 1950
and 1951, the revised subsidy policy, the increase in the sales tax,

[20] See the fuller discussion of this point in Chapter 12.

rising prices, and the lag of wages behind prices, all contributed to holding down personal disposable incomes. In general, tax receipts continued to be high and public savings large. The private banks were beginning to feel a reserve pinch. All these factors contributed to the virtual elimination of inflationary pressure in the consumer sector by 1951. They were especially important in explaining the fact that consumption did not increase in 1951.

But the first task had been to increase the supplies of certain basic consumer items. The government was determined in 1949 and 1950 to import much greater quantities of basic consumer goods. Goods of high import content had been scarce and they had to be made available, gradually, in greater quantities. Pressure on Norway by the Organization for European Economic Cooperation to liberalize import restrictions may also have had some effect on the speed with which supplies were increased.

Considerable progress was made in 1949 in improving the composition of consumption and in reducing price controls and rationing in the consumer sector. Supplies of domestically produced food improved, some rations were increased, and some were eliminated.[21] Textile supplies were better.[22] A further substantial increase in the supply of basic consumer goods occurred in 1950.[23] Imports of textiles were increased sharply, partly to prepare for future liberalization of textile imports. By mid-1950, textiles, coffee, meat other than pork, cheese, sugar, and certain minor or luxury imports were the only significant areas of unsatisfied consumer demand, except for electricity and housing.

A large proportion of all consumer goods imports was freed from controls in 1951. Most textiles and shoes were admitted freely, but imports of automobiles, of certain consumer durables, and of fruits were still restricted. Meat and textiles were removed from rationing; at the end of 1951, textiles began to accumulate on the shelves. During 1952 the last important commodities were removed from rationing —

---

[21] Early in 1949, bread, flour, and soap rationing were ended and milk and egg rationing eliminated in most districts. Meat, sugar, and fat rations were increased.

[22] There was no official increase in the ration. For the first time since the war, however, goods of poorer quality began to pile up on the shelves.

[23] In April rationing of fats, chocolate, and rubber boots was ended.

cheese in July and coffee and sugar in September.[24] Commodities that had been rationed previously did not tend to disappear from the shelves in 1952.

The virtual elimination of consumer rationing and the stability of total private consumption suggest that by 1951 the government already had substantially achieved its goal of eliminating inflationary pressure in the consumer goods sphere. By 1952 the goal had clearly been met. The only important scarcities remaining were in electricity and in housing, both available at subsidized or artificially low prices.[25] The fact that prices and wages were rising during 1951 and 1952 cannot be taken as an indication of persisting inflationary pressures in the consumer goods sector. The devaluation, the rise in world prices, and the cut in subsidies were largely responsible for the actual price rises which occurred during these years.[26]

The shift in the pattern of consumption beginning in 1949 indicates a much more normal supply situation (Table 23). Until 1949, expenditures on food, household goods, and clothing had been relatively low, compared with the prewar average; expenditures on beverages and tobacco, travel and transport, and education, literature, and entertainment had been relatively high. While food expenditures continued to be relatively low in 1949, the percentage share for beverages and tobacco fell sharply and that for clothing and footwear rose substantially. Expenditures on durable household goods continued low.[27]

The changes in consumption in the period from 1949 to 1951 are shown clearly by volume indices for consumption in the various com-

[24] Rice, dried fruits, and coal for domestic use were also temporarily lifted from rationing. The only consumer goods still subject to rationing were coke and fuel oil for domestic use, but some imports of consumer goods were still restricted.

[25] Certain "luxury" items could not be imported freely, such as cars, washing machines, and electric mixers. The prices of these imports were not high enough to restrict demand to the available supplies. Informal customer rationing or special import licensing procedures allocated supplies. The fact that these commodities were scarce in 1952 does not indicate any significant degree of general inflationary pressure in the consumer field.

[26] See the discussion in Chapter 8.

[27] Within this group, purchases of radios and furniture fell, and purchases of pots and pans and previously scarce necessities rose.

Table 23. Percentage distribution of private consumption by types of goods and services at 1938 prices, 1938 and 1946–1952

	1938[a]	Average 1946–48	Average 1949–51	1952
Food..................................	31.1	28.3	29.1	28.3
Beverages and tobacco.................	6.4	7.9	6.5	6.4
Dwellings, light, and fuel...............	15.9	15.6	15.9	16.3
Durable household goods................	9.3	8.7	8.4	8.9
Clothing and footwear.................	12.7	11.2	12.3	12.7
Health services and medical care.........	4.6	4.8	4.5	4.5
Travel and transport..................	5.5	6.6	7.0	7.3
Education, literature, and entertainment..	5.1	6.8	6.7	6.4
Hotel and other personal services........	3.3	3.5	3.3 ⎫	9.3
Other................................	6.1	6.7	6.3 ⎭	
Total[b].............................	100.0	100.0	100.0	100.0

Source: Central Bureau of Statistics. Data are for percentage distribution of total specified consumption before some minor corrections to the total. Figures through 1948 are from *National Accounts, 1930–39 and 1946–51;* from 1949 on from *National Accounts, 1938 and 1948–53.* Somewhat revised data for 1952, available in a slightly different form in *National Accounts, 1949–1955* show 29.0 per cent for food, 17.0 for dwellings, light, and fuel, 7.9 for travel and transport, and 12.4 for clothing and footwear.

[a] The pattern of consumption was remarkably stable in the late thirties, and virtually unchanged from 1937–39.

[b] Details may not add to 100 per cent because of rounding.

modity groups (Table 24).[28] The consumption of both household goods and clothing increased sharply in 1952, and the pattern of consumption was about as close to prewar as it was likely to be, in view of the rise in the standard of living.[29] During 1952, the only

[28] The substantial increases in total consumption in 1949 and 1950 were more than accounted for by increases in food, clothing, and footwear, and in dwellings, lights, and fuel. Consumption in all other groups except durable household goods was virtually constant in 1950. In 1951, there was little change in any group, except for a decline in clothing and footwear. In 1952, this decline was more than made up, and the consumption of durable household goods increased sharply. The consumption of beverages and tobacco also rose again. By 1952, the volume of consumption in every group except food and durable household goods was about as high, compared with prewar, as total consumption. Travel, transport, education, literature, and entertainment had risen much more than total consumption.

[29] Expenditures on food and durable household goods continued to be relatively lower, and expenditures on dwellings, light, and fuel, travel and transport, education, literature, and entertainment relatively higher. Presumably the habits acquired in the immediate postwar years were not to disappear, and they reinforced the effect of rising incomes in maintaining expenditures in some areas.

Table 24. Indices of volume of private consumption
by commodity groups, 1946–1952 (1938 = 100)

	1946	1947	1948	1949	1950	1951	1952
Food...........................	103	109	114	120	126	125	129
Beverages and tobacco..........	147	147	144	138	132	132	138
Dwellings, light, and fuel........	115	118	120	126	134	138	148
Durable household goods........	93	118	121	113	123	122	131
Clothing and footwear..........	90	118	107	121	135	126	138
Health services and medical care.	123	126	126	124	127	141	136
Travel and transport............	134	145	150	162	162	178	199
Education, literature, and entertainment....................	144	161	167	173	173	178	173
Hotel and other personal services.	121	123	126	130	133	135 ⎫	136
Other.........................	127	135	134	137	139	134 ⎭	
Total consumption...........	109	120	122	130	135	135	142
Population..................	108	109	110	111	112	113	114
Per capita consumption.......	103	111	112	118	122	120	125

Source: Central Bureau of Statistics. Data through 1948 from *National Accounts, 1930–39 and 1946–51;* from 1948 on, from *National Accounts, 1938 and 1948–53,* except for 1952. For this year revised estimates for most of the groups from *National Accounts, 1949–1955* have been used as well as the revised total. Volume indices at 1938 prices.

Table 25. Index of consumer prices, total index and indices by groups of goods
and services, 1946–1952 (1938 = 100)

	1946	1947	1948	1949	1950	1951	1952
Food...........................	167	170	169	169	189	217	246
Beverages and tobacco..........	197	232	251	258	267	287	300
Dwellings, light and fuel........	111	115	120	120	121	132	142
Durable household goods........	189	201	210	229	233	272	291
Clothing and footwear..........	219	235	242	251	275	343	356
Health services and medical care.	167	183	198	218	224	226	256
Travel and transport............	153	157	156	162	181	189	209
Education, literature and entertainment....................	149	153	158	158	168	181	189
Hotel and other personal services.	157	172	182	185	193	207	...
Other.........................	135	150	158	168	184	220	...
Total consumer prices........	163	175	180	185	199	224	244

Source: Central Bureau of Statistics. Data through 1948 from *National Accounts, 1930–39 and 1946–51;* from 1948 on, from *National Accounts, 1938 and 1948–53.*

controls over consumption were those over certain luxury imports.
Compared with prewar years, there were marked shifts in the relative prices of consumer goods in the various groups; but for the postwar period there was comparative stability. The groups containing either substantial imports or luxury goods, durable house-

hold goods, beverages, tobacco, and clothing and footwear were relatively high priced, compared with prewar; rents, travel and transport, food, hotel and other personal services, education and literature and entertainment, and health services and medical care were relatively low (Table 25). Price changes relative to prewar are not closely correlated with changes in the volume of consumption. For travel and transport, education, literature, and entertainment, prices were low and consumption high. The consumption of beverages and tobacco was high in spite of high prices. For clothing and footwear, lack of supplies rather than high prices held back consumption. Price differentials within the various commodity groups presumably had substantial effects on consumption, although availabilities and rations were also important until 1951.[30]

The increases in consumption in 1949 and 1950 were undoubtedly necessary. Investment and exports probably could not have been speeded up by more severe restrictions on consumption during these years. Most of the resources going into increased domestic production of consumer goods and services could not be shifted to investment or to exports. The increased consumption which involved a drain on foreign-exchange resources was essential if inflationary pressure in the consumer goods sector was to be eliminated. The steady increase in the labor force probably would not have occurred if workers had not been able to obtain better food and cothing. The 48-hour week would have been hard to maintain. Labor turnover and absenteeism would have been more pressing problems. The consumption increases in 1949 and 1950 could hardly have been postponed.

The consumption of domestically produced goods and of services showed little or no tendency to fall as the scarcer imported goods became available. The big increases over the prewar average, which had occurred from 1946 to 1948, were not reversed. There had not been an excessive development of travel, restaurant, or entertainment facilities in the sense of expansion which would not be justified when other goods became available; in fact, there had been little investment in such facilities. If the increased production of such consumer goods

[30] With low prices for domestic milk, cream, cheese, margarine, and eggs, the per capita consumption of these products in 1951 was much greater than in 1939. With higher prices for meat and imported fruit, per capita consumption was much lower than in 1939.

and services represented some misallocation of resources from 1946 to 1948, the continued high output could hardly be considered excessive by 1951 or 1952.

On the whole, consumption policy seems to have been well timed. Developments from 1949 to 1952 conformed closely to the government's plans in 1948. The fact that the revised data indicate a volume of consumption much higher, compared with prewar years, than was estimated at the time is in a sense irrelevant, as it was in the period from 1946 to 1948. Even so, it is anomalous that a country which, in order to release resources for investment, was continually aiming at austerity — at least when it came to imported food, to clothing, and of course to housing — should have achieved in some sense a rather high consumption standard.

From 1946, the aim had been to restrict the use of resources for public as well as for private consumption.[31] The 1948 plan did not set a specific goal for public consumption, but it emphasized the importance of restricting increases.[32] Public consumption nevertheless tended in most of the postwar years to take 3 or 4 per cent more of the national product than before the war.[33] Most of this increase, however, was in the use of goods and services for defense.[34] The volume of public consumption is estimated to have risen by 25 per cent from 1948 to 1952, to a level over twice the prewar level. Civilian public consumption, however, only rose 10 per cent from 1946 to

[31] The immediate goal in 1946 had been a sharp cut in expenditures from the 1945–46 budget level of about 1.5 billion 1946 kroner. When the 1948 plan was worked out, the fundamental idea was the same. No special goal was set up for public investment. Sectors under public jurisdiction, such as roads and schools, were given definite limited investment quotas. From the time of the original publication of the plan, efforts were made to reduce this type of "nonproductive" investment below the originally planned level.

[32] By 1948 military expenditures had been sharply reduced and were expected to remain small. Some defense "investment" was planned, amounting to 210 million kroner a year, or 100 million kroner a year more than budgeted for in 1948.

[33] The revised national accounts data treat all defense expenditures as public consumption.

[34] The increase in defense consumption after the Korean war was, of course, not expected when the fall of 1948 plan was made. Defense consumption has averaged 3 per cent of gross national product at current prices, compared with 1 per cent in 1938 and 2 per cent in 1948. In 1952, defense took 4 per cent of gross national product. Civilian public consumption absorbed only 6½ per cent of gross national product from 1949 to 1952, compared with 6 per cent in 1938.

1951.[35] When the expanded functions of the government after the war are taken into account, the increase from 1946 to 1951 was remarkably restrained.[36]

The plans for 1949 to 1952 were substantially carried out for both investment and private consumption. The volume of investment was higher than planned. The distribution of investment corresponded reasonably well with the plans. Private consumption increased about as much as expected over the whole period. More important, consumption of basic necessities increased sharply, rationing of consumer goods was abolished, and inflationary pressure in the consumer sector apparently was eliminated. Available resources from domestic output and import surpluses had exceeded expectations, as they had from 1946 to 1948, thus permitting a greater total domestic use of resources than had been planned.

[35] It was then 70 per cent above prewar (see *Current Economic Trends*, 1952). Defense consumption is estimated to have been three or four times the prewar volume in 1946, to have fallen sharply before the Korean war, and then to have risen again in 1951, to about four times prewar.

[36] In general, it seems that the public administrative offices suffered severely from shortages in personnel. On the other hand, the waste of excessive bureaucracy was avoided. The National Budget Office for years had a staff of only five or six persons, including the director and the secretary.

10

Output and the Foreign Balance: 1949–1952

The 1948 plan called for a heavy investment program and for large import surpluses to help provide resources for investment in order to build up productive capacity. Expansion of output, and relatively rapid expansion in sectors earning foreign exchange, would make it possible to achieve at least the prewar standard of living. The plan was developed sector by sector and commodity by commodity. The increase in net national product from 1948 to 1952–53 would be from 15 to 20 per cent.[1] The government was convinced that there were two principal ways by which output could be increased: (1) by investment to expand and modernize productive capacity and (2) by policies to achieve full use of resources. Unemployment, work stoppages, and plant operation at less than full capacity had to be avoided if possible.[2]

Certain questions should be considered when analyzing the actual increase in output from 1949 to 1952. Did output increase as fast as it should have, in view of the high level of investment and employment? Or did full employment and inflationary pressure lead to high turnover, absenteeism, and inefficiency? Did over-all output, output by sectors, and the output of individual commodities tend to behave in accordance with the government's plans?

[1] The output and balance-of-payments estimates in the 1948 plan referred to the fiscal year 1952–53 as the year in which the hoped-for viability would be achieved. A small capital inflow would continue in 1952–53, however. This was in accordance with the planning of the Organization for European Economic Cooperation and the Marshall Plan authorities. The government plans for increases in investment and output included many projects which could be begun but not necessarily be completed by 1952–53. The investment goals by sector were on a four-year (1949–52) basis.

[2] In the pulp and paper industry, there was excess capacity compared with the available supplies of timber. In certain of the "ash tray" industries, also, operation at full capacity was not desirable. Generally speaking, however, plant operation at full capacity was the goal.

Gross national product in fact increased by 16.9 per cent from 1948 to 1952 (Table 26). As pointed out above, the goal for 1952–53 was a

Table 26. Indices of volume of gross and net national product at 1938 prices, and yearly percentage increases, 1946–1952

	Gross national product		Net national product	
	Index (1938 = 100)	Percentage increase over previous year	Index (1938 = 100)	Percentage increase over previous year
1946............	107.6		109.4	
1947............	122.0	13.4	124.3	13.6
1948............	127.3	4.3	129.5	4.2
1949............	131.8	3.5	133.6	3.2
1950............	137.7	4.5	139.4	4.3
1951............	143.0	3.9	144.4	3.6
1952............	148.8	4.1	149.9[a]	3.8[a]

Source: Central Bureau of Statistics. Data through 1947 are from *National Accounts, 1930–39 and 1946–51;* for 1948–51, from *National Accounts, 1938 and 1948–53;* for 1952, from *National Accounts, 1949–1955* (Oslo, 1956), a mimeographed document. See Table 16 for reasons for not using other more recent data relating to 1952.

[a] Estimated by the author on the basis of the relation between gross and net national product in previous years.

15–20 per cent increase in net national product. The annual average increase in net national product from 1949 to 1951 was 3.7 per cent, compared with the 3.5 per cent rate implied by a 15 per cent increase in four years. For 1952 comparable revised data are not available but, on the basis of gross national product compared with net national product in the years 1949–51, the increase in net national product may be estimated at about 3.8 per cent. Output expanded about as fast as expected in the 1948 plan.

Output projections in the annual budgets tended to be more estimates than goals and tended also to err deliberately on the pessimistic side. During the period of the Marshall Plan, one factor of uncertainty was the amount of aid that would be received in the next fiscal year; the amount received was bound to affect investment and output. The budget's pessimistic estimate of output did not turn out to be justified in any year.[3]

Whether gross and net national product increased as fast as they

[3] The forecast for 1949 was a 2½–3½ per cent increase in gross national product; for 1950, 2–3 per cent; for 1951, 2–2½ per cent; and for 1952, 3 per cent.

might have, or perhaps should have, must be considered in terms of the numbers employed and the amount of unemployment. Unemployment was negligible in the period 1946–52 — considerably less than 1 per cent of the labor force on the average each year, compared with 4–5 per cent in the late thirties[4] (Table 27). Two thirds

Table 27. Employment and unemployment, 1938 and 1946–1952
(thousands)

	Employment, full-time man years[a]	Monthly average of registered unemployed[b]
1938.....................	1330	60[c]
1946.....................	1394	12
1947.....................	1444	9
1948.....................	1456	9
1949.....................	1478	8
1950.....................	1489	9
1951.....................	1507	11
1952.....................	1522	12

Source: Employment data from *National Accounts, 1938 and 1948–53*, and mimeographed document *National Accounts, 1949–1955*. Unemployment data from *Statistiske Meldinger*.

[a] Includes all workers whether self-employed or hired workers
[b] Registered unemployed at government employment offices.
[c] This is a very rough estimate cited in many official documents, including the long-term program of 1948. It seems to be consistent with figures on the percentage of trade union members unemployed.

of the unemployment was seasonal unemployment in the winter months. Work stoppages also were negligible.[5] In 1946, less than 1 per cent of the labor force was unemployed; from then on employment increased at a faster rate than the additions to those in the 18–64 year age group who were seeking work. Large numbers were drawn into the labor force.[6] There was also a marked shift of labor to more productive employment.

[4] Since 1946, the average percentage of certain trade union members unemployed has been 3 per cent, compared to 21 per cent in the late thirties. This series is published in *Statistiske Meldinger*.

[5] Work stoppages involved a loss of about 74,000 man days or 250 man years of work on the average each year from 1946 through 1952.

[6] In this context, employment includes self-employed as well as hired workers. From 1947 to 1951, the average increase in employment was 15,000 a year; in 1946 the increase was 50,000; in 1952, only 4,000. The government estimates that less than 9,000 a year would ordinarily have been added to the labor force from the increase in the population in the 18–64 age group. Owing to a cycle in population growth, the increase in the population in the 18–64 age

The productivity of Norwegian workers during the occupation, as measured by changes in the volume of gross national product per full-time employed worker, must have been well below the prewar level. In 1946 and 1947, with the return to more normal conditions, productivity increased sharply[7] (Table 28). During the years 1948 to

Table 28. Indices of volume of gross national product and of employment, and yearly percentage increases in gross national product per employed worker, 1946–1952

	Indices (1938 = 100)		Percentage increase over previous year in gross national product ÷ percentage increase in employment
	Gross national product[a]	Employment[b]	
1946.................	107.6	104.8	2.7
1947.................	122.0	108.6	9.3
1948.................	127.3	110.4	2.7
1949.................	131.8	111.1	2.9
1950.................	137.7	112.0	3.5
1951.................	143.0	113.3	2.7
1952.................	148.8	114.4	4.0

Source: See Tables 26 and 27.
[a] Volume index based on 1938 prices.
[b] Full time equivalent man-years of employment, including both self-employed and hired workers.

1952, the annual average increase in productivity was 3.2 per cent. This is a good record. Presumably there was some tendency from 1948 to 1952 for the rate of growth in output to be high because of the increasing availability of supplies and better use of capacity, but this could not have been a very important factor.

The increase in output per man was sufficiently high to suggest that full employment and inflationary pressure did not exert a significant drag on productivity and output. A high level of absenteeism and a high rate of labor turnover undoubtedly existed. Offsetting the

---

group was about 14,000 a year in the postwar period, compared with 30,000 in the late thirties. Since about one third of the women were seeking employment, the increase in the number seeking work would be about 9,000. According to one estimate less than half of the increase in employment from 1946 to 1952 was due to increases in the population of working age. See Leiserson, "Wages in a Controlled Economy," and *Stortingsmelding, nummer 62, 1954*.

[7] In 1946, output per man year was about 3 per cent above the 1938 level in spite of postwar dislocations, lack of materials, and war damage. In 1947, it increased by 9.3 per cent. In 1947, repairs and restoration permitted better use of capacity, and materials were available to raise output closer to capacity.

tendency of absenteeism and high turnover to reduce productivity were two other factors. High wages and labor scarcity tended to stimulate employers to seek more efficient use of labor. And the workers themselves were clearly under no compulsion to use slow-down tactics or to attempt to make jobs last longer for fear of unemployment.

Comparisons of the increase in output in this short period from 1948 to 1952 with increases in past periods, either in Norway or in other countries, are dangerous. Cyclical fluctuations in output and employment lead to sharp shifts in the rate of growth of productivity. A period during which stocks accumulate and firms operate below capacity is one of little increase in productivity; and during the recovery from such a period, the increase may be rapid. Terminal years are important in any comparisons.

From 1900 to 1930, gross national product in Norway increased by about 3 per cent a year; and gross national product per person in the 18–64 year age group increased, on the average, only 1.7 per cent a year. Employment data are lacking for years prior to 1930. From 1930 to 1939, gross national product increased by 2.8 per cent per year, and gross national product per person in the 18–64 year age group, by 1.2 per cent.[8] But gross national product per employed worker during this period increased by 2 per cent a year.

A comparison of the 1948–52 period with the years 1936–39 is of considerable interest (Table 29). The gross investment rate for the 1936–39 period was not far below that for 1948–52, though the net investment rate was much lower. The increase in output per employed worker averaged only 1.9 per cent per year from 1936 to 1939, compared with an average of 3.2 per cent per year from 1948 to 1952. The postwar record seems satisfactory, and does not suggest that inflationary pressure and full employment were seriously interfering with labor efficiency. The increase in productivity in the postwar period is higher than the average over long periods in the United States.

But the investment rate in the postwar period was unprecedentedly high in Norway. Whether the increase in output was reasonable in view of the level of investment is difficult to determine. The immediate postwar years were abnormal. The capital-output ratio for some

[8] Data from *Economic Survey, 1900–1950*.

Table 29. Percentage increases in volume of output, in employment, and in output per worker, and investment rates: annual averages for selected periods, 1931–1952

	1931–35	1936–39	1947–52	1948–52
Average annual percentage increases in				
Gross national product[a]	1.6	4.5	5.6	4.1
Net national product[a]	1.9	4.9	5.2	3.6
Percentage increase in employment	0.9	2.3	1.5	1 0
Percentage increase in gross national product per worker	2.1	1.9	4.2	3.2
Investment rates				
Gross	20	25	29	29
Net	4	12	18	17

Source: Central Bureau of Statistics. Investment, output and employment data up to 1947 from *National Accounts, 1930–39 and 1946–51.* Data since 1947 from *National Accounts, 1938 and 1948–52.* The 1952 figures are from mimeographed document *National Accounts, 1949–1955,* except for unpublished estimates of net investment and net national product. See Table 16 for explanation of failure to use revised data for 1952 in *Economic Survey, 1956.*
[a] Volume indices based on constant 1938 price data.

time after the war was undoubtedly affected by the fact that net investment had been reduced to zero by the end of the occupation and that there was substantial war damage. Also, fishing and forestry output as well as agricultural output fluctuate widely with weather conditions.

The incremental capital-output ratio in Norway was well above 4 to 1 from 1948 to 1952. Although this is not far out of line with incremental capital-output ratios in other industrial economies, it is somewhat high.[9] The stage of development of a country presumably affects the capital-output ratio. Investment in a country already highly industrialized with fully developed basic facilities may yield larger increases in output than in a relatively unindustrialized economy. For a time, the basic tendency toward diminishing returns as the supply of capital increases may be more than offset by other influences. Norway is relatively unindustrialized, compared with countries like the United States, the United Kingdom, and Germany.

The character of a country's undeveloped resources also affects the capital-output ratio. Investments in certain sectors, such as power

[9] See William Arthur Lewis, *The Theory of Economic Growth* (Great Britain: Irwin, 1955), chapter V, for a review of the available information and a discussion of the factors affecting the capital-output ratio to be expected in less developed countries compared with industrial countries. For industrial countries, incremental capital-output ratios seem to vary from 3 to 1 to 4 to 1.

development and shipping, require large expenditures for each percentage increase in annual output; and these investments yield results only over a long period. Norway's investment program was heavily weighted by shipping, and power development was not unimportant. There were also many projects in the Norwegian investment program such as the reconstruction of the iron ore mines and the building of a new steel mill and a new aluminum plant — projects that cannot yield a net increase in output during the years in which they are being completed. Transport facilities and housing, which necessarily yield only indirect returns over long periods of time, were also very important in Norway's investment program.

The Norwegian program was not designed to yield the maximum increase in output per unit of investment from 1949 to 1952. Although shipping was expected to yield quick returns in foreign exchange, the annual returns were small when compared with the investment. Power, electrochemical, and electrometallurgical development were bound to be slow. The composition of investment was determined chiefly by long-run economic considerations; and, in view of the

Table 30. Percentage distribution of net national product at 1938 prices by sector of origin, selected years, 1938–1951

Sector	1938	1946	1948	1951
Agriculture	6.9	4.6	4.6	4.9
Forestry	4.0	3.0	2.8	2.5
Fishing	1.3	0.4	1.1	1.3
Whaling	0.8	0.2	0.2	0.2
Mining	1.2	0.4	0.4	0.4
Manufacturing	24.4	22.5	25.8	28.4
Construction	6.2	7.8	7.0	7.3
Electricity, gas, and water	1.8	4.0	3.4	4.5
Wholesale and retail trade	17.9	17.8	17.5	17.3
Banking and insurance	2.6	2.9	2.7	2.4
Ownership of buildings	7.0	6.4	6.1	5.6
Water transport	8.3	3.8	5.6	6.6
Other transport and communications	4.3	7.2	7.6	7.1
Government services	1.8	3.6 ⎫	9.6	9.2
Community and business services	6.8	8.2 ⎭		
Personal services	4.5	3.7	3.1	2.6
Statistical discrepancy	0.0	3.6	2.4	0.0
Total[a]	100.0	100.0	100.0	100.0

Source: Calculated from data in *National Accounts, 1930–39 and 1946–51*.
[a] Details may not add to 100 per cent because of rounding.

actual composition, the capital-output ratio seems reasonable.[10]

The effect of the investment program on the distribution of ouput is striking. In 1946, electric power, construction, and inland transport were already contributing relatively more to output than in 1938, and most of the other basic producing sectors were contributing relatively less (Table 30). By 1948, shipping and also fishing had recovered somewhat, but they were still not as important as in 1938. By 1948 manufacturing, however, was more important than in 1938; and by 1951 manufacturing accounted for 28.4 per cent of net national product, compared with 24.4 per cent in 1938. By 1951 construction, electric power, and inland transport were contributing a much higher proportion of output than in 1938. Shipping and fishing were contributing about the same proportion as in 1938. But the other traditional export sectors, forestry, whaling, and mining, were lagging relatively, as were agriculture and personal services; the investment program had been aimed at reducing the dependence of Norway on these export sectors and on agriculture.

The shifts in employment, most of which had already begun in 1946, were even greater than those in output (Table 31). The two outstanding declines in the share of total employment were in agriculture and personal services. In 1952, agriculture accounted for only 20 per cent of total employment compared with 29 per cent in 1938; and personal services 8 per cent compared with 12 per cent in 1938. Employment in fishing, forestry, whaling, and mining was relatively less than before the war. The biggest increase in the share of total employment was in manufacturing, from 18 per cent in 1938 to 24 per cent in 1952. By 1946 the percentages for construction, inland transport and communications, and government services were already much higher than in 1938 and they remained high through 1952.[11]

The question of whether increases in output, on the whole, cor-

[10] The fact that investment was much higher than planned might suggest that the over-all production goals also should have been greatly exceeded. The unplanned investment was mostly in buildings or in repairs and maintenance of buildings and equipment, however, not in machinery and equipment which would lead to immediate increases in output. Also, there undoubtedly was some real underestimation of construction and equipment needs.

[11] The government service figure reflects the large numbers in the armed services as well as increases in civilian personnel.

Table 31. Percentage distribution of full-time employment by sectors,
selected years, 1938–1952

Sector	1938	1946	1948	1952
Agriculture.............................	28.7	25.2	23.1	20.4
Forestry................................	2.7	1.9	2.3	2.6
Fishing.................................	4.0	3.6	3.5	3.4
Whaling................................	0.6	0.3	0.4	0.5
Mining.................................	0.9	0.6	0.6	0.7
Manufacturing..........................	18.1	20.1	22.7	23.8
Construction...........................	6.0	9.1	8.6	8.6
Electricity, gas, and water..............	0.7	0.8	0.8	0.9
Wholesale and retail trade..............	9.1	8.6	8.9	9.1
Banking and insurance..................	0.9	1.0	1.0	1.1
Ownership of buildings.................	0.3	0.3	0.3	0.3
Water transport........................	3.9	2.6	3.2	3.6
Other transport and communications......	4.5	5.2	5.4	5.6
Government services....................	1.8	4.2	3.9	4.9
Community and business services........	5.6	6.9	6.7	6.4
Personal services......................	12.2	9.4	9.0	8.1
Total[a]...............................	100.0	100.0	100.0	100.0

Source: Central Bureau of Statistics. Data for 1938, 1946, and 1948 calculated
from data in *National Accounts, 1930–39 and 1946–51*, and data for 1952 from
National Accounts, 1938 and 1948–53.
[a] Details may not add to 100 per cent because of rounding.

responded with the 1948 plans can be approached from several angles.
The planning estimates by sectors and for output as a whole were
rough; the principal emphasis was on estimates by commodity. As
pointed out above, the increase in gross national product was within
the rough 15–20 per cent goal. For the various sectors, a recent
government document indicates that the goals were met in mining and
manufacturing and exceeded in the other sectors, except in agriculture (Table 32). Volume indices for net national product by sector
of origin confirm this general impression of increases in output.[12]

The output goals in the 1948 plan were really rough estimates of
shipping tonnage, kilowatt hours, cubic meters of timber cut, square
feet of building. Comparisons of goals for a hundred or more individ-

[12] Net national product of merchant shipping increased 31 per cent from
1948 to 1951, electric power 50 per cent, manufacturing 24 per cent, construction
18 per cent, and fishing 26 per cent (Table 33). But depreciation estimates and
shifting weather conditions alter the picture in other cases, for example, in
agriculture and forestry. For electric power, inland transport, and construction,
output from 1946 to 1948 was already considerably above 1938. Comparable
data are not available for 1952.

Table 32. Actual percentage increases in output by sectors from 1948 to 1952, compared with 1948 program goals for 1952–1953

Sector	1948 program goals for 1952–53[a]	Actual increase by 1952
Agriculture..........................	20	15
Forestry.............................	10	12
Fishing..............................	15	24
Mining and manufacturing............	20–25	24
Building and construction.............	10	24
Electric power output................	30	48
Shipping tonnage....................	35	36
Other...............................	—	9

Source: Data from *Om et langtids program for 1954–57, Stortingsmelding nummer 62, 1954*.
[a] Very rough estimates. Those for fishing and forestry were based on normal weather conditions. Slight adjustments in some of these goals were made for statistical reasons, according to the source document.

Table 33. Indices of the volume of net national product by sector of origin, selected years, 1946–1951, and percentage changes from 1948 to 1951

Sector	Indices (1938 = 100)				Percentage change, 1948 to 1951
	1946	1948	1950	1951	
Agriculture......................	74	87	115	105	27
Forestry.........................	81	91	88	90	−1
Fishing..........................	32	110	103	138	26
Whaling.........................	21	33	31	31	−6
Mining..........................	41	45	40	47	4
Manufacturing...................	101	137	162	170	24
Construction.....................	138	147	178	173	18
Electricity, gas, and water.........	235	237	355	355	50
Wholesale and retail trade.........	108	126	147	142	13
Banking and insurance............	123	135	135	135	0
Ownership of buildings............	100	112	114	116	4
Water transport..................	50	88	109	116	31
Other transport and communications	183	230	242	243	6
Government services..............	216	180 }	148	154	—
Community and business services...	132	134 }			
Personal services.................	89	90	85	85	−6
Total..........................	109.4	129.4	143.9[a]	146.7[a]	13

Source: *National Accounts, 1930–39 and 1946–51*.
[a] The indices are based on 1938 constant price data. Revised data show total net national product at 1938 prices at 139.4 and 144.4 for 1950 and 1951. The revised data are not available by sector of origin.

ual commodities for 1952–53 with actual output in 1952 or 1953 present some statistical difficulties, and the results are hard to interpret. Two or three facts stand out, however. Electric power output was 19.5 million kilowatt hours in 1953, compared with 12.3 million in 1948 and the goal of 16 million for 1952–53. The merchant fleet tonnage increased by 35 per cent from 1948 to 1952, precisely the goal for 1952–53. These were the central output goals of the 1948 plan. It is more difficult to compare the 1952 electrochemical and electro-metallurgical output with the goals.[13] Electrochemical output as a whole appears to have increased about as much as planned, if not more, and electrometallurgical output less. In agriculture, output of milk, potatoes, meat, butter, and eggs tended to lag behind the goals set for 1953, but this was not true for grain. Forestry and fishing vary from year to year, but seem to have exceeded the goals. There were delays in the reconstruction of the iron ore mine and the building of the steel mill.

The absolute level of output before 1952, compared with the level in prewar years, was much greater than realized at the time.[14] Although the over-all rate of increase from 1948 to 1952 was about as expected in the 1948 plan, the absolute amount of resources made available for investment and consumption was much greater. The level of output was higher than realized and the absolute volume of the increases was also greater.

The 1948 plan had relied heavily on resources to be provided by import surpluses. Surpluses of 1.1 billion kroner a year, on the average, were to finance half the planned net investment at 1948 prices. The balance-of-payments position was expected to improve sharply by 1952–53; and the government believed that from then on a capital inflow of 200 million kroner a year would be reasonable to help finance the continued development of Norway's economic resources.

Although the 1948 plan deliberately aimed at huge import surpluses, the annual budget each year thereafter until 1952 aimed at reducing them. The government was pessimistic each year about the Marshall Plan aid that would be allocated to Norway and the credits that could be raised; and the defense program placed an added burden on the balance of payments. It was partly because the balance-

---

[13] The program referred in some cases to eventual goals, such as 95 thousand tons of aluminum, but listed 50 thousand as the goal for 1952–53 in a tabular summary.

[14] The long-term plan estimated that output in 1948 would be 10 per cent above 1938. Revised data indicate that output was 27 per cent above 1938, and 21 per cent higher in current prices than estimated at the time.

of-payments deficits seemed likely to be excessive that the government attempted to cut investment and to restrict increases in consumption.

The attempts to cut the deficits were not very successful in 1949 and 1950. In 1949, Marshall Plan aid financed more than half of the 1.2 billion kroner deficit at current prices; nevertheless the use of reserves and credits was at a rate which could not be maintained. In 1950, aid permitted a substantial increase in reserves, despite a deficit of 800 million kroner at current prices. In a sense, then, Norway would only have delayed its development and recovery if it had reduced investment and consumption more sharply. The aid received in 1951, plus a small export surplus at current prices as a result of a sharp shift in the terms of trade, permitted an even greater increase in reserves.[15] In 1952, there was approximate balance at current prices, although in the second half of 1952 the position was deteriorating rapidly as freight rates weakened.

The original 1948 plan assumed a steady flow of Marshall Plan aid at over $100 million per year, perhaps at $150 million. The United States program for tapered aid, tapered as sharply as possible, was therefore a blow to the Norwegian government. Actually, however, the dollar value of aid to Norway rose in 1949–50 and remained high through June 1951, largely because Norwegian deficits, especially in intra-European trade, continued high (Table 34). On balance, Norway did not draw on reserves and credits from 1949 to the end of 1952.[16]

The original 1948 plan for annual deficits of 1.1 billion kroner meant current deficits of $220 million a year at the 1948 exchange rate. Only in 1949, however, was the deficit of approximately this dollar

[15] In the first half of 1951, the position was believed to be much less favorable than it actually was. This explains in part the aid allocation through June 1951, and the continual concern of the government with the balance-of-payments situation. The sharp shift in the terms of trade was due to the post-Korean rise in freight rates.

[16] After a serious decline in 1949, Norway's reserve position was restored in 1950 and 1951. Calendar-year data in kroner (from *National Accounts, 1938 and 1948–53,* converted into dollars show net aid from abroad, including private aid, of $122 million in 1949, $150 million in 1950, $54 million in 1951, and $15 million in 1952. Net use of reserves and credits was $109 million in 1949; but the increase in reserves, plus a net decline in indebtedness, amounted to $27 million in 1950, $80 million in 1951, and $3 million in 1952.

Table 34. Marshall Plan aid to Norway, 1948–1953 (millions of dollars)

	Direct dollar aid	Net intra-European drawing rights[a]	Initial position in the European Payments Union[b]	Total
April–June 1948...	20			20
1948–49..........	81	44		125
1949–50..........	90	80		170
1950–51..........	46		60	106
1951–52..........	17			17
1952–53..........	21			21
Total.........	275[c]	124	60	459

Source: Quarterly reports of the Norwegian government.
[a] Financed by conditional dollar aid.
[b] Financed by dollar grant to European Payments Union.
[c] Of the total, 49 million dollars was in loans.

magnitude.[17] Import prices rose so quickly after devaluation that the import surpluses would have had to be much greater than 1.1 billion kroner at current prices to finance purchases of real goods and services worth 1.1 billion in 1948. The shift in the terms of trade in favor of Norway worked in the other direction. It meant that total imports of goods and services could reach the planned levels without such large import surpluses.

The actual import surpluses tended to be smaller than implied in the 1948 plan. At current prices, the average was less than 450 million kroner; at 1948 prices, the surplus was about 1.1 billion kroner in 1949 and 500–600 million kroner in the next three years.[18] Import surpluses also tended to be smaller than estimated in the annual budgets.

The failure to achieve import surpluses of the intended 1.1 billion

[17] After devaluation, $220 million would have financed a deficit at current prices of 1.5 billion kroner; and $160 million a deficit of 1.1 billion. The deficit at current prices was much less in 1950; and in 1951 and 1952, there was a surplus or balance at current prices.

[18] At current prices, the import surplus of goods and services was 1,186 million kroner in 1949 and 800 million in 1950; there was an export surplus of 258 million in 1951, followed by an import surplus of 23 million in 1952. At 1948 prices, the surpluses were 1,120 million kroner in 1949, 484 million in 1950, 597 million in 1951, and 471 million in 1952. Current price data from *National Accounts, 1938 and 1948–53,* except for revised unpublished estimate for 1952. The calculations at 1948 prices are based on Central Bureau of Statistics price indices from the same publication.

kroner at 1948 prices might be more an indication of success than of failure in carrying out the plan. The plan aimed at equilibrium in the current balance by 1952–53; it was achieved by 1951. But the equilibrium was due to the shift in the terms of trade and was likely to be short-lived. From 1948 to 1950, the terms of trade were about 10 per cent less favorable than they had been in 1938; in 1951 they were 5 per cent more favorable; and in 1952 they were at about the 1938 level (Table 35). The terms of trade deteriorated sharply in the

Table 35. Price indices for total imports and exports of goods and services and terms of trade, 1946–1952 (1938 = 100)

	Exports of goods and services	Imports of goods and services	Terms of trade
1946...................	275	242	114
1947...................	295	293	101
1948...................	300	324	93
1949...................	288	315	91
1950...................	313	351	89
1951...................	441	419	105
1952...................	433	431	100

Source: Central Bureau of Statistics, *National Accounts, 1930–39 and 1946–51, National Accounts, 1938 and 1948–53,* and mimeographed document *National Accounts, 1949–1955.*

second half of 1952.

The original 1948 goals for the volume of exports of goods and services were achieved. The 1948 plan assumed that by 1952 exports of goods and ships could be increased to at least 10 per cent above the 1938 level, and that the merchant fleet could be raised 18 per cent above the 1938 level. The goal set for 1952 for exports of goods and ships was exceeded in 1950; and in 1951 and 1952, exports of goods rose sharply[19] (Table 36). Exports of shipping services in 1952 reached the goal called for in the plan.

The 1948 plan assumed that the imports of goods and ships which could be financed by 1952–53 would exceed the 1938 level by 10–12 per cent; the import of goods alone was expected to be only 5 per cent above 1938. For both goods and ships, however, imports were

[19] In 1951, exports of goods alone were 22 per cent above 1938; and in spite of a drop in exports of both goods and ships in 1952, the 1952 total for goods and ships was 19 per cent above 1938. Ship exports consist mostly of second-hand ships.

Table 36. Indices of volume of imports and exports of goods and ships and of exports of shipping services, 1946–1952 (1938 = 100)

	Exports				Imports		
	Goods	Ships	Goods and ships	Net exports of shipping services[a]	Goods	Ships	Goods and ships
1946	63	40	62	49	78	74	78
1947	82	75	81	68	104	166	112
1948	86	32	83	90	94	126	98
1949	91	30	88	100	107	140	111
1950	113	70	111	113	113	136	116
1951	122	213	127	116	125	135	126
1952	119	118	119	118	129	81	123

Source: Central Bureau of Statistics. Data for 1946 and 1947 from *National Accounts, 1930–39 and 1946–51*. Data from 1948 to 1951 from *National Accounts, 1938 and 1948–1953*. Unpublished revised data for 1952.
[a] Volume of gross earnings minus volume of operating expenditures abroad.

substantially above the planned level. In 1950, imports of goods and ships were already 11 per cent above 1938, but investment imports were to be cut in 1952 and 1953. Actually, imports of goods continued to rise sharply. In 1951, because of the favorable terms of trade, increases in import sectors still subject to control were deliberately allowed.[20] In 1952, imports of ships fell sharply, but imports of goods rose. The continued favorable terms of trade made it difficult to control imports, but there is little evidence of a burst in imports of consumer goods.

The increases in imports in 1951 and 1952 were due partly to the continued liberalizing of import restrictions. The full 75 per cent liberalization goal of the Organization for European Economic Cooperation was reached by 1952 in all three categories of goods. Dry cargo ship contracting was freed, so that certain types of machinery and equipment could still be controlled. Many textile goods were finally freed early in 1952.[21]

[20] There were also sudden imports of trucks and busses, apparently for defense reasons.
[21] There was no tendency toward sharp increases in imports of particular goods after liberalization. The government tried to increase supplies gradually prior to liberalization, to avoid a sudden impact and buying for stocks.

The high volume of imports reflected increases in imports of investment goods rather than of consumer goods;[22] in 1951 and 1952, the increases were much greater for investment goods than for consumer goods.[23] The low level for finished consumer goods reflects partly the development of domestic production and partly the continued severe restrictions of luxury imports, such as fruit, passenger cars, and special types of household equipment.

On the whole, the facts indicate that output and export goals were met from 1949 to 1952. Total output rose about as fast as expected. Targets for increases in output were mostly met, sector by sector and commodity by commodity. The volume of exports rose more than planned or expected. Also, it seems reasonably clear that output rose at a satisfactory rate. Output per worker increased more than in any preceding period. Inflationary pressure did not hinder output seriously. Although the absolute level of output was much higher than assumed in 1948, and the expected percentage increases in output provided more resources, import surpluses did not play anything like the role contemplated in 1948.

[22] Imports of finished investment goods, including ships, averaged 23 per cent of the value of total imports from 1936 to 1938, 33 per cent from 1947 to 1950, and 30 per cent in 1951. Imports of finished consumer goods represented 18 per cent in 1936–38, 11 per cent in 1947–49, 9 per cent in 1950–51. Other groups showed relatively small changes. Data from *Current Economic Trends*.

[23] The index of the volume of imports of finished investment goods, including ships, rose from 160 (1938 = 100) in 1947–49 to 200 in 1951; for imports of raw materials for production of investment goods, from 122 to 138; imports of raw materials for consumer goods, from 100 to 121; and imports of finished consumer goods fell from 76 to 75. Source: *Current Economic Trends*.

11

Total Resources and Uses: 1946–1952

The plans for the whole period from 1946 to 1952 were esentially homogeneous. The goal was the same throughout the period — rapid increases in the volume of output, especially in export sectors — and the means relied on to achieve these goals were also the same. An ambitious investment program required restrictions on increases in private and public consumption. Foreign capital was needed to finance about half the net investment program. On the whole, it seems clear that the two basic long-term plans of 1946 and 1948 worked out well.

Attention should be directed to some important questions, however. What proportion of total output was devoted to investment and what proportion to consumption in the postwar period? How did the allocation of resources compare with that in prewar years? When compared with the prewar period, how much of the change in the distribution of total output at current prices was due to changes in the relative prices of consumer and investment goods? How much did total real available resources increase year by year? How were the increases distributed among various uses? How did the program for resource uses contribute to the elimination of inflationary pressures? How did output increases and resource uses compare with those in other European countries?

For the period as a whole, data at current prices present a picture which corresponds to the broad outlines of both the 1946 and the 1948 plans.[1] Investment rates were phenomenally high. Gross investment averaged 35 per cent of gross national product, and net investment averaged 22 per cent of net national product. In 1938 the gross investment rate had been 25 per cent and the net rate 12 per cent. The average net investment rate in the 1946–52 period, therefore, was

[1] See Tables 37, 38, and 39.

Table 37. Total resource availabilities and uses at current prices,
1938 and 1946–1952 (millions of kroner)

	Gross national product	Import surplus[a]	Total resources	Gross invest-ment	Private consump-tion	Public consump-tion
1938	5,857	−139	5,718	1473	3,827	418
1946	11,030	612	11,642	3472	6,816	1354
1947	12,995	1240	14,235	4835	8,087	1313
1948	14,092	741	14,833	5099	8,396	1338
1949	15,015	1186	16,201	5593	9,174	1434
1950	16,647	800	17,447	5640	10,275	1532
1951	20,706	−258	20,448	7004	11,581	1863
1952	22,810	23	22,833	7642	12,905	2286

Source: Central Bureau of Statistics. Data up to and including 1948 from
National Accounts, 1930–39 and 1946–51. Data from 1949 to 1951 from *National
Accounts, 1938 and 1948–53.* The 1952 figures are from *National Accounts, 1949–
1955.* The 1952 figures published in the *Economic Survey, 1956* are not used (see
Table 16). The import surplus figures are for goods and services, excluding interest
and dividends.
[a] Minus sign indicates export surplus.

Table 38. Private and public consumption, gross investment, and import surplus
as per cent of gross national product at current prices, 1938 and 1946–1952

	Private consumption	Public consumption	Gross investment	Import surplus[a]
1938..............	65	7	25	−2
1946..............	62	12	31	5
1947..............	62	11	37	10
1948..............	60	10	36	5
1949..............	61	10	37	8
1950..............	62	9	34	5
1951..............	56	9	34	−1
1952..............	57	10	34	0
Average, 1946–52...	60	10	35	5

Source: See Table 37.   [a] Minus sign indicates export surplus.

almost double the prewar rate.[2] Conversely, the percentage of gross
national product devoted to consumption from 1946 to 1952 was
low. Private consumption, at current prices, averaged 60 per cent of
gross national product compared with 65 per cent in 1938. While

[2] See the discussion on the Norwegian definition of gross investment below
on page 156. A net investment rate of 22 per cent probably has not been sur-
passed by any democratic country in modern times. See Tables 45 and 46
for comparisons with Europe, the United States, and Canada.

Table 39. Net national product, net investment, net investment as per cent of
net national product, and import surplus as per cent of net investment
at current prices, 1938 and 1946–1952

	Net national product	Net investment	Net investment as per cent of net national product	Import surplus[a] as per cent of net investment
	(millions of kroner)			
1938.	4,994	610	12	−23
1946.	9,286	1728	18	35
1947.	10,963	2803	25	44
1948.	11,756	2763	24	27
1949.	12,402	2980	24	40
1950.	13,758	2751	20	29
1951.	17,314	3612	21	−7
1952.	18,843	3675	20	1
Average, 1946–52.			22	24

Source: See Table 37.   [a] Minus sign indicates export surplus.

public consumption averaged 10 per cent of gross national product
in contrast to 7 per cent before the war, defense accounted for most
of the increase.[3]

A considerable part of the expansion in investment was made
possible by import surpluses. Over the entire period, import surpluses
averaged almost 5 per cent of gross national product; and prior to
1951, they averaged 7 per cent of gross national product and 35 per
cent of net investment. Although they did not finance half of total
net investment, as had been hoped in 1946 and 1948, they were
vitally important in fulfilling the basic objectives of the plans.

Comparisons of prewar and postwar years at current prices are
strongly affected by the shifts in relative prices between the two
periods (Table 40). These shifts resulted partly from the stabilization
program. Prices of investment goods, largely imported, rose much
more than prices of consumer goods.[4] The effect on current price

[3] The percentage of gross national product at current prices devoted to public
plus private consumption was on the average only 2 per cent below 1938.
[4] The relative shifts from the prewar period were fairly stable throughout
the postwar period. In 1952, import and export prices were more than four
times 1938 levels; the price index for gross national product and domestic use
of resources more than two and one half times 1938; for gross investment,
three and one fourth times 1938; and private consumption, less than 2 and
one half times 1938.

Table 40. Price indices of components of gross national product, imports, net national product, and domestic use of resources, selected years, 1948 to 1952
(1938 = 100)

	1948	1950	1952
Private consumption	180	199	238
Gross investment, excluding stocks	231	261	324
Exports	300	313	433
Imports	324	351	431
Net national product	182	198	258
Gross national product	189	206	262
Domestic use of resources	196	216	268

Source: Data from *National Accounts, 1938 and 1948–53,* except for the revised indices for consumption, exports, imports, and gross national product in 1952, which are from *National Accounts, 1949–1955.* These revised indices may not be strictly comparable to the other indices for 1952.

data is to make the percentage of resources devoted to investment in the postwar period seem larger, and the percentage devoted to consumption smaller, compared with the prewar years.

Data at constant prewar (1938) prices present a different picture and presumably indicate more clearly the real changes in resource availabilities and uses.[5] The investment rate in the postwar period as indicated by these data is somewhat lower than the rate indicated by the data at current prices and the proportion of total resources devoted to consumption is higher.[6] Gross investment averaged 29 per cent and private consumption 64 per cent of gross national product. Net investment averaged 18 per cent of net national product. The change from the prewar to the postwar period appears much smaller than that indicated by data at current prices. The net investment rate is only about 50 per cent higher than before the war. Gross investment compared with gross national product is only about 4 per cent higher than before the war and private consumption only 2 per cent lower. Import surpluses at 1938 prices average only 3 per cent of gross national product and 22 per cent of net investment from

[5] Any such calculations may be misleading and must be considered as giving only some indication of orders of magnitude. The particular year chosen affects the results. The Central Bureau of Statistics has calculated that at 1948 prices and weights the volume of private consumption in 1948 was 16 per cent above 1938, while at 1938 prices and weights, consumption was 22 per cent above 1938. Volume indices based on 1938 prices have been referred to in previous chapters.

[6] See Tables 41, 42, and 43.

Table 41. Total resource availabilities and uses at 1938 prices,
1938 and 1946–1952 (millions of kroner)

	Gross national product	Import surplus[a]	Total resources	Gross investment	Private consumption	Public consumption
1938	5857	−139	5718	1473	3827	418
1946	6334	385	6719	1755	4187	777
1947	7144	435	7579	2227	4608	744
1948	7458	121	7579	2209	4674	696
1949	7718	238	7956	2256	4965	735
1950	8068	18	8086	2160	5165	761
1951	8374	45	8419	2440	5165	814
1952	8718	14	8732	2451	5413	868

Source: Central Bureau of Statistics. Data up to and including 1947 from
National Accounts, 1930–39 and 1946–51. Data for the years from 1948 to 1951
from *National Accounts, 1938 and 1948–53.* The figures for 1952 are from *National
Accounts, 1949–1955.* [a] Minus sign indicates export surplus.

Table 42. Private and public consumption, gross investment, and import surplus
as per cent of gross national product at 1938 prices, 1938 and 1946–1952

	Private consumption	Public consumption	Gross investment	Import surplus[a]
1938.	65[b]	7	25[b]	−2
1946.	66	12	28	6
1947.	65	10	31	6
1948.	63	9	30	2
1949.	64	10	29	3
1950.	64	9	27	0
1951.	61	10	29	1
1952.	62	10	28	0
Average, 1946–52...	64	10	29	3

Source: See Table 41.
[a] Minus sign indicates export surplus.
[b] The 1935–39 average for consumption was 66 per cent and investment 25
per cent.

1946 to 1950. Import surpluses appear to have provided a less substantial part of the real resources needed for the investment program.

The import surpluses and the aid that made them possible were of
vital significance, however, even though they seem relatively less important at constant 1938 prices. Imports had to be financed at current prices. World prices rose fast, and prices of ships rose even
faster. Norwegian foreign-exchange reserves were totally inadequate
to finance the required imports. The import surpluses, though small

Table 43. Net national product, net investment, net investment as per cent of net national product, and import surplus as per cent of net investment at 1938 prices, 1938 and 1946–1952

	Net national product	Net investment	Net investment as per cent of net national product	Import surplus[a] as per cent of net investment
	(millions of kroner)			
1938.............	4994	610	12	−23
1946.............	5464	885	16	44
1947.............	6209	1292	21	34
1948.............	6469	1220	19	10
1949.............	6671	1209	18	20
1950.............	6964	1056	15	2
1951.............	7211	1277	18	4
1952.............	7398	1241	17	3
Average, 1946–52...			18	17

Source: See Table 41 for sources of data prior to 1952. Data for 1952 are from the *Economic Survey, 1955*. More recent estimates are not available on a comparable basis with data for earlier years. *National Accounts, 1949–1955* does not contain estimates for net investment and net national product at 1938 prices.

[a] Minus sign indicates export surplus.

compared with total resources, provided marginal amounts of machinery, materials, and food, which were necessary for recovery.

Although constant 1938 price data indicate that the allocation of resources in the postwar years did not differ from the prewar allocation as much as would appear from current price data, they also indicate that both the volume of investment and the volume of consumption were much higher than before the war and as high as or even higher than planned. These volume increases were achieved in spite of the fact that import surpluses tended to be less important than expected. The explanation is that the plans were based on output estimates for the postwar period which were much too low in comparison with prewar output, and the plans also underestimated increases in output. The picture presented is, nevertheless, rather different from the long-term plans.

The constant 1938 price data on resources and uses provide a significant year-by-year account of increases in the volume of resources available and of the source of the increases. The increase in total available resources was tremendous in 1947; and in 1949,

1951, and 1952 the increases were substantial (Table 44). In 1948 and in 1950, however, the increases were negligible. Output increases were satisfactory throughout the period. The variations from year to year in the additions to total available resources were due for the

Table 44. Increases or decreases in resource availabilities and resource uses, and per cent increase or decrease in resource availabilities and resource uses over previous year at 1938 prices, 1946 to 1952

	1946[a]	1947	1948	1949	1950	1951	1952
Increase[b] in resource availabilities							
(millions of kroner)							
Gross national product.	477	810	314	260	350	306	344
Import surplus........	524	50	−314	117	−220	27	−29
Total...........	1001	860	0	377	130	333	315[c]
Increase[b] in resource uses							
(millions of kroner)							
Public consumption....	359	−33	−48	39	26	53	54
Gross investment......	282	472	−18	47	−96	280	11
Private consumption...	360	421	66	291	200	0	248
Total...........	1001	860	0	377	130	333	313[c]
Per cent increase in resource availabilities over previous year...........	18	13	0	5	1	5	4
Per cent increase[b] over previous year in resource uses							
Public consumption....	86	−4	−6	6	4	7	6
Gross investment......	19	27	−1	2	−4	13	1
Private consumption...	9	10	1	6	4	0	5

Source: Calculated from data in Table 41.
[a] Increases over 1938.
[b] Minus sign indicates decrease.
[c] Details do not add to equal totals because of rounding.

most part to changes in the amounts contributed from abroad. Import surpluses added substantially to total available resources in 1946, 1947, and 1949; but from 1950 on, the contributions were negligible.

The added resources were used in almost equal amounts for investment and for consumption in 1946 and 1947, when total availabilities increased rapidly (Table 44). In 1948, when there was no net increase in resources, there was a slight cut in investment and a slight rise in consumption. Most of the substantial increase in resources in 1949 was devoted to consumption. There was only a small increase in resources in 1950, but a cut in investment made possible a consumption increase that was somewhat larger. During these two years, great progress was made in eliminating inflationary pressure in the consumer goods sector. In 1951 consumption was virtually constant, although controls on consumption were already unimportant. In 1952 investment rose very slightly and consumption rose 5 per cent.

On the whole, the share of increases in resources devoted to consumption from 1946 to 1952 was high, especially in 1949 and 1950 and again in 1952. The rise in consumption from 1948 to 1950 was possible because investment was held almost constant or decreased. In these years, direct controls managed to keep gross investment more or less at or slightly below the 1947 level. To put it another way, the fact that investment was held fairly constant from 1947 to 1950 was an important factor in making it possible to eliminate inflationary pressure in the consumer goods sphere.

It would not be correct to consider the changes in output and consumption as induced by independent changes in investment and public consumption. Changes in these resource uses were not the active factors determining the level of output and consumption. The government did not plan on or permit a given level of investment and then let output and consumption find their own levels. Both total investment and total consumption were strictly controlled until 1951. The government believed that investment should have priority, but when resources were available it permitted higher consumption increases than originally planned.

The level of output reflected the government's plans for and controls over both investment and consumption. The size of the import surpluses was also controlled. The government considered output possibilities, before deciding on plans for consumption and investment, so that the causal relationship sometimes went from expected output to planned and actual investment and consumption. Increases in investment did, of course, affect consumption and output within certain limits. The consumption of many domestically produced goods and services was not as strictly controlled as the consumption of imported goods, and responded to changes in income, which in turn depended partly on changes in, or on the level of, investment. Consumption of domestically produced goods and services rose sharply in 1946 and 1947, along with the rapid increase in investment. From 1947 to 1950 investment was either virtually constant or falling, but consumption rose sharply in 1949 and 1950. The free-economy type of reaction to a levelling off in investment did not take place.

By 1951 and 1952 controls over consumption were virtually eliminated except for luxury imports. In 1951 gross fixed investment increased slightly, and in 1952 it increased substantially. Stock accumulations were large in 1951 and presumably involuntary for the most part. They fell sharply in 1952. The stability of consumption in 1951 reflects mostly the effect of the upward price adjustment on real wage rates. In 1952 real wage rates and consumption both rose sharply.

It is tempting to try to compare Norway's experience during the recovery program with that of other European countries. A few rough statistical comparisons can be made on the basis of the national accounts estimates of the Organization for European Economic Cooperation (OEEC). These estimates have been made for all member countries and for the United States and Canada, as far as possible on a comparable basis according to OEEC standard definitions. The principal adjustment made in Norwegian official data is the exclusion of ordinary repairs and maintenance from gross investment and gross national product. This adjustment reduces the percentage of gross national product devoted to gross investment at current prices by about 6 per cent of gross national product. It also raises consumption as a percentage of gross national product by 3 or 4 per cent of gross national product.[7]

In spite of the substantial reduction of gross investment estimates for Norway, the OEEC data indicate that Norway was outstanding among member countries in the proportion of output devoted to investment (Table 45); Iceland is the only country which had a higher investment rate. Norway on the average devoted 29.5 per cent of gross national product to investment from 1947 to 1952, according to current price data, and Iceland 30.8 per cent. Germany, next highest to Norway, averaged 22.4 per cent from 1949 to 1952,

[7] For a fuller explanation of the adjustments made in the official Norwegian data see *National Accounts Studies, Norway* (Paris: OEEC, 1953).

Table 45. Private consumption and gross domestic capital formation as per cent of gross national product at current prices, selected countries, 1938, 1948, and 1952

Country	Private consumption			Gross domestic capital formation		
	1938	1948	1952	1938	1948	1952
Austria	76[a]	76	69	7[a]	21	22
Belgium	n.a.	76	70	n.a.	17	16
Denmark	77	72	69	13	19	18
France	74[b]	73[b]	67	14[b]	19[b]	18
Germany	57[b]	n.a.	56	20[b]	n.a.	24
Iceland	64[b]	66[b]	68[b]	25[b]	30[b]	28[b]
Italy	65	72	72	17	18	20
Netherlands	74	70	59	11	24	18
Norway	70	64	61	19	30	28
Portugal	83[b]	90[b]	79	13[b]	13[b]	16
Sweden	71	69	63	19	19	21
United Kingdom	76	71	66	11	13	13
Canada	72	67	61	15	21	23
United States	75	68	62	12	18	18

Source: All the percentages were calculated from data in the OEEC study, *Statistics of National Product and Expenditures, No. 2, 1938 and 1947 to 1955.* The table includes data for all the member countries for which data are available except Greece, Ireland, and Luxembourg.

[a] 1937.   [b] Unofficial estimates of the OEEC secretariat.

and Austria 22.2 per cent from 1948 to 1952. The Netherlands came next, averaging 20.1 per cent from 1947 to 1952.

In the early postwar years Norway and Iceland devoted the smallest proportion of gross national product to private consumption, according to current price data, but no data are available for Germany. In the later postwar years the proportion of output devoted to private consumption in Norway was among the lowest, but higher than in Germany and the Netherlands (Table 45).

A somewhat different picture is presented when the OEEC data for investment, consumption, and gross national product for the postwar years are converted to 1938 prices (Table 46). The proportion of postwar output devoted to investment appears to be much lower and the proportion devoted to consumption much higher in Norway (as indicated by official Norwegian data) and in certain other countries, notably Austria.[8] Even so, the estimates at 1938

[8] Relatively high prices after the war for imported capital equipment account for much of the difference in Norway. The shift from postwar prices to 1938 prices makes very little difference in the cases of the United States, the United Kingdom, France, and Germany.

Table 46. Private consumption and gross domestic capital formation as per cent of gross national product at 1938 prices, selected countries, average for 1947 to 1952

Country	Private consumption	Gross domestic capital formation
Austria[a]	71.0	12.3
Denmark	70.8	16.9
France[b]	77.4	20.0
Germany[b,c]	60.2	20.0
Italy	69.5	17.2
Norway	67.9	23.1
United Kingdom	70.1	10.8
Canada	67.6	19.7
United States	69.0	14.0

Source: The percentages were calculated from 1938 data at 1938 prices, and volume indices based on 1954 prices, from the OEEC study cited as the source for Table 45. No data are available for Iceland, the Netherlands, or Sweden.
[a] Average for 1948 to 1952 calculated at 1937 prices.
[b] Unofficial estimates of OEEC secretariat.
[c] Average for 1949 to 1952.

prices indicate that Norway devoted a larger proportion of output to investment than any other European country for which data are available. If data for Iceland were available, however, they most

Table 47. Volume of per capita private consumption and gross domestic fixed capital formation in selected countries in 1952 compared with 1938 and 1948

Country	Per capita private consumption		Gross domestic fixed capital formation	
	1938 = 100	1948 = 100	1938 = 100	1948 = 100
Austria	112[a]	128	247[a,b]	188
Belgium	n.a.	104	n.a.	113
Denmark	102	103	169	131
France	110[c]	120[c]	150[c]	115[c]
Germany	92[c]	n.a.	126[c]	n.a.
Italy	113	119	119[b]	154[b]
Netherlands	n.a.	92	n.a.	119
Norway	126	111	166	113
Portugal	120[b,c]	93[b,c]	135	117
Sweden	n.a.	103	n.a.	110
United Kingdom	95	101	105	114
Canada	156	107	307	124
United States	143	105	223	116

Source: See Table 45. The table presents data for all countries for which data are available except Ireland and Greece. No data are available for Iceland.
[a] 1937 = 100.
[b] Data in these cases are not strictly comparable because data for earlier years include changes in stocks.
[c] Unofficial estimates of OEEC secretariat.

probably would show a slightly higher investment rate. The gross investment rate in Norway averaged 23 per cent, compared with 20 per cent for France and Germany, and 17 per cent for Denmark and Italy. Germany devoted the lowest share of output to private consumption, 60 per cent on the average, and Norway was next lowest at 67 per cent.

Volume indices of per capita private consumption and gross fixed investment, as calculated by the OEEC, present another and a slightly different picture (Table 47). Gross fixed investment in Norway in 1952 was not as high, compared with 1938, as it was in Austria and Denmark. But both of these countries had relatively low investment rates in 1938 whereas Norway had a high investment rate. The increase in Norway was greater than in the other European countries for which data are available. From 1948 to 1952 gross investment rates rose less in Norway than in most other European countries.

Per capita consumption increased more in Norway from 1938 to 1952 than in any other European country for which data are available (Table 47). The increase in per capita consumption was especially rapid in the early postwar years; from 1948 to 1952 the rate of increase in consumption was about average. There is no indication in these over-all volume indices of comparative austerity in Norway. The severe scarcities of basic consumer goods in the early years were accompanied by substantial increases in the consumption of other non-basic consumer goods. The United Kingdom and Germany are the countries which stand out as having the smallest increases in per capita consumption from 1938 to 1952. In the United Kingdom the rate of increase in consumption was especially low from 1948 to 1952.

The relatively rapid growth of private consumption at the same time that investment in Norway was also relatively high compared with prewar suggests that the rate of increase in output in Norway must also have been greater than in other European countries. In fact, the volume of gross national product increased more in Norway from 1938 to 1952 than in any other European country with the exception of Iceland (Table 48). The results are the same whether indices of total gross national product or of per capita gross national product are compared. The rate of increase in total output was almost as high in Portugal and Sweden. The rate of increase in per capita out-

Table 48. Volume of gross national product in selected countries in 1952
compared with 1938 and 1948

Country	Gross national product		Per capita gross national product	
	1938 = 100	1948 = 100	1938 = 100	1948 = 100
Austria.................	132[a,b]	148	129[a,b]	148
Belgium................	131[b]	114	127[b]	113
Denmark...............	132	112	114	108
France.................	128[b]	129[b]	125[b]	127[b]
Germany...............	116[b]	172[b]	93[b]	162[b]
Iceland................	300[b]	113[b]	236[b]	96[b]
Italy..................	116	126	106	122
Netherlands............	133[b]	116	111[b]	111
Norway................	148	117	131	112
Portugal...............	140[b]	113[b]	122[b]	108[b]
Sweden................	143[b,c]	113	126[b,c]	109
Switzerland............	131[b]	109[b]	114[b]	103
United Kingdom........	116[b]	110	109[b]	108
Canada................	223	126	178	114
United States...........	200	122	166	114

Source: See Table 45. The table presents data for all member countries for which
data are available except Greece, Ireland, Luxembourg, and Turkey.
  [a] 1937 = 100.
  [b] Unofficial estimates of the OEEC secretariat.
  [c] 1938/1939 = 100.

put was almost as high in Austria, Belgium, and Sweden. The OEEC
data on output increases seem to indicate that Norwegian postwar
economic policies not only did not prevent rapid recovery and development but were well designed to achieve these goals.

From 1948 to 1952 the rate of increase of total and per capita
output in Norway was well below that in Germany, Austria, France,
and Italy, but these countries had achieved relatively small increases
in output by 1948 compared with prewar levels. The rate of increase
in per capita output in Norway from 1948 to 1952 was just slightly
below that in Belgium, the United States, and Canada; it was above
that in Sweden, the United Kingdom, the Netherlands, Denmark,
Switzerland, and Portugal. The Norwegian record in these years
sems to be a good one.[9]

  [9] The fact that the investment rate was higher in Norway than in other
European countries during these years of recovery might be expected to result
in a higher rate of increase in output (see Chapter 10). It must be remembered,
also, that Norway's war losses were relatively high, and replacement of war
losses, especially in shipping, accounted for a substantial share of investment.
Also, the rate of increase in Norway of the population of working age was lower
than that of the total population.

The facts reviewed in this chapter on the postwar recovery of Norway during the entire period up to 1952 may be summarized as follows:

1. Norwegian investment rates, according to official Norwegian data, were phenomenally high, measured at current prices; they were also high when calculated at 1938 prices, but considerably lower than at current prices, and not so much above the prewar level. Converse statements apply to the proportion of output devoted to private consumption. The real rate of development, which had been rapid in prewar years, increased only moderately in the postwar period.

2. Import surpluses were relatively small compared with net investment, measured at 1938 prices. They averaged 22 per cent of net investment from 1946 to 1950 and were negligible thereafter. This does not mean that the import surpluses, financed partly by aid, were not of vital importance.

3. Increases in output provided the largest source of increase in total available resources.

4. Private consumption absorbed a substantial share of the increases in available resources from 1947 to 1950, while total gross investment was held constant or cut slightly.

5. Compared with other European countries, according to the OEEC data at current prices, Norway has devoted a relatively large proportion of output to investment since the war and a relatively small proportion to private consumption. The OEEC data show that Norway's investment rate, calculated at prewar prices, though less spectacularly high than when calculated at current prices, has also been relatively high compared with other European countries. The volume of investment was also relatively high compared with prewar.

6. The volume of private per capita consumption increased more in Norway between 1938 and 1952 than in other European countries; and, disregarding problems of choice and quality, consumption had already increased more in Norway than in other European countries by 1948.

7. According to the OEEC data, output, both total and per capita, increased more in Norway than in any other European country except Iceland.

Norway's recovery program not only worked out according to

plan but was more ambitious than the programs carried out in most other European countries, and was more successful, if success is measured by increases in output and in consumption in comparison with 1938. The substantial and steady increase in consumption no doubt helped to maintain the high rate of increase in output. But the steady rise in consumption probably could not have been maintained if output had not risen continuously.

12

Savings and Inflationary Pressure: 1946–1952

Domestic savings financed much more of the investment program than had been expected. In the period from 1946 to 1952, domestic savings averaged 79 per cent of net investment (Table 49). Even in

Table 49. Net investment, domestic savings, and domestic savings as per cent of net investment and of net national product, at current prices, 1938 and 1946–1952

	Net investment	Domestic savings[a]	Domestic savings as per cent of	
			Net investment	Net national product at factor cost
	(millions of kroner)			
1938...........	610	689	123	14.7
1946...........	1728	1081	65	12.5
1947...........	2803	1516	56	14.7
1948...........	2763	1959	73	17.2
1949...........	2980	1735	60	14.6
1950...........	2751	1884	71	14.2
1951...........	3612	3793	107	23.8
1952...........	3675	3604	99	21.2

Source: Central Bureau of Statistics. Data for the years up to and including 1947 from *National Accounts, 1930–39 and 1946–51*. Data for the years 1948 through 1951 from *National Accounts, 1938 and 1948–53*. Data for 1952 from *Economic Survey, 1955*. The latest revised data for 1952 in *Economic Survey, 1956* raise the estimates for net investment and net domestic savings substantially. These data cannot be used in connection with data for earlier years since they are not comparable.
[a] Derived by subtracting from net investment the import surplus of goods and services, including net interest and dividends.

the years of big import surpluses from 1946 to 1950, domestic savings amounted to almost two thirds of net investment. The average net investment rate at current prices of 22 per cent from 1946 to 1952 clearly indicates that the rate of domestic savings was very high.

The question of how such a level of domestic savings was maintained throughout the period remains to be answered. How much of the total domestic savings were public savings and how were the public savings achieved? What about private savings? Were they at or above prewar rates? If private savings were substantial, were they entirely business savings or partly personal savings? How were consumer incomes brought into line with the supply of consumer goods by 1951 or at least by 1952?

Some of these questions can be answered quite fully and easily. Others cannot be answered in terms of the data now available. The financial statistics in Norway have not yet been developed as completely as the production accounts. Income cannot be separated, for example, into personal as distinct from corporate income. Private disposable income, therefore, cannot be divided into personal and corporate disposable income, and private savings into personal and corporate savings. It is possible, however, to measure total domestic savings and also public savings as distinct from private savings. It is also possible to guess at the sources of private saving and obtain some general idea of the relative importance of personal and corporate savings.

Domestic savings averaged 17 per cent of net national product at factor cost from 1946 to 1952, which was above the 1938 rate of about 15 per cent (Table 49) which in turn was above the average in prewar years. Domestic savings averaged about 15 per cent from 1946 to 1950.[1] In these early years, import surpluses were not accompanied by a cut from the prewar level in the total domestic savings rate; therefore, import surpluses made it possible to finance a higher rate of net investment during these years than before the war. In 1951 and 1952, a sudden spurt in domestic savings permitted Norway to continue financing a high level of net investment even though the import surpluses disappeared.

The fact that from 1946 to 1950 domestic savings were at approximately the prewar rate is explained mostly by the very high rate of public savings. Public savings as a percentage of net national product were at almost twice the prewar rate from 1947 to 1949 and above the prewar rate each year thereafter (Table 50). Private savings were at about the prewar rate in 1946, but averaged substantially below the prewar rate in the period 1947–50. High public

---

[1] The rate was 14.7 per cent in 1938, 16.9 per cent from 1946 to 1952 on the average, and 14.6 per cent from 1946 to 1950 on the average.

Table 50. Public and private savings in absolute amounts and as per cent of total domestic savings and of net national product at current prices, 1938 and 1946–1952

	Public savings			Private savings			Total savings as per cent of net national product[a]
	Millions of kroner	As per cent of		Millions of kroner	As per cent of		
		Domestic saving	Net national product		Domestic saving	Net national product[a]	
1938	171	25	3.6[b]	518	75	11.1	14.7
1946	86	8	1.0	995	92	11.5	12.5
1947	588	39	5.7	928	61	9.0	14.7
1948	789	40	6.9	1170	60	10.3	17.2
1949	776	45	6.5	959	55	8.1	14.6
1950	1026	55	7.6	858	45	6.6	14.2
1951	1384	36	8.7	2409	64	15.1	23.8
1952	1419	39	8.4	2185	61	12.8	21.2

Source: See Table 49 for source of data on domestic savings and net national product. For public savings, see Table 51. Public savings include savings of the state and the municipalities. Private savings were derived by subtracting public savings from total domestic savings.

a At factor cost.

b The 1935–39 average was 4 per cent.

savings offset low private savings during these years. Public savings rose even higher in 1951 and 1952, but private savings also increased sharply during these years. For the whole 1946–52 period, public savings averaged about 40 per cent of total domestic savings.

In normal times, high taxes and high public savings might be expected, other things being equal, to reduce private savings by some fraction of the reduction in private disposable incomes. In the actual Norwegian situation from 1946 to 1948, different policies might have led to higher private savings. Lower public savings would have meant that individuals and businesses had larger disposable incomes. But allocations, rationing, and price controls limited expenditures rather effectively. If higher private savings had resulted, they would have been forced on the public against their wishes. The pressure on the price-control system at the time, and also later, would have been greater. High public savings were preferable for these reasons, and they also tended to bring sharp reductions in private bank reserves.

Lower public savings would probably have necessitated a revision of certain other policies to avoid excessive strain on the price-control system and price-stabilization policy. Stricter control of bank credit, higher interest rates, or stricter wage controls might have been adopted. Or the government might have had to abandon the stabilization line. On the whole, the high public savings policy seems to have been a wise one, and eminently successful.

The high public savings were possible only because of a tremendous increase in tax receipts (Table 51). Current tax revenues had to

Table 51. Public current revenues and expenditures and public consumption, public savings, and public net investment, 1938 and 1946–1952 (millions of kroner)

	1938	1946	1947	1948	1949	1950	1951	1952
Current revenues								
Direct taxes...........	526	1365	1859	2438	2454	2540	2802	3072
Indirect taxes..........	377	1208	1544	1524	1642	1832	2403	2804
Other.................	50	40	44	16	50	79	63	39
	953	2613	3447	3978	4146	4451	5268	5915
Current transfer expenditures								
Subsidies..............	65	569	865	1127	1145	1020	1039	1099
Grants................	210	446	536	586	648	733	847	975
Interest...............	89	158	145	138	143	140	135	136
	364	1173	1546	1851	1936	1893	2021	2210
Available current revenues[a]	589	1440	1901	2127	2210	2558	3247	3705
Public consumption........	418	1354	1313	1338	1434	1532	1863	2286
Public savings...........	171	86	588	789	776	1026	1384	1419
Public net investment......	122	264	416	512	605	687	749	905
Public savings minus public investment.............	49	−178	172	277	171	339	635	514

Source: Central Bureau of Statistics. Data for the years up to and including 1947 from *National Accounts, 1930–39 and 1946–51.* Data for the years from 1948 to 1952 from unpublished revisions of data in the *Economic Survey, 1953.* Slight revisions have been made in the direct tax figures for the years 1948 to 1952 since these calculations were made. The revised figures reduce direct tax receipts by about 40 million kroner from 1948 to 1951 and raise the 1952 figure by about that much. See *Economic Survey, 1954.* The revision amounts to only 1/3 of 1 per cent of net national product at factor cost. It does not materially alter the tables which follow. Another set of revised figures, for 1952 only, in *Economic Survey, 1956,* raises net national product and direct taxes both by more than one per cent. These data are not comparable with data for earlier years.
[a] Total current revenues minus current transfer expenditures.

finance a sharp rise in transfer expenditures and also in public consumption.[2] Even so, the public savings rate was much higher than

[2] Including defense expenditures, public consumption ran from 65 per cent to 100 per cent above the prewar volume; when compared with gross national product at current prices, it was about 3 per cent higher than before the war. Current transfer expenditures rose from about three times the prewar level at current prices in 1946 to six times prewar in 1952.

before the war; and public saving exceeded public net investment each year after 1946. The excess reached a peak of 4 per cent of net national product in 1951, but fell to 3 per cent in 1952 as a result of rising defense expenditures. Most of the excess public savings were accumulated by the state rather than by the municipalities. At the same time, the state accumulated large counterpart funds from foreign aid and credits.[3] Both direct and indirect taxes as a percentage of net national product were much higher than in 1938 (Table 52).

Table 52. Total public current revenues, net available current revenues, public savings, and public savings minus public net investment as per cent of net national product at factor cost, 1938 and 1946–1952

	Total public current revenues	Net available current revenues	Public savings	Public savings minus public net investment
1938	20.4	12.6	3.6[a]	1.0
1946	30.2	16.7	1.0	−2.1
1947	33.5	18.5	5.7	1.7
1948	35.0	18.7	6.9	2.4
1949	34.8	18.6	6.5	1.4
1950	34.4	19.8	7.6	2.6
1951	33.0	20.4	8.7	4.0
1952	34.8	21.8	8.4	3.0

Source: See Table 51.
[a] The 1937–39 average was 4 per cent.

Indirect taxes were relatively more important than before the war and amounted to almost half of total revenues except from 1948 to 1950. Offsetting sudsidy payments averaged about half the value of indirect taxes. Grants in the form of family allowances and social insurance payments also rose rapidly. The net burden of taxes, or current revenues available to the public sector after meeting these transfer payments, nevertheless ran from 17 to 22 per cent of net national product each year, compared with 13 per cent in 1938.

The direct tax burden was from 50 to 100 per cent higher than before the war during the whole period from 1947 to 1952. Direct

[3] Until 1952 the state revenue surpluses led mostly to the accumulation of idle deposits. Some tax receipts, as well as most of the counterpart funds, were used to reduce the occupation account, or occupation debt, at the Norges Bank. This was purely a bookkeeping transaction. The state also borrowed to help reduce inflationary pressures. In 1952, idle deposits were used to make loans to the state banks.

taxes rose to a peak of 20 per cent of private factor income plus grants in the three years 1948–50, but then fell somewhat (Table 53). The capital-levy and war-damage taxes contributed to the especially high direct tax receipts from 1948 to 1950. Personal and business income tax payments were both a much higher percentage of private factor income plus grants than before the war.

Table 53. Private factor income, public grants, factor income plus grants, total direct taxes and direct taxes as per cent of factor income plus grants, and private disposable income, 1938 and 1946–1952 (millions of kroner)

| | Private factor income | Public grants to private sector | Private factor income plus grants | Direct taxes | | Private disposable income |
				Total	As per cent of private factor income plus grants	
1938	4,658	210	4,868	526	11	4,342
1946	8,629	446	9,075	1365	15	7,710
1947	10,253	536	10,789	1859	17	8,930
1948	11,317	586	11,903	2438	20	9,465
1949	11,814	648	12,462	2454	20	10,008
1950	12,800	733	13,533	2540	19	10,993
1951	15,852	847	16,699	2802	17	13,897
1952	16,953	975	17,928	3072	17	14,856

Source: See Table 51.

Much of the increase from the prewar level was due to the higher money incomes rather than to changes in rates of the progressive personal income tax although personal income tax rates were increased somewhat. The fact that state and local income taxation are of almost equal magnitude makes comparisons difficult. Taxes on business incomes are also levied by both the state and the municipalities. The basic rate paid to the state on business income in the 1946–52 period was 30 per cent, and up to another 20 per cent was paid to municipalities. The state also levied a 10 per cent tax on undistributed profits.

Since the government believed that the direct tax burden was as high as it could be by 1950, it did not raise direct tax rates to help finance increased defense expenditures. Rising incomes in 1951 and 1952, as a result of the revision of the stabilization policy, put personal taxpayers in even higher brackets. In 1952, some relief was given by the state to personal taxpayers in the lowest income brackets, and the rates were made less progressive up to 20,000 kroner. The relief to medium-income receivers was greater than to the lower income group.

High direct taxes kept private disposable incomes from rising as fast as private factor incomes, in spite of large social insurance payments to the private sector. Private disposable incomes were from 12 to 14 per cent below private factor incomes from 1950 to 1952, compared with 7 per cent in 1938.[4] The policy of high public savings and the efforts to reduce private disposable incomes were designed to help reduce inflationary pressures; but all of the fiscal policy decisions did not reflect this aim. Another important goal was to help redistribute income in favor of low-income groups. The direct tax structure was heavy and progressive, and undoubtedly led to some redistribution of personal disposable incomes in comparison with the years before the war.[5] Indirect taxes and subsidies, furthermore, tended to redistribute real income; luxuries were highly taxed and high in price, while necessities were subsidized and low in price.[6] In general, redistribution of income might be expected to add to inflationary pressures.

To the extent that the redistribution was of real incomes, through indirect taxes and subsidy policies, it did not have the same inflationary effect as a redistribution of disposable money incomes. Indirect taxes and subsidies were not used indiscriminately, irrespective of supply and demand conditions. High indirect taxes were imposed on imported luxuries, the supply of which was to be restricted. Subsidies were granted on essentials, whether imported or

[4] The index (1938 = 100) for private factor incomes plus grants rose from 220 in 1947 to 275 in 1950 and 364 in 1952. The index of private disposable incomes was 206 in 1947, 253 in 1950, and 342 in 1952. For basic data, see Table 53.

[5] Comparable up-to-date data on the distribution of disposable income do not exist. Direct taxes plus grants appear to have led to some slight redistribution of total disposable incomes, in comparison with the distribution of factor incomes, in favor of the wage and salary group from 1948 to 1950, and presumably earlier. But the huge profits of 1951 and 1952 tended to make the effect less important. See *Economic Survey, 1952* (Oslo: Central Bureau of Statistics, 1953).

[6] A recent study shows that the net effect of the indirect taxes and subsidies was highly progressive in the personal income brackets covered. See Helge Seip, *Det Norske Skattesystems virkninger paa den personlige inntektsfordeling* (Oslo: Central Bureal of Statistics, 1954).

domestically produced, the supply of which was being increased as fast as possible. In general, therefore, the redistribution of real income through indirect taxes and subsidy policies did not add to suppressed buying pressure but rather tended to rearrange demands to fit supplies.[7]

Fiscal policies, however, were not the only policies leading to a redistribution of money incomes. There was a deliberate policy of reducing inequalities in wage incomes. A redistribution of incomes within low income groups with similar marginal propensities to consume, however, would not add much to consumption pressure. Much of the equalization of wage incomes which was taking place may have been of this nature, especially during the early years of pent-up demands. Rents, interests, and dividends probably went mostly to higher income groups, on the other hand, and these types of income were controlled and, as a percentage of total factor incomes, were sharply below the prewar levels. Half of the cut, relatively, in these factor incomes was balanced by an increase in the wage share; the other half went to the "all other" category, which includes incomes of self-employed businessmen and corporations, and to self-employed farmers, foresters, and fishermen (Table 54). The self-employed businessmen, and some of the self-employed farmers and foresters were in relatively high income groups, but many of the self-employed farmers, foresters, and fishermen were not. On the whole, the increase in consumption pressure was probably not as great as if the entire cut in the share of rents, interest, and dividends had gone to relatively low income receivers. From 1946 to 1952, the proportion of total factor incomes going to wages and salaries was remarkably stable, averaging about 3 per cent above the 1938 rate.

In spite of government policies designed to redistribute income in favor of lower income groups, the increase in profits between the prewar and postwar years apparently was as great as the increase in wages. Profits may be roughly defined as incomes in the "all other" category plus some part of the incomes of the self-employed farmers, foresters, and fishermen. In four of the seven postwar years, the index (1938 = 100) of the incomes of the "all other" category was higher than the index of total wages and salaries (Table 55). Only

---

[7] The actual subsidy payments, of course, added to private money incomes and inflationary pressures, just as indirect taxes reduced private incomes.

Table 54. Percentage distribution of private factor income
by types of income, 1938 and 1946–1952

	Wages and salaries	Self-employed farmers, foresters, fishermen	Self-employed profes-sional service	Interest to house-holds	Divi-dends	Rents	Bank serv-ices	All other	Total[a]
1938	49[b]	9[c]	3	2	3	4	2	27	100
1946	54	10	3	1	1	1	1	28	100
1947	53	10	3	1	1	1	1	30	100
1948	53	11	3	1	1	.5	1	30	100
1949	54	11	3	1	1	.5	1	27	100
1950	54	10	3	1	1	.6	1	29	100
1951	50	10	2	1	1	.4	1	34	100
1952	53	11	2	1	1	.1	1	31	100

Source: Central Bureau of Statistics. Calculated from data through 1948 in *National Accounts, 1930–39 and 1946–51.* Data from 1948 on from *National Accounts, 1938 and 1948–53.* The most recent revised data for 1952 in the *Economic Survey, 1956,* which are not used in this table because they are not comparable with data for earlier years, raise the share of wages and salaries to almost 55 per cent and reduce the share of the "all other" category.

[a] Details may not add to 100 per cent because of rounding.
[b] The total varied from 47–50 per cent in the last few prewar years.
[c] The total varied from 8–9 per cent in the last few prewar years.

Table 55. Indices of private factor income by types of income, 1938 and 1946–1952
(1938 = 100)

	Wages and salaries	Self-employed farmers, foresters, fishermen	Self-employed profes-sional service	Interest to house-holds	Divi-dends	Rents	Bank serv-ices	All other	Total
1946	204	199	206	118	60	41	124	190	185
1947	236	235	221	112	80	31	143	246	220
1948	262	274	237	117	82	25	156	267	243
1949	280	305	244	133	91	31	166	258	254
1950	302	300	243	142	94	38	189	293	275
1951	344	375	250	146	108	31	238	429	340
1952	391	417	267	152	127	12	263	413	364

Source: See Table 54.

in 1949 was the "all other" group index much lower than the wage and salary index; and in 1951 and 1952 the "all other" group index was substantially higher. The index of incomes of self-employed farmers, fishermen, and foresters approximately equaled or exceeded the wage and salary index in all years except 1946. Although data on the distribution of factor income cannot measure changes in the distribution of disposable incomes, or real incomes, which may have taken place, they do point to a high level of profits before taxes. There is every indication that profits were high even after taxes, and that the high level of profits accounts for the high level of private savings.

In the period from 1946 to 1952, private savings as a percentage of net national product at factor cost were below the prewar rate in only 1947, 1949, and 1950 (Table 56). From 1946 to 1950, however,

Table 56. Private savings as per cent of net national product, private factor income plus grants, and private disposable income, 1938 and 1946–1952

	Private savings as per cent of		
	Net national product at factor cost	Private factor income plus grants	Private disposable income
1938...............	11.1	10.6	11.9
1946...............	11.5	11.0	12.9
1947...............	9.0	8.6	10.4
1948...............	10.3	9.9	12.4
1949...............	8.1	7.7	9.6
1950...............	6.6	6.3	7.8
1951...............	15.1	14.4	17.3
1952...............	12.8	12.2	14.7

Source: Based on data from previous tables in this chapter.

the average was 2 per cent below 1938; in 1951 and 1952 the rate was above that in 1938, and presumably it did not include forced personal savings in the sense of amounts saved only because direct controls limited the consumer goods available. During these last two years, rationing was of negligible importance. Private savings as a percentage of private factor income plus grants and as a percentage of private disposable incomes followed the same pattern as far as comparisons with prewar rates are concerned.

To eliminate inflationary pressures, it was necessary to achieve a relation between personal disposable incomes and consumption such that personal savings represented amounts which individuals did not wish to spend at current prices. Also, business savings had to be brought into line with the amounts that business firms wished either to invest or to accumulate as reserves. As long as detailed and strict price controls were in force, inflationary pressures could not auto-matically resolve themselves in price increases but could lead to involuntary accumulation of liquid assets by individuals and business firms. Under such circumstances, the degree of inflationary pressure and progress in eliminating it could be properly determined only by finding out either how much of actual private savings was voluntary (in the sense defined above) or the amount by which direct controls were still restraining consumption and investment expenditures. Neither of these questions can be answered quantitatively.

It would be somewhat easier to consider the problem of the amount of private savings that were voluntary if it were possible to determine how much of the private savings were personal savings. Ever since the war government officials have believed that personal savings have been small. Up to 1950, when total domestic savings were thought to be much lower than later estimates have indicated, personal savings were believed to be negative.[8] Rough estimates by the government in recent years have suggested that personal savings were very small in 1951 and that they amounted to 300–500 million kroner in 1952.[9]

Although quantitative estimates are not available, speculation on the sources of private savings suggests certain qualitative conclusions. Rough evidence indicates that corporate savings probably were at or above prewar rates during most of the period from 1946 to 1952, and that personal savings probably were below prewar rates at least from 1946 to 1950 if not in later years. Total private savings from 1946 to 1950 were at about prewar ratios to disposable incomes. This is entirely consistent with the presumption in favor of a higher rate of business savings and a lower rate of personal savings. High profits undoubtedly account for the fact that from 1946 to 1948, when personal savings were probably low, the ratio of private savings to disposable income was at the prewar level. Also, high profits probably

[8] See the national budget discussions in the years 1948 to 1950.

[9] In the 1953 national budget, 300–400 million was mentioned for 1952. Some calculations in the *Economic Survey, 1954* implied about 200 million in 1951 and 500 million in 1952. In the *Economic Survey, 1955* this implication was reversed. The rough estimates for personal disposable income were reduced so that the implied savings were lower in both years. Also, use of the data to derive estimates of personal savings was specifically rejected as unwarranted.

caused the very sharp rise in private savings in 1951 and 1952.[10] Rather strict limitation of dividend payments also tended to keep corporate savings high.

But there is some evidence that personal savings may have been positive in 1946–48. Private savings decreased more sharply in 1949 than would seem to be accounted for by the decline in profits as a result of the slight recession, and private savings continued low in 1950 despite much higher profits. This suggests a sharp drop in personal savings in 1949 and 1950, possibly even personal dissaving.

There are other reasons for assuming that personal savings were probably positive from 1946 to 1948 even if the few very high-income recipients are excluded. There probably had been no substantial accumulation of assets by the middle-income groups during the occupation. Wages, salaries, and rents had been frozen at much lower levels than prices. Even in 1946, prewar savings were worth only about half as much as before the war. Tax rates were higher because absolute earnings were higher. The most needed goods were not easy to obtain. Middle- and low-income receivers, therefore, in spite of pent-up demands, probably did not want to dissave much in the first postwar years.

There were good reasons for positive personal savings even from 1946 to 1948. Some self-employed persons saved to restore farm, fishing, and workshop equipment; some saved in order to be able to buy needed basic commodities when they became available and to buy or build houses. In certain cases, these personal savings were used currently to finance investment in equipment and housing; in others they were accumulated for future use. Some of those workers who were newly drawn into the labor market, or who moved to urban centers from the farms, probably saved a substantial amount. But there were, of course, some who had suffered considerably during the war, or some who did not care to look far ahead, and who un-

---

[10] All indications are that business profits have been high ever since the war. Domestic wages have lagged behind export prices, so that export profits have been great. The demand for domestic consumer goods has led to output at full capacity, and prices have been controlled at rates which led to good profits. The continued high investment demand in both domestic and export sectors is evidence of a good profits position. The dividend limitation policy may have led to some involuntary business savings, but this was probably not too significant quantitatively.

doubtedly wanted to spend their entire incomes or more. There may also have been some tendency for the more adequate insurance benefits and full employment to lower savings; but the change in insurance benefits probably was not drastic enough to alter savings habits quickly, and full employment was probably not regarded as sufficiently permanent to be considered seriously in this connection.

Although the middle and lower income groups as a whole probably did some personal saving from 1946 to 1948, it seems reasonable to assume that personal savings in these years were below the prewar rate. Part of the saving was involuntary in the sense that the money was saved only because the basic goods needed were not available. The spill over to available domestic goods and services was important, but did not necessarily absorb all of the money which would have been spent on basic goods. In 1949 and 1950, when the supplies of basic scarce goods were sharply increased, it seems doubtful that the middle and lower income groups saved anything out of current income. More probably they dissaved.

Even if it seems probable that there was some involuntary personal saving from 1946 to 1948, and if it also seems possible that there was some personal dissaving in 1949 and 1950, the amounts involved probably were relatively small. Accumulated assets did not grow fast enough from 1946 to 1948 to be a problem after one or two years of increased supplies of basic commodities and of relatively constant real incomes. The steady rise until 1950 in total consumer prices, if not in the cost-of-living index, and a considerable rise in both thereafter helped to mop up any pressure from accumulated assets that might have existed. But even in 1951, when the big upward adjustment was just getting under way, consumption did not increase, although total wages and salaries earned, deflated by the consumer price index, did rise a little.[11]

As mentioned above, the evidence points to positive voluntary personal savings in 1951 and 1952. The rise in private savings was extremely sharp in those years and recent official estimates suggest positive savings. Also, it appears that data on savings deposits, insurance policies, and new mortgages on houses would support an estimate of about 600 million kroner of personal savings in 1952, or about one fourth of total private savings. Whether personal savings

[11] See Table 57.

were 300 million or 600 million kroner in 1952, it seems reasonable to assume that most of the factors cited above as operating from 1946 to 1948 to produce positive savings were present in a greater degree. Pent-up demands had mostly been met. More housing was beginning to be available, and mortgage payments had mounted in the whole postwar period. The availability of durable household goods was also becoming greater. Rising prices in 1951 and falling real wages tended to cut into saving, but by 1952 real wages increased again.

In any case, it seems fairly certain that there were some positive personal savings by 1952 and that whatever personal savings were made in 1951 and 1952 were voluntary. In 1951, direct controls on the volume of consumption were relatively unimportant, and by 1952 they had been eliminated. It may be said that during 1951 no important consumer goods were being held at controlled prices which were below the levels needed to equate current supply and demand.

The elimination of inflationary pressure in the consumer sector by 1951, or at least by 1952, reflects the success throughout the recovery period of over-all government policies designed to restrain increases in wages and salaries and in total private disposable incomes at the same time that substantial increases in the supply of consumer goods were made available. In 1951, the government's decision to revise the subsidy policy to permit some price increases and to raise the sales tax, combined with restrained wage increases, completed the job of eliminating inflationary pressures in the consumer sector.

The subsidy, tax, and wage-price policies described in earlier chapters were ultimately reflected in the relation between total wages and salaries, or total private disposable incomes, and consumption. When these totals are deflated by the consumer price index, the picture is fairly clear. During the period from 1946 to 1948, the index (1938 = 100) of total wages and salaries, deflated by the consumer price index, was much higher than the index of the volume of consumption (Table 57). The index of private disposable incomes was much lower than the wage and salary index in 1946, but it rose as fast as wages and salaries in 1947, though not in 1948.[12] The level

---

[12] Use of the cost-of-living index as a deflator would indicate much greater increases in private disposable incomes and total wages and salaries. But the fact was that consumption of higher priced nonbasic items was very important in the early years.

Table 57. Indices of volume of consumption, private disposable incomes, and total wages and salaries at 1938 consumer prices, 1946–1952 (1938 = 100)

	Volume of consumption	Private disposable incomes	Total wages and salaries
1946...................	109	109	125
1947...................	120	118	135
1948...................	122	121	146
1949...................	130	124	151
1950...................	135	127	152
1951...................	135	143	154
1952...................	142	140	160

Source: See Table 16 for volume of consumption, Table 53 for private disposable income, Table 54 for total wages and salaries, and Table 11 for consumer price index.

of total wages and salaries reflected the increases in hourly money earnings in mining and manufacturing and also in other sectors, the shift to higher paid jobs, and increases in employment (Table 58).

Table 58. Indices of hourly money and real earnings in manufacturing and of average money and real wages paid per man year for all workers, 1946–1949 (1938 = 100)

	1946	1947	1948	1949
Hourly earnings in mining and manufacturing				
Money earnings...........................	155	171	180	189
Real earnings deflated by				
Cost-of-living index.....................	100	108	113	119
Consumer price index....................	95	98	100	102
Average wages per man year, all hired workers				
Money wages.............................	188	206	221	229
Real wages, deflated by				
Cost-of-living index.....................	121	130	138	144
Consumer price index....................	115	118	123	124

Source: For sources of the basic data, see Tables 11–15.

In 1949 and later years, the rate of increase in total wages and salaries deflated by consumer prices slowed down, and the volume of consumption goods made available rose sharply. In 1950, total real wages and salaries, deflated by consumer prices, were virtually stable, and consumption rose almost as sharply as in 1949. Private disposable incomes rose very slowly in both these years. In 1951, total real wages and salaries increased slightly, but consumption was constant in spite of government plans for an increase and in spite of very few direct controls. Huge profits, particularly in export sectors, led to a sharp rise in total private disposable incomes in 1951. Total real wages and salaries rose somewhat faster in 1952 as the government again planned an increase in consumption, and an increase in fact occurred. Private disposable incomes fell slightly as export profits were lower.

The comparative stability of total real wages and salaries during most of 1949, virtual stability in 1950, and a very slight rise in 1951 reflect the stability of real hourly earnings and average real wages per man year (Table 59). This was the period of upward price

Table 59. Indices of hourly money and real earnings in manufacturing and of average money and real wages paid per man year for all workers, 1950–1952 (1949 = 100)

	1950	1951	1952
Hourly earnings in mining and manufacturing			
Money earnings...................................	106	121	135
Real earnings deflated by			
Cost-of-living index............................	101	99	102
Consumer price index..........................	98	99	104
Average total wages paid per man year, all hired workers			
Money wages....................................	106	119	134
Real wages deflated by			
Cost-of-living index............................	101	98	101
Consumer price index..........................	98	98	103

Source: Except for the adjustment of the wages-paid data to a per man year basis, all data are from *Nasjonalbudsjettet, 1955, Stortingsmelding nummer 1, 1955,* Tables 29 and 30.

and wage adjustment after devaluation. The revised subsidy policy and the increase in the sales tax raised prices. The tendency for wages to lag behind prices helped to keep real wage rates stable in 1950 and to bring a slight fall in 1951. But trade union responsibility was an important factor limiting actual money wage increases, and government efforts to restrain increases were undoubtedly successful. In 1951 the slight fall in real wage rates, as a result of the lag of wages behind prices and the resulting redistribution of income in favor of profits, reinforced the effect on consumption of resistance to the domestic price increases and expectations of falling world prices. The volume of private consumption was stable.

The decision to permit large increases in the consumption of basic items in 1949 and 1950, together with subsidy, tax, and price-wage policies to restrict increases in personal real income, resulted in the successful elimination of inflationary pressure in the consumer sector. But inflationary pressure continued in the investment sector in 1951 and 1952. No data are available on the level of unsatisfied investment demands, but the fact that the government had a constant struggle in 1950 and 1951 to keep private investment within the planned amounts is well known.[13]

There were still quantitative restrictions on construction, and detailed allocation procedures for the most important building materials, and controls on most machinery imports. By 1952, the restrictions were somewhat less severe and the situation had eased a little; but applications for many equipment imports and for building and construction licenses were still far in excess of those granted. The rate of housing construction was increased sharply, and heavy new ship contracts were licensed, both steps helping to reduce the investment pressure.

Domestic savings large enough to finance most of the investment program from 1946 to 1952, and meanwhile permit the elimination of inflationary pressure in the consumer sector, are explained partly by the high level of public savings and partly by the high level of business savings. Government tax policy and the price stabilization policy explain the high level of public and business savings. Personal savings were probably below the prewar rate at least until 1950. The elimination of inflationary pressure in the consumer sector is explained in part by the fact that taxes held down the rate of increase in private disposable incomes. But the substantial increases in private consumption in 1949 and 1950 and the successful handling of the revised subsidy policy and the upward price-wage adjustment from 1950 to 1952 were also extremely important.

The emphasis in this chapter has been on the successful elimination of inflationary pressures in the consumer sphere. It was abundantly clear even in 1952, however, that inflationary pressures persisted in the investment sphere. Investment demand substantially exceeded financing possibilities. Balance-of-payments equilibrium could not have been achieved in 1951 and 1952, even at the favorable

---

[13] Data such as published for 1947 on the extent to which private plans were cut in preparing the annual budget would be very useful.

terms of trade which prevailed, if there had not been strict controls
on investment. Inflationary pressures could not be considered to be
fully eliminated until equilibrium in the current balance of payments could be achieved without the help of strict controls on investment and at terms of trade which were not unusually favorable.

13

Transition Period

At the end of 1952 there were many indications that the ambitious recovery program had been quite successfully carried out. Output and export goals had been met. A large proportion of output was still going into investment; but domestic savings were high, in part because of huge export profits. Rationing of consumer goods had been abolished, and previously rationed commodities were in good supply at controlled prices. Inflationary pressures had apparently been eliminated in the consumer sphere.

The outlook, however, was not altogether bright. The years 1951 and 1952 presented too favorable a picture. Current balance-of-payments equilibrium had been achieved but freight rates had been unusually high. They were falling at the end of 1952 and a deterioration in the over-all terms of trade seemed probable. Less favorable terms of trade would lead to large current balance-of-payments deficits unless the volume of exports rose sharply or imports could be cut. If export prices and profits should fall substantially, private savings also would decline. Public savings were expected to decrease because of rising defense expenditures.

The demands on available resources were continuing to grow. Defense would take more manpower and materials. A steady increase in private consumption not only would be desirable but was considered to be a political necessity. Investment had to continue at a very high rate to expand exports and also to provide sorely needed housing, schools, and hospitals. These problems were not likely to be unmanageable, but careful budgeting of resource availabilities and resource uses would continue to be necessary.

The government stated in the 1953 budget that it would have to use measures other than direct controls for the most part, to ensure that resource uses conformed to targets. Consumer rationing had ended, 75 per cent of imports had been freed, and some specific price regulations had been eliminated. Detailed price regulations would be abolished in the near future, except those on subsidized commodities. Direct controls over investment would be maintained, but they would be made broader and less rigid. Tendencies toward over-full employment, excessive aggregate demand, and excessive imports would have to be restrained by over-all policies rather than by direct controls.

The political and psychological environment strongly influenced the economic policy decisions made in 1953. A large defense effort, after years of reconstruction and recovery, would not be welcomed with enthusiasm. Some relaxation of pressures and some indulgence — for example, more housing and freedom from detailed restrictions — would help win support for the increased defense appropriations. The defeat of the Labor Party in the United Kingdom, the huge housing program of the Conservative Party in the United Kingdom, and the elections scheduled in Norway for 1953 and 1957 all had some effect on Norwegian policies.

The 1953 national budget was optimistic in spite of tendencies toward recession in Europe, less favorable terms of trade, and the expanding defense effort.[1] Actually, the terms of trade fell sharply in 1953, fixed investment rose much more than planned, exports rose less, and the current balance-of-payments deficit was almost 900 million kroner. Output rose only 2.6 per cent. For the first time in the postwar period the rate of increase was below 3.5 per cent, and also below the 3 per cent budget estimate. Defense consumption did not rise as much as had been expected, and private consumption increased just about as planned (Table 60).

In the spring of 1953, a new long-term program for the years 1954–57 was presented to the Storting.[2] It did not have the sense of urgency, of emphasis on one or two goals, and of sacrifice to achieve those goals, of the 1946 and 1948 plans. It was a political document, a statement of principles and policies for a normal period of growth and stability.[3] Full employment, a reasonable distribution

---

[1] *Nasjonalbudsjettet 1953, Stortingsmelding nummer 1, 1953.*

[2] *Om et langtidsprogram for 1954–57, Stortingsmelding nummer 62, 1953.*

[3] The election was coming in the fall of 1953. The program stated that the government's plans did not include further nationalization or government import

of income, rising standards of living, and increases in output were still the basic objectives.[4] A high rate of investment was necessary, and the stabilization policy would be continued. Imports of capital were

Table 60. Plans for percentage increases in volume of output, resource uses, exports, and imports compared with actual percentage increases or decreases, 1953–1956

	1953		Plan for 1954–57: average increase per year	1954		1955		1956	
	Budget	Actual		Budget	Actual	Budget	Actual	Budget	Actual
Gross national product......	3.0	2.6	3.0	3.0	4.1	2.0	3.1	3.8	3.9
Gross fixed asset formation....	1.2	7.2	0ᵃ	2.8	4.0	−1.5ᶜ	4.1	0	0.7
Total gross investment...		2.6			4.0		6.2	2.7	3.1
Private consumption.....	1.5	1.5	3.5ᵇ	1.1	5.9	2.2	3.5	2.3	3.4
Government consumption..	16.6	7.2	3.5ᵇ	8.1	3.6	−0.6ᶜ	−2.9ᶜ	0.1	0
Exports of goods and services ..	5.2	4.0	3.5ᵇ	7.5	10.5	5.6	4.5	6.0	9.8
Imports of goods and services ..	4.8	5.2	2.3ᵇ	4.8	12.4	2.0	5.9	2.8	6.5

Source: Percentage increases based on actual data at 1950 prices are those furnished the author by the National Budget Office in June 1957. The planned changes from the 1953 plan and the annual budgets are at different prices from the actual changes at actual prices. See precise references in Chapter 13 to the 1953 plan and the budgets.

ᵃ The goal was no increase in net investment and a very slight increase (almost negligible) in gross investment owing to higher repairs and maintenance.

ᵇ Roughly based on the goals which were 15 per cent for four years for consumption and exports, and 10 per cent for imports.

ᶜ Minus sign indicates decrease.

still needed for the next two or three years but, on the assumption that the terms of trade would not become too unfavorable, not at

monopolies, that consumer rationing would not be reintroduced, that full employment would be maintained at all cost, that private consumption would increase steadily, and that prices would be kept stable.

[4] The fact that a little more unemployment had occurred in late 1951 and 1952 led to great emphasis on full employment. Most of the unemployment was concentrated in the winter months and reflected the higher rate of construction, especially in northern Norway. But some unemployment reflected falling foreign and domestic demand. From 1946 to 1951, successive plans and programs mentioned full employment as an obvious goal. After 1952 there was extended discussion of measures to maintain demand and employment.

the rate in the 1946–52 period.[5] The aim was a small export surplus by 1957.[6]

The program called for an average increase of 3 per cent a year in gross national product. The rate of increase would be lower than it had been since the war for several reasons. The annual increase in the population of working age would tend to be ½ per cent rather than 1 per cent as in previous years. The drain of manpower from the farms could not continue at the postwar rate. Most important, the areas of development most suitable for Norway — electric power, and electrochemical and electrometallurgical plants — involved very high capital-output ratios, and a substantial amount of investment in housing and public buildings was necessary. Furthermore, output increases might be held back by declining export demand if there should be a world recession.[7]

Most of the resources made available by increases in output were to be used for private and public consumption. Net investment was to be kept approximately stable at the level contemplated in the 1953 budget. The gross investment rate was to continue at about 33 per cent.

The new long-term program, like the 1953 budget, stressed the shift from direct controls to over-all monetary and fiscal measures. It discussed at length the problem of how it might be possible to maintain full employment and also avoid price and wage increases.

[5] For the period as a whole, deficits totaling one billion kroner were considered necessary. The over-all terms of trade (including shipping services) assumed were the same as the 1947–52 average, or 4 per cent below 1938. In 1952 the terms of trade were 2 per cent below 1938; and in 1953 they were expected to be much lower. The assumption was fairly optimistic.

[6] By 1957, exports of goods and services were expected to increase by 15 per cent and imports by 10 per cent, compared with the national budget estimates for 1953.

[7] A decrease in exports, in comparison with plans, had been partly responsible for output increasing by only 2.6 per cent in 1953. The figures cited so far were not the only estimates in the program. A second set of estimates was based on the assumption that exports would not increase by 15 per cent because of world conditions. In that case, output would not increase by 3 per cent a year, private consumption could not increase by more than 6–7 per cent, and there would be an import surplus of 300 million kroner in 1957, not an export surplus of 200 million kroner. Both private and public consumption in 1957 were expected to be about 15 per cent above the planned 1953 volume. The use of resources for defense was expected to be very high in the early years, but to decline slightly by 1957.

Because of bottlenecks, direct control measures might be necessary to avoid price increases. Monetary and fiscal policies should be flexible enough and selective enough to maintain aggregate demand at about the right level and also to maintain price stability. Price-wage stability was essential to keep costs in Norway low and to avoid deflation in the event of a world recession and falling world prices.

The investment program stressed power, industries based on cheap power, and merchant shipping because they offered the greatest possibilities for increased export earnings. The merchant fleet, already 20 per cent higher than before the war, would be expanded another 25 per cent. Power development would continue at the same rate as in the earlier postwar years. Some slight increase in investment in agriculture and forestry would be justified. In fishing, whaling, and mining, physical limits on possible increases in output were close to being reached. More investment than in previous years in schools, hospitals, public buildings, transport, and housing was considered feasible.

The long-term program of 1953 provided the general framework for the economic policy decisions of the next four years. At the election in the fall of 1953 the Labor Party was returned to power. The national budgets presented to the Storting from 1953 to 1957 have been generally consistent with the long-term program.[8] It is not yet possible to make a full or a final comparison of the results achieved during these four years with the 1953 plan. Data now available, including preliminary estimates for 1956, indicate certain rough conclusions on the carrying out of the program in the first three years (Table 60). Output has increased somewhat faster than expected and the volume of exports of goods and services has increased about twice as fast as assumed in the long-term plan. In these respects the record is extremely good. But investment and imports have also both risen much more than planned. In 1954 private consumption increased at a rate much faster than implied in the program, but not in 1955 and 1956. Defense has been less of a drain on resources than expected.

Current balance-of-payments deficits were much larger than estimated in the years 1953 to 1955, but approximate current

[8] The budget for each year was published as *Nasjonalbudsjettet* (with the year), *Stortingsmelding nummer 1* (with the year).

balance was restored in 1956 and is expected for the full year 1957.[9] Current deficits in the neighborhood of 100 million kroner in 1956 (and in 1957 according to the latest estimates) are explained by net deficits in the balance of interest and dividend payments. Goods and services transactions have either balanced or shown a slight surplus. The over-all terms of trade on commodity and service transactions were very much less favorable than assumed in the long-term program in 1954, but they improved substantially in 1955 and have been much more favorable than assumed in 1956 and 1957.

The extreme variability of the terms of trade, especially if shipping services are taken into account, suggests that the 1956 and 1957 balance-of-payments equilibrium cannot be expected to continue.[10] Unless investment and imports are cut, huge deficits will recur if the terms of trade deteriorate. Large foreign loans financed the 1953–55 deficits, but the possibilities seem slight that future big deficits can be met by such large credits and loans as characterized those years.[11]

The efforts of the government since 1952 to keep investment from increasing have not been entirely successful. Investment in 1953 rose much faster than contemplated in the 1953 budget, and in both 1954 and 1955 investment rose sharply. The long-term program had called for no increase in investment during the whole four-year period, and the budgets in 1954, 1955, and 1956 aimed at holding fixed invest-

[9] Current deficits are now estimated at 1.2 billion in 1954, 1.0 billion in 1955, 150 million in 1956, and about 100 million in 1957. See *Economic Survey, 1956* for data relating to the balance of payments and the terms of trade.

[10] The government has stressed this point recently, arguing that a surplus should be earned in good years even if average small deficits are planned over a period of years. The terms of trade (1949 = 100) have fluctuated as follows in recent years (taking into account only commodity exports and imports, excluding ships): 1952, 104; 1953, 95; 1954, 97; 1955, 102; 1956, 107. The over-all terms of trade, including exports and imports of ships and exports of shipping services, have fluctuated even more violently.

[11] The large government loans raised abroad in 1954 and 1955 presumably cannot be raised year after year. In the first half of 1955, $25 million was borrowed from the International Bank for Reconstruction and Development, $15 million on the United States market, and another $15 million or so in the Netherlands and in Switzerland. In 1954, $25 million was borrowed from the International Bank and about $10 million in Sweden. The U.S. loan for the Sunndalsora aluminum plant was also being used and drawings on EPU were important. Private borrowing on ship contracts was also substantial. Total foreign indebtedness is lower, when compared with national income, than before the war, and foreign exchange reserves are higher than prewar, although much lower in comparison with imports.

ment constant or even decreasing it. In 1954 an exception was made
because of an expected increase in ship deliveries, and in 1956 it was
assumed that total investment would increase due to stock accumulations. Until 1956 the plans to hold fixed investment approximately
constant did not succeed. The difficulties in controlling investment resulted from the fact that direct controls over investment were less
strict, and monetary and fiscal policies were not sufficiently strengthened to take over the job.

The failure of the government to take stronger steps in 1954 and
1955 may be explained partly by the fact that the long years of
gross investment at about 35 per cent of gross national product, and
the accompanying shift of labor from the farms to construction,
tended to freeze investment plans. Apparently, fear of unemployment had some influence in keeping the government from planning
bigger cuts in investment. Seasonal unemployment in construction
reached a peak of 31,000 in 1953, and there was discussion
of a possible world recession in the years 1952 to 1954. Unemployment in Norway averaged less than 1 per cent of the labor force
throughout these years, as it had ever since the war. The average
in 1953, however, was 14.4 thousand unemployed compared with an
average of 10 thousand from 1946 to 1952. Unemployment decreased
somewhat in 1954 and 1955, but rose again to about the 1953 level
in 1956.

Investment in building and construction tended to exceed planned
levels after 1952 partly because controls were left in local hands
until 1955. Local authorities were less strict than state in authorizing
new building and construction. They were supposed to license housing
on the basis of available manpower and supplies, but no fixed national
or local quotas were set. This relaxation of controls reflected strong
political pressures for more housing and public building. In 1954
and 1955 much stricter controls were reinstated. Licenses for new
houses have been sharply cut from almost 40,000 in 1953 to 25,000
in 1956 and 1957. In 1954 and 1955, somewhat fewer licenses were
issued than in 1953 but the number of houses completed remained
very high through 1955 and 1956.

Controls over investment have been less effective since 1952 partly
because import restrictions have been relaxed. Most machinery has
been on the free list, and contracts for dry cargo steamers have not

been restricted.[12] Tanker contracts were freely licensed provided the foreign-exchange cost was self financed either through credits or ship sales. Ship contracts and ship deliveries have been at phenomenal rates.

The reinstatement of more rigid controls on building and construction in 1955 presumably would not have been necessary if monetary and fiscal policies had been more restrictive. During the years from 1952 to 1955 there was a gradual move in the direction of tighter monetary and fiscal policies, but the effects of the measures taken were not strongly felt until 1956. A few important steps were taken in 1954 but a much more important series of measures was adopted in early 1955.[13] The government believed rather drastic action was necessary. Excessive investment demand was leading to tremendous imports and current balance-of-payments deficits. It was also an important factor in the continued upward pressure on wages and prices. Import prices were lower from 1953 to 1955 than they had been in 1952, but even so the cost of living was being held fairly stable only with the help of increased subsidies, and wage rates were rising steadily.

Until early 1955, in spite of difficulties in financing the state banks at the 2½ per cent rate, the official rate was not raised. The effective rate on government securities was well above the official rate, and other interest rates were tending to rise also. The government insisted until 1955 that it did not intend to raise the official long-term rate and considered that a higher interest rate would raise the cost of priority investment in power and housing and would not reduce total investment demand or bank loans significantly. In February 1955, after numerous attempts to persuade the private banks to

---

[12] There was little interest in dry cargo ships until mid-1954, however.

[13] In January 1955 former Prime Minister Gerhardsen became Prime Minister again and there was quite a Cabinet shift. The new Cabinet announced many measures in February 1955. A series of articles in the *Bank of Norway Bulletin* (in English) contain an excellent summary of economic developments and policies in Norway since 1954. See the general survey in the issue of January 31, 1955; the addresses of Finance Minister Lid and Governor Erik Brofoss of the Bank of Norway in the March 23, 1955, issue; the Prime Minister's address in the July 15, 1955, issue; and the general surveys and special articles in later issues. The discussion in this chapter is based largely on these articles and the *Economic Surveys* published by the Central Bureau of Statistics for 1955 and 1956.

finance the state banks, the official long-term government bond rate and the discount rate were raised to 3½ per cent.[14] In March the government floated a 20-year loan at 4 per cent. Rates charged by private and state banks, except for state bank housing loans, were raised.

Much emphasis was placed on direct dealings with both the private banks and the state banks to control bank credit expansion. Private banks were urged to restrict bank credit expansion and especially loans for nonpriority projects. Up to 1955, the efforts at moral suasion were apparently not too successful (Table 61). In 1955 the rate of

Table 61. Bank loans outstanding, private bank reserves, and private bank deposits, end of year, 1952–1956 (billions of kroner)

	1952	1953	1954	1955	1956
Loans outstanding					
Private banks......................	7.0	7.5	8.1	8.5	8.6
Other private lending institutions....	1.0	1.1	1.3	1.3	1.3[a]
State banks.......................	2.8	3.3	3.8	4.4	4.8[a]
	10.8	11.9	13.2	14.2	14.7
Private bank reserves					
Net increase[b]...................	0	0	−.3	0	0
Private bank deposits					
Time............................	7.2	7.6	8.1	8.5	9.1
Demand.........................	2.6	2.5	2.5	2.5	2.4
Total deposits.................	9.8	10.1	10.6	11.0	11.5

Source: *Statistiske Meldinger,* 1957.
[a] End of September data.
[b] Minus sign indicates decrease.

increase in private bank loans outstanding slowed down. Also in 1955 the private banks agreed to keep their total loans outstanding constant in 1956 and 1957. At the end of 1956 loans outstanding were at the end of 1955 level, but the expansion in the early months

[14] Ever since 1952 the government had borrowed to finance the expansion of loans by the state banks. Attempts to persuade the private banks to buy the state bank 2½ per cent securities guaranteed by the government were quite unsuccessful. In 1954, the government itself borrowed at rates higher in reality than the official long-term 2½ per cent rate. The government issued 40-year bonds at 3½ per cent and 10-year bonds at 2½ per cent for subscription only by private banks and insurance companies. New government domestic borrowing totaled 530 million kroner.

of 1956 was somewhat greater than in the early months of 1955. Budgets for state bank loans and commitments have been prepared ever since 1952. The steady expansion of state bank loans since 1952 has been largely to finance the big housing program. In 1954 the budgets for commitments were cut substantially and the budgets were made binding; in 1955 a further cut in commitments was required. In 1956 loans outstanding continued to increase, however.

Private bank reserves were constant or decreased slightly each year.[15] Early in 1955, at the time the discount rate was raised, the government for the first time used the 1952 law and required new reserves in the form of deposits at the Norges Bank. The requirements were relatively low and apparently did not have much effect.[16] A few of the big banks still seemed to have large liquid reserves, while the others did not. The Norges Bank is now considering revisions of the bank reserve requirements in order to include time deposits and also perhaps special reserve requirements against increases in deposits. The Bank is also trying to make possible effective open-market operations.[17]

When the series of measures designed to cut inflationary pressure was announced in February 1955, the Norges Bank was given power to approve or disapprove of all bond issues, including municipal issues.[18] At the same time, efforts to raise private savings were announced. The interest payable on savings deposits was raised, and plans for a premium bond issue were made.

It is not surprising that monetary policy was not too effective in

[15] Government borrowing and net sales of foreign exchange from reserves and government credits, and increases in notes in circulation, offset the effects of government financing of the state banks. Demand deposits have been approximately constant, but time deposits increased by about as much as private bank loans outstanding.

[16] Private banks with capital of more than 100 million kroner were required to keep deposits at the Bank of Norway at 10 per cent of demand deposits; banks with capital of 10 to 100 million kroner, at 5 per cent. There were no new requirements for banks with capital of less than 10 million kroner.

[17] Open-market operations have never been effective. There is no important open market for treasury bills or notes, and the Norges Bank has no portfolio of government securities. The Norges Bank is planning for a number of different types of short-term government securities, and trying to arrange for an initial holding of government securities by the Norges Bank.

[18] The law had been proposed in 1953 in connection with the new law on interest rates giving the government the power to regulate maximum and minimum rates.

restraining investment demand. The high profits in export sectors, especially in shipping, were keeping up the demand for investment. Shipping investment was financed largely with foreign credits. Housing loans continued to be made at 2½ per cent by the state banks. And public investment was rising.

Fiscal policy was less of an anti-inflationary influence after 1952 than it had been before. In 1953, when public consumption, mostly

Table 62. Public and private net investment, domestic savings, the current deficit, and public and private savings, 1952–1956 (billions of kroner)

	1952	1953	1954	1955	1956
Net investment					
Public...................................	0.9	1.1	1.1	1.2	1.3
Private..................................	3.2	3.1	3.4	3.6	3.5
Total.....................................	4.1	4.2	4.5	4.8	4.8
Current deficit[a]..............................	0	0.9	1.2	1.0	0.2
Domestic savings...............................	4.1	3.3	3.4	3.8	4.6
Public....................................	1.4	1.1	1.3	1.5	1.7
Private...................................	2.7	2.2	2.1	2.3	2.9
Available public revenue..........	3.6	3.6	4.0	4.2	4.7
Public consumption..............	2.2	2.5	2.7	2.7	3.0
Excess of public saving compared with public investment.........	0.5	0	0.2	0.3	0.4
Private savings as per cent of private disposable income.......	18	15	13	13	15

Source: From *Economic Survey, 1956*, except for public investment and public savings data, which are from *Nasjonalbudsjettet, 1956, Stortingsmelding nummer 1, 1956*, and *Nasjonalbudsjettet, 1957, Stortingsmelding nummer 1, 1957.*
[a] Includes net interest and dividends and grants.

for defense, increased, public savings were considerably lower than they had been in 1952.[19] However, they returned to about the 1952 level in 1954 and 1955 and rose further in 1956. But even in 1956 the excess of public saving over public investment was lower than in 1952 (Table 62), and much lower than in 1952 compared with net national product at factor cost. Total tax receipts rose steadily. The increase in direct tax receipts occurred in spite of a cut in the income tax rates in 1953–54 and a cut in export profits which was reversed in 1955. The tax cut was expected to help restrain wage increases. The cut in rates also seemed necessary because rising in-

[19] In 1953, while public investment was 200 million kroner higher than in 1952, public savings was 300 million kroner lower.

comes were putting workers in higher brackets and there was some belief that the rates were interfering with work incentives. Indirect tax receipts fell in 1953 because of declining export tax receipts, but they rose again to the 1952 level in 1954, and rose steadily thereafter. Subsidies were about constant until 1955 but rose somewhat in 1955 and 1956. Social insurance payments rose steadily, primarily as a result of higher allowances for children and of increased pensions, which were intended to reduce the pressure for wage increases.

The combination of almost steadily rising public and private net investment and lower or fairly stable public savings from 1953 to 1955 was especially unfortunate because it coincided with a fall in private savings. Private savings decreased sharply in 1953, and were well below the 1952 level until 1956. Even in 1956 they were lower compared with private disposable income than they had been in 1952. The huge export profits in 1951 and 1952 had been responsible for the very high rate of private savings in those years, and it was not surprising that the lower export profits of 1953 to 1955 would be accompanied by a decrease in private savings. Total domestic savings, both public and private, were much lower in 1953 and 1954 and somewhat lower in 1955 than they had been in 1952. There was a sharp rise in 1956, however.

It appears that the government, under the circumstances, should have tried to increase public savings. One doubtful decision seems to have been the cut in income tax rates for 1953–54. While the decrease may have seemed justified at the time, it is hard to raise taxes once they have been cut, and it soon seemed clear that the cut should be reversed. Raising indirect taxes or cutting subsidies would tend to lead to increases in prices and costs. Social insurance payments could not be cut without more pressure for wage increases.

The government finally decided to impose some new indirect taxes designed to cut investment, and in March 1955 it announced a number of new measures: a sales tax on all building and construction work other than housing and farm buildings, a 10 per cent tax on new ship contracts,[20] a 10 per cent tax on imports of motor vehicles and tractors, and some tax exemption on funds blocked as depreciation re-

[20] The tax did not apply to self-financed ship contracts.

serves. The increase in public savings in 1955 reflected the new tax measures as well as a rise in export prices and profits.

The series of measures taken in 1954 and 1955 to cut investment seemed to be having a real effect in 1956. Employment in building and construction declined. There were fewer buildings under construction, and imports of machinery and investment goods declined sharply. Unemployment in the first three months of 1956 was considerably higher than in previous years. Monetary and fiscal measures were accompanied by much stricter direct controls over building and construction activity. On the whole, the tightening of direct controls over building licenses had probably been the most important single factor in reducing investment.

Throughout the period from 1953 to 1956 there was strong upward pressure on wages and prices. Wage rates rose steadily year after year. Hourly money earnings in industry rose by 5–6 per cent each year from 1952 to 1955 and by almost 8 per cent in 1956 (Table 63). Although there were no general cost-of-living adjustments, in-

Table 63. Indices of money wages and prices and of money wages deflated by the cost of living, 1952–1956 (1949 = 100)

	1952	1953	1954	1955	1956
Cost of living.....................	133	136	142	143	148
Import prices[a].....................	136	127	120	124	130
Hourly earnings in industry					
Money earnings..................	135	141	148	156	168
Real earnings (money earnings deflated by cost-of-living index)....	102	104	105	110	114

Source: *Statistiske Meldinger, nummer 6, 1957*, except for real hourly earnings index for 1952, from Table 59.

[a] Excluding ships.

creases were granted under industry contracts; and upgrading, shifts to piece work, and rates above those stipulated in industry contracts led to the steady increase in wage rates.

Early in 1953, the trade unions and employers had agreed to have no industry contract revisions in 1953. This seemed to be a victory for the stablilization policy, but rates rose in 1953 by about 5 per cent. The cost of living rose only slightly that year. In early 1954, the government eliminated most detailed individual price controls, except on subsidized commodities and rents.[21] As a result of the elimination of controls and also as a result of the 1953 wage increases, the cost of living was expected to rise somewhat in 1954.

The government strongly urged that wage increases should not be demanded in industry contract revisions in 1954 since they would only lead to further pressure on prices. At the end of 1953 the trade union association stated that the unions should not ask for general increases in 1954 but should concentrate on fringe benefits. The negotiations in 1954 were long and difficult. The Employers' Association pressed for a general settlement, and in May a complicated agreement was reached. The result was widespread increases in rates of about 3 per cent as well as in fringe benefits. Most of the industry contracts were renewed for two years, so that the next major revisions would not take place until 1956. But a semi-automatic cost-of-living adjustment arrangement was reintroduced.[22] Partly by increased subsidies and partly by price decreases negotiated with domestic firms, the index was kept just below the critical cost-of-living adjustment level of 146 (1949 = 100) until the end of 1954, and was reduced somewhat in early 1955.

The increases under industry contracts in 1954 were granted over a period of months, and the full effect on wage rates was not felt until early 1955. A few industry contracts which expired in 1955 led to further wage rate increases. In forestry and agriculture, negotiations were still going on at the end of the year. At the end of 1955 the cost-of-living index was at 143 (1949 = 100), below the red line, but an increase in 1956 was almost certain.

The wage and price negotiations in 1956 were difficult. Most industry wage contracts expired in the spring, and the agreement on farm prices expired in June 1946. A special committee was appointed, under the chairmanship of the Ministry of Finance, with representatives of employers, the unions, and the farmers, to consider the entire problem. The government announced in March the general policy that

[21] In 1954, a permanent price-control act was passed with widespread powers. It aims to give the government control over individual prices in order to eliminate excessive monopoly profits and also to give the government powers to control the general price level in periods when such controls seem necessary.

[22] The critical dates were September 15 and March 15, and the red line 7 points above the 139 (1949 = 100) level of March 15, 1954. Any increase would be negotiated.

it believed should be followed, i.e., to raise milk prices, to cut subsidies somewhat, and to limit wage increases to about 20 öre per hour (or about 4 per cent) on the average. Altogether, the effect of these measures would be about a 5 point rise in the index, bringing it well above the red line. It actually rose to 147 in April and to 150 in May. The rise in April was due to the elimination of subsidies on coffee, sugar, and margarine in March.

At the time the government announced the cut in subsidies, pensions and allowances for children were increased, and a temporary price freeze was ordered for all prices established by private agreements. In April 1956, farm negotiations were concluded with a rise in milk prices. Farm prices were to be reconsidered at such time as the wage agreements were reopened, and immediately if the average increase agreed on in the 1956 wage agreements should be more than the 20 öre (or about 4 per cent) recommended by the government.

Efforts to arrive at an over-all wage settlement had begun in February but had failed. Separate negotiations were carried out on individual industry contracts and the agreements reached called for different rates of increase in money wages. The Central Bureau of Statistics has estimated that the increases granted averaged about 4 per cent as recommended by the government.[23] But increases in earnings due to upgrading and other factors also averaged about 4 per cent. The new agreements reached in the spring of 1956 provided for a semi-automatic cost-of-living adjustment again if the index should go above 156 in March or September. The government announced it would try to stabilize the cost of living at 150. Early in 1957 the government raised the stabilization line to 153.

The problem of price and wage stability has seemed more difficult to handle since 1952 than in the period of upward adjustment from 1950 to 1952. Increases in hourly money earnings were not much larger, except in 1956, but money earnings rose faster relative to the cost of living. In the earlier period, real hourly earnings in industry rose only 2 per cent above the 1949 level; by 1955 they were 10 per cent above the 1949 level, and in 1956 14 per cent above. In 1954 money hourly earnings rose only about as fast as the cost of living, but in 1953 and 1955 they rose much faster (Table 63).

The problem of maintaining full employment and price-wage

[23] See the *Economic Survey, 1956.*

stability is one which has no simple solution. Unemployment of less than 1 per cent of the labor force may not be consistent with price-wage stability on the one hand and the absence of tight direct controls over investment on the other hand. The decision to experiment with selective monetary and fiscal measures and in the meantime to loosen direct controls over investment involved considerable risk. The return to stricter direct controls and at least a temporary price freeze suggests that monetary and fiscal policies alone cannot be relied on to achieve wage and price stability.

The upward pressure on wages and prices in Norway, however, has not been very much greater than that experienced in several other countries in which the percentage of the labor force unemployed has been considerably more than 1 per cent. Wages and prices have been rising steadily in the United Kingdom and even in Denmark in spite of higher unemployment (especially in Denmark). Roughly 4 per cent unemployment in the United States has been accompanied recently by wage and cost-of-living increases. The exceptionally low unemployment rate in Norway undoubtedly added to the problem of controlling inflation. But it probably is true that wage-price pressures would have existed with much greater unemployment.

Monetary and fiscal policies do not seem to be very effective in dealing with inflationary pressures arising primarily from wage increases. The Norwegian government has made it clear that it believes monetary and fiscal policies alone could only stop the inflation if carried far enough to bring considerable unemployment. Policy makers have tended to insist that workers' and employers' organizations must assume some of the responsibility for maintaining price stability. They must agree on less rapid increases in money wages.

On the whole the years 1953 to 1956 tend to bear out the impression that the recovery program of earlier years was sound. Total output, output per worker, and exports have continued to increase at satisfactory rates. Approximate current balance in international payments was reached again in 1956. The balance-of-payments situation cannot yet be considered satisfactory, however, since a current surplus of considerable magnitude would be suitable in a period of exceptionally favorable terms of trade. Reserves should be built up to tide over periods of less favorable terms of trade.

The transition to more reliance on monetary and fiscal policies was not smooth or entirely successful. Neither monetary nor fiscal policies were as restrictive as they might have been. However, by 1956 bank credit expansion was under control, interest rates had been raised, and instruments for more effective monetary policy were being developed. Public savings rose sharply in 1956.

The Norwegian government intends to continue the basic program of a very high investment rate. The latest four-year program for the years 1958 to 1961, published in May 1957, calls for maintenance of the present investment rate.[24] The program is expected to lead to a 3 per cent a year increase in output and a continued rapid expansion of exports. The terms of trade are assumed to be less favorable than in 1956 and 1957, but current import surpluses of less than 100 million kroner a year are estimated on the average for the four years. The rate of increase in imports is not expected to be as great as in recent years.

The program puts great emphasis on the need for continued restrictive monetary and fiscal policies to help fight against the dangerous tendency of wages and prices to rise. The program is similar in most respects to the 1953 program. But it seems to be a stronger program in the sense that it emphasizes difficulties and problems, calls for very little increase in consumption, and insists that sufficiently restrictive monetary and fiscal policies will be carried out to keep balance-of-payments deficits from again reaching the proportions of 1953 to 1955.[25]

---

[24] *Om langtidsprogrammet for 1958–1961, Stortingsmelding nummer 67, 1957.*

[25] The description in this chapter of developments since 1952 could not take into account the data in the 1958 budget, *Nasjonalbudsjettet 1958, Stortingsmelding nummer, 1, 1958.* Nothing in the budget seems to alter substantially the conclusions reached in this chapter. In 1957 wage rates again rose faster than the cost of living. Revised estimates of the volume increases in gross national product and consumption from 1953 to 1956 considerably alter the year-to-year changes but not the increases for the period as a whole. Volume estimates of investment for past years are not presented. Total gross investment is estimated to have increased 3.6 per cent in 1957, private consumption 2.8 per cent, and gross national product 2.9 per cent. Investment is expected to increase 7 per cent in 1958 because of huge ship imports, gross national product 3 per cent, and consumption about 2½ per cent. Current price data are generally consistent with those presented in this chapter for 1953 to 1956. A small current balance-of-payments surplus is estimated for 1957 but a deficit of over a billion kroner is expected in 1958 due to lower freight rates and huge ship imports.

14

Conclusion

When World War II finally ended, Norway, like most other European countries, was faced with the difficult job of rebuilding an economy both devastated and dislocated by long years of war and occupation. Its problems were similar to those of other European countries, but they were perhaps more intense.

Extreme dependence on imports combined with wartime destruction of much of its foreign-exchange earning capacity made Norway's situation exceptionally difficult. The investment needed to restore export earnings would be a serious drain on foreign-exchange earnings and would compete with imports of food and raw materials which were sorely needed. Productive capacity had to be expanded, especially foreign-exchange earning capacity, to support a growing population at prewar living standards. This would require even more investment. Norway had to choose between rapid reconstruction and development and rapid restoration of the prewar standard of living.

The internal financial situation was also precarious. Inflationary occupation financing had vastly expanded the liquid assets of the banks and the public. Prices and incomes had been controlled at levels well below those consistent with the inflated monetary system. Norway had to decide how to handle this situation. The excess liquidity could either be wiped out by a strict monetary reform or be allowed to work itself off in an inflationary price and wage spiral, or gradually be eliminated over a period of years with increases in output and with appropriate policies to restrain increases in disposable incomes.

The Norwegian government made the basic decisions on these problems rather quickly. Investment to restore and also further to develop productive capacity, especially in foreign-exchange earning sectors, would be given priority over a rapid rise in living standards. Private consumption would be allowed to increase very gradually, but the use of foreign exchange for consumption purposes would be kept to an absolute minimum. The proportion of output devoted to investment would be higher than that ever attempted by any democratic country over a long period of years.

The ambitious recovery and development program would require careful economic planning. Output would have to be increased as fast as possible and import surpluses would have to be relied on to contribute significantly to current available resources. Resources for consumption and investment would have to be used according to a consistent plan. Direct controls would be needed to ensure that resource uses were in accordance with the plans.

The government also decided to aim at price and wage stabilization, with the help of price controls, even though the excess liquidity of the banks and the public was not substantially reduced by the very mild monetary reform which was carried out in 1945. This meant that inflationary pressures were to be eliminated gradually over a period of years. Inflationary pressure does not appear to have been deliberately or positively sought as a desirable environment for carrying out a big investment program, but it was not expected to interfere with the program. Direct controls would be relied on heavily for some period of time. The program to eliminate inflationary pressures over a number of years meant that direct controls would be relied on longer than would otherwise have been necessary, but this was not considered serious.

The history of Norway's postwar economic development shows that the early plans were essentially followed throughout the recovery period. The basic policy lines were the same in each successive long-term program and annual budget. Economic planning for resource availabilities and uses played a very important role.

The great weight of statistical and factual data, furthermore, shows that the plans were quite successfully carried out. The basic goals throughout the period were for increases in output and exports; and output and exports increased in accordance with the planned targets. By 1952 the expansion of output over the prewar level was greater than in any other European country. Output and productivity increased at rates which must be considered satisfactory even when the very high rate of investment is taken into account.

The proportion of output devoted to investment from 1947 to 1952 was remarkably high, above that in any of the other western European countries except Iceland. The expansion of output and especially of exports was the direct result of a heavy investment program. The plans for the distribution of investment were essentially carried out and the decisions on the sectors to be given priority were reasonable. The big expansion in shipping and in electrochemical and electrometallurgical output did not encounter export marketing difficulties.

The plans to restrict consumption, however, were not realized. In the sense that scarce resources were not used to any substantial extent to permit rapid increases in consumption, the plans were carried out. But total private consumption increased rapidly, and throughout the postwar period it has been high in comparison with prewar years. Apparently, private consumption in 1952 was higher in Norway, when compared with the prewar level, than in the other European countries. This reflected, for the most part, the rapid increase in output. Domestically produced goods and services, using resources that were not scarce, were responsible for much of the increase in consumption. However, for many years the pattern of consumption was not in accordance with the desires of the Norwegian people. Basic food and clothing items were very scarce until 1951; and it is in this sense that the Norwegian program can still be considered an austerity program.

The planning for resource uses was implemented primarily by direct controls until 1951 and 1952. Such controls were extremely effective, both in limiting total investment and consumption and in ensuring that the distribution of investment and consumption accorded with the plans. The high dependence on imports made direct controls effective in many areas. Although unplanned investment in small building and construction jobs and unplanned increases in output of domestically produced consumer goods and services did occur, the misallocation of resources involved does not appear to have been serious.

The unplanned increases in output of domestically produced consumer goods and services probably helped to eliminate inflationary pressures in the consumer goods sphere. By 1951 and 1952 rationing had been abolished, and consumer goods other than certain imported luxuries were in plentiful supply at controlled prices. This result was achieved primarily by a combination of fiscal, price-wage, and re-

source policies. Very high taxes produced large public sav   The
stabilization policy led to high profits and, therefore, large   less
savings. The price-wage adjustment after 1949 was so hand   hat
real wages were virtually stable for two or three years. During this
period, supplies of basic imported consumer goods were sharply increased. The result was that supplies of consumer goods at controlled
prices were in line with consumer incomes by 1951 and 1952.

Since investment demand continued to be excessive in 1952, direct
controls over investment were still essential. Very favorable terms of
trade and balance-of-payments equilibrium tended to make the situation seem less difficult than it actually was. Investment and imports
were both higher than they could have been without serious balance-
of-payments deficits if the terms of trade had not been much more
favorable in 1951 and 1952.

An adverse shift in the terms of trade in 1953 and 1954 combined
with rapid increases in investment and imports led to big deficits
again from 1953 to 1955 in spite of very sharp increases in exports.
Much more favorable terms of trade led to approximate balance
again in 1956. During most of the period since 1952, Norway has
been struggling with balance-of-payments deficits and renewed inflationary pressures. The defense program, political factors connected
with financing that program, and pressures for housing and public
buildings, all have contributed to the difficulties. Direct controls over
building and construction were loosened for two or three years, chiefly
because of these factors.

The intention was, in any case, to rely primarily on monetary and
fiscal policies in the period after 1952 to control the demand for
resources. Direct controls over consumption and imports were not
reasonable as a long-run policy, but some direct controls on investment seemed to be necessary.

Monetary and fiscal policies from 1952 to 1955, however, were
not very effective. Fiscal policy was relatively less restrictive than it
had been before 1952, probably in part for political reasons. In 1956,
monetary policy began to be quite effective. Wage policy has presented difficulties, and wage increases have been much less restrained
than in earlier years. Both prices and wages have been rising, wages
much faster than prices. Since 1955 direct controls on housing have
been tightened, and a temporary price freeze has been ordered.

One of the obvious problems facing Norway is how it is possible to keep unemployment at less than 1 per cent of the labor force and also maintain price-wage stability. This problem is a difficult one. Possibly tight direct controls on investment will be the only answer. It may be that the upward pressure on wages and prices would be equally great with 4 or 5 per cent unemployment. Other countries with more unemployment than Norway's are having similar difficulties. There is growing emphasis in Norway on the idea that it will be essential, somehow, to slow down wage increases.

Although Norway's record with economic planning has been good, it does not follow that there were not some failures, evasions of controls, mistakes, and problems. This was inevitable, and it would be unrealistic to pretend that the results were otherwise. It would be equally unrealistic, however, to be so impressed by the difficulties and problems as not to recognize the fact that the recovery program accomplished its broad objectives in spite of them.

Norway's experience since 1945 suggests that it is possible to promote a rapid rate of economic growth and a reasonable pattern of economic development by means of overall economic planning for resource availabilities and uses. It also suggests that suppressed inflationary pressures combined with direct controls may tend to promote rather than to hinder a rapid rate of growth. Inflationary pressures seem to make the job of ensuring investment in priority sectors relatively easy and the job of controlling total investment and consumption relatively difficult.

Norway's experience also suggests that economic planning and direct controls need not be accompanied by interference with political or civil liberties. Norway's economic planning has been accompanied by a substantial and detailed set of government controls. Individual consumers and businessmen were not free during much of the postwar period to buy or to build just as they wished. It has never been suggested, however, that the detailed control system has been extended or used in any way to interfere with civil liberties. The Norwegian people are traditionally freedom loving and they have not lost any of their freedom of speech, of religion, or of the press.

Norway's economic planning has not deprived the people of their private property in homes, farms, or business firms. The only resemblance between planning in Norway and planning in eastern

European countries has been in the investment rates achieved. There has been little or no extension of nationalization; most of the output and investment has been private. The few major undertakings by the government are more on the order of the TVA project in the United States than anything else.

The high rate of investment has not been accompanied by a lower standard of living for the majority of workers. Although profits have been very high, living standards have improved sharply when compared with the prewar years. Furthermore, there has been a leveling out of living standards and a redistribution of personal money and real incomes. Rapid economic development apparently can be consistent with a program for expanding social services, for increasing social welfare, and for achieving a more equitable distribution of incomes.

Economic planning in Norway has not even led to a great development of civilian bureaucracy. Vast jobs are being carried out by small, understaffed offices and bureaus. Private organizations of bankers, shipowners, exporters, farmers, and foresters have cooperated with the government even in preparing the national budgets. The essential simplicity of life in Norway has prevented bureaucratic expansion.

If the above conclusions are correct, Norway's experience should provide useful clues for many countries which are trying to raise living standards rapidly. The countries usually defined as underdeveloped, say with incomes of less than $300 per capita, undoubtedly have problems quite different from those of Norway. Social, medical, educational, religious, political, and other institutional barriers to economic development clearly did not exist in Norway. Nevertheless, underdeveloped countries could profit from Norway's planning experience. Many countries in Europe and some in South America come close to resembling Norway; they are modern, semi-industrialized, and normally well off. But they are anxious to develop rapidly and approach the standard of living of the most highly industrialized countries in the world.

Many countries are relying heavily on aid of some sort or on credits to help finance rapid growth and development. The lending countries should be concerned that loans, or aid, really promote a faster rate of growth. From this point of view, also, Norway's experience seems well worth review.

During the period of the Marshall Plan, there was a tendency to believe that United States aid was being used effectively if it was accompanied by a rapid elimination of import restrictions and of all types of direct control over domestic economic activity. The opposite seems more likely to be the case on the basis of the Norwegian experience, however, if effectiveness is judged by restoration and expansion of productive capacity accompanied by rising living standards, demonstrating the capacity of a free society to meet serious economic problems without impairment of political liberties.

Norway's experience indicates that a country which relies on overall economic planning and direct controls can use aid effectively to promote growth and development. The Norwegian authorities made certain that aid-financed import surpluses were used to supplement a high rate of domestic savings and thus finance more investment and more rapid growth than would have been possible without aid. Furthermore, the import surpluses fitted into an over-all plan for development of Norway's resources and foreign-exchange earning capacity.

The existence of an over-all program for resource uses and a firm intention to ensure that it is carried out would seem to be a prerequisite for the constructive use of foreign aid. Willingness to use direct controls for a short period of time, if found necessary to carry out the development program, would seem to be a favorable rather than an unfavorable condition for effective use of aid.

Undoubtedly some of the factors which accounted for the success achieved in Norway might not be present to the same extent in other countries. Norway had, and still has, large undeveloped resources. The unused power potential helped to provide a field for very profitable development of productive facilities. The restoration of war damage, especially to the merchant, whaling, and fishing fleets, was also an important and proven area for productive investment. While reconstruction is to some extent less risky than development, the reconstruction even in these areas was about completed by the end of 1948, and the continued expansion of shipping and the modernization of the fishing fleet since then has been equally successful.

The fact that Norway is not fully developed industrially, in the sense of having a vast array of secondary industries manufacturing for the domestic market, has not provided an area for extensive investment. The domestic market is too small to support large-scale industries catering only to the domestic market. In this sense, there-fore, Norway's problems have been no less difficult than those of underdeveloped countries with such low living standards that the domestic market is small in spite of a large population and area. In fact, Norway's problem has been more serious. A rising standard of living for a normally homogeneous population with a rather even distribution of income has led to great import pressure from both producers and consumers, partly because of the lack of domestic industries. The government is convinced that the solution is not to develop such industries and protect them from more efficient foreign competitors.

A source of real strength may have been that Norway had re-sources that could be developed profitably and could help produce goods and services in great demand on world markets. A number of underdeveloped countries and also many semi-industrially developed countries are in the same position. In one respect, Norway may have had an unusual advantage; the legal, institutional, and educational structure is similar to that of highly developed industrial western economies. The average underdeveloped region is not in a position to use the same techniques for promoting a big development program; and many semideveloped countries in southern Europe and South America also are limited by institutional factors.

One institutional factor which contributed to the success of Nor-way's postwar planning was the stability of the government. The Labor Government kept the support not only of the majority of trade union members, but also of a majority of farmers, fishermen, and foresters. As a stable government with broad political support, it could follow a number of unpopular courses of action. Rationing and import controls, price controls and wage restraint, all call for broad political backing. An extensive program of education within the Labor Party contributed to maintaining support for postwar economic policies. The fact that the Labor Party worked closely with the Trade Union Federation, and that the trade unions are highly disciplined and have a strong national organization, also helped to make it possible to restrain wage increases.

The character of the Norwegian people aided the government in making all sorts of detailed direct controls effective over a number of peacetime years. The Norwegian people, like the British, though individualistic, are highly disciplined. As there was little attempt to evade rationing and price controls, it was possible to restrict consumption of basic consumer goods which would have used scarce foreign exchange in the early years. There was a tendency for wage rates to exceed those stipulated in the contracts, but this was not illegal.

One more noneconomic factor was certainly of great importance. Norway's economic planning was farsighted and technically sound. A small number of key officials were responsible for the broad policy lines, the adjustment of plans to changes in the world situation, and the important decisions on methods of carrying out the plans. A larger group of trained economists and officials helped to administer the program and develop the detailed budgets and regulations. The Norwegian recovery program undoubtedly succeeded partly because competent economic policy makers were available.

The fact that a large number of well-trained economists were available for the job was due largely to the work of Professor Ragnar Frisch of the economics department at the University of Oslo. Of the considerable number of economists who were trained at the University, only a few were absorbed by the University; most of the others, whether Conservatives, Liberals, or Labor Party members, were drawn into government service. In many countries, the scarcity of highly trained economists and administrators is a serious bottleneck in attempts at over-all economic planning. The success of any economic plan is bound to depend on the individuals available to carry it out.

Strictly economic factors also made economic planning and direct controls more effective in Norway than they might be in certain other countries. Norway's extreme dependence on imports, though of itself leading to constant problems, made controls over consumption and investment relatively easy to administer and relatively effective in the early years. Import controls were remarkably effective in limiting the use of foreign exchange for consumption and in controlling the amount and composition of investment. The only substantial area in which investment controls were not very effective was in small building and construction jobs which did not require imported materials. Controls over consumption were evaded only insofar as domestic materials could be used.

Import controls regulated investment in ships, inland transport equipment, and most types of machinery, as well as construction steel. They also regulated consumption of many foods, feeding stuffs, rubber, leather, and textile materials. There are many difficulties connected with the administration of import controls, but the possibilities of actual evasion are very limited. In countries less dependent on imports, it seems clear that control is more difficult.

The simplicity and smallness of the Norwegian economy probably made it relatively easy to administer controls intelligently. The farms, forests, and fisheries produce a limited array of basic commodities. Although there are many small producers, they are highly organized. Manufacturing on a large scale is confined to a few large plants. Price determination and import licensing and allocation problems are relatively simple. Government officials can become well informed on production plans and costs in a short time and can easily keep in touch with the major individual producers or the organizations representing them. In the policy sense, of course, it may be more difficult to deal with a single large producer than with hundreds of small competing producers.

The success of the Norwegian recovery program is partly due to the fact that it was carried on in a period of world economic stability and of steady economic progress in Europe. Although steadily rising world prices led to difficulties, a world depression would undoubtedly have interfered more with carrying out the Norwegian investment program. Comparisons with other European countries, equally favored by world prosperity and European progress, indicate that Norway's planned recovery was as successful as any, if not more successful.

The Korean war interfered with European recovery programs in some respects, but the effects were not all adverse. The war led to a greatly increased demand for Norwegian shipping and to special aid for developing electrometallurgical output. The defense effort, on the other hand, absorbed resources in men and materials which might well have been used to carry the recovery program even further.

A country trying to achieve a rapid rate of growth within the framework of an over-all economic plan might well be impressed by certain features of the Norwegian postwar experience. There are some lessons to be learned about the planning process and the problems of planning as such. There is also important evidence of the advantages and disadvantages of suppressed inflation as a stimulus to rapid economic growth.

Successful economic planning must start with a basic analysis of the economy and a careful estimate of its potential. Plans covering a period of at least four or five years are essential. Planning on a year-to-year basis, while necessary, is of limited usefulness unless it is geared to a long-range program in which all the important economic magnitudes can be considered as variables rather than determined by the actual situation. Once a long-term plan involving a firm program for the rational use of potential available resources has been developed, annual budgets for available resources and uses play a very useful, if not an absolutely essential, role. A careful review from month to month of the actual situation in terms of whether or not it is consistent with long-term and annual plans is also essential. And the review process must provide the background for continuous policy decisions aimed at more successful implementation of plans or revisions.

Although the United States clearly is not interested in economic planning, as usually defined, the President's economic reports and reports on long-term growth prospects are similar to the Norwegian annual budgets and programs in some respects. It is intended that policy recommendations be geared to achieving the objectives of the Employment Act of 1946. Developments in the course of a year are carefully watched and, as a result, important policy recommendations are occasionally made.

The similarities end here, however. The annual reports of the United States do not set forth targets in line with long-term growth targets. And the United States is inclined to take the attitude that economic policies can only avoid extremes of depression or inflation. Day-by-day government action to help make output, investment, or employment conform to a clearly defined minimum target is not considered appropriate.

It is precisely the setting up of firm long-run targets and continuous action to try to meet the targets which makes for successful economic planning. This means that economic planning must be taken seriously by the administration and the parliament. The task of developing, proposing, defending, and winning support for an economic plan must be given priority. Two or three times a year, the over-all economic program must be considered at length, and every aspect of economic policy making, including monetary, fiscal, price-wage, and trade policies, must be consistent with plans for resource availabilities and uses.

This means that firm political support is essential for the program. Plans can be completely thrown off by parliamentary decisions on particular aspects of economic policy which are inconsistent with the program. Since 1952, there has been a tendency in Norway for political decisions to interfere with rational economic policy making. It is useless to imagine that such problems can be avoided entirely, but it is important to realize how essential it is to have the necessary political support for a long-term plan for economic development.

Norwegian experience suggests that too much emphasis cannot be placed on the need for developing the statistical background for economic planning. Full knowledge provides a much sounder basis for planning than rough estimates provide. On the other hand, fairly rough preliminary estimates can be used without entirely throwing off the program. Rough estimates are presumably better than none. If it is assumed that aggregate demand tends to be excessive, plans must be based on conservative estimates of available resources. There is bound to be a margin of error, and even tight controls are likely to fall short of full effectiveness. A series of targets for resource uses based on optimistic estimates of available resources is likely to cause trouble. There has been some tendency in Norway since 1952 to depart from the policy of conservative targets which was extremely successful before 1952. Oddly enough, this seems to reflect in part the fact that much more complete data on output have been available since 1952.

In estimating available resources, one of the greatest problems for a country with a large foreign trade is forecasting the terms of trade. Available resources from import surpluses may be small in real terms even when a country is managing to finance huge foreign deficits. Generally speaking, resources made available by import surpluses are likely to be small in comparison with output. Domestic savings must finance the greater part of a heavy investment program. In planning for resource uses, probably one of the most difficult problems is that of determining how to control or to estimate changes in stocks.

In a sense, Norway's experience with economic planning for rapid development is closely related to the simultaneous, and yet distinct, experiment with suppressed inflation over a period of years in peacetime. Countries not interested in planning in peacetime have found it necessary in a time of war. Huge defense efforts have been carried out at relatively low cost and in an atmosphere of relative price and wage stability by using controls to prevent inflationary spending from driving up prices and wages. Norway's postwar experience is unusual primarily because the same sort of program was carried out in a time of peace.

The fact that Norway's experiment with peacetime suppressed inflation was effectively handled is noteworthy. Controls were reasonably efficient. Black markets were not important. Increases in output proceeded at a satisfactory rate. High domestic and export profits and low domestic prices and wages provided a violent stimulus to investment. And after five or six years, and some upward price adjustment, most of the suppressed inflationary pressures had apparently been worked off.

Other countries, perhaps, would do well to avoid the extremes of suppressed inflation that Norway inherited from the occupation, and the extremes reached in keeping domestic prices below export prices. Norway's ability to handle this situation to date probably reflects a number of the factors in the Norwegian political, educational, psychological, and institutional situation which are least likely to exist to the same degree in other semi-industrialized countries, not to mention underdeveloped areas. But countries trying to devote a large share of output to investment in order to expand productive capacity rapidly are likely to develop inflationary pressures. They might find it useful to have a relatively short period of price controls and suppressed inflation rather than to allow actual inflation to develop. And domestic prices somewhat below world prices, even though requiring subsidies, may be a very potent stimulus to necessary investment in export sectors.

One obvious fact is that Norway eliminated inflationary pressures in the consumer sector only by a strong combination of fiscal policy, price-wage policy, and policy on the use of resources for consumption. The heavy reliance on fiscal and price-wage policies to keep the controlled price system from getting too far out of line with disposable incomes, and gradually to bring it more into line, was of the utmost importance. Fiscal and wage policies are less manageable in many countries. Even in Norway since 1952, the situation has become more difficult.

One resource problem appears to be of critical importance when an attempt is made to stimulate rapid increases in output. Some improvement in living standards and some kind of steady increase in consumption probably should accompany any heavy investment program. The consumption increases allowed in the early years may be limited to certain types of goods and services. Steps can be taken to conserve scarce resources for investment. But a rise in consumption of some kind must be provided in a period of very full employment and long working hours if productivity and incentives are to be maintained. Furthermore, after a few years, the rise in consumption must be in the type of goods most strongly wanted.

The Norwegian consumption program seems to have been particularly successful. It is certainly not a coincidence that total and per capita consumption rose more in Norway than in other European countries at the same time that the increase in output above the prewar level was greater and the investment program was heavier.

One last point to be made in connection with the progress toward elimination of suppressed inflation in Norway is that over-all economic planning clearly helped in meeting a difficult situation. When the whole period from 1946 to 1956 is considered, national budgeting for resource uses appears to have contributed to the handling of a series of difficult problems and critical situations. The remaining unsolved problem is whether unemployment can be kept below even 1 per cent of the labor force without steady inflationary pressure.

National budgeting for resource uses by itself cannot solve the problem, but it may well help to preserve an atmosphere in which a considerable amount of useful experimenting can be carried on. How far over-all monetary and fiscal policies can be used to keep aggregate demand in line with continuous really full employment is uncertain. Less than 1 per cent may be far too high a target for Norway. Permanent direct controls over investment may be accepted as preferable to 3 to 5 per cent unemployment. Whatever the level of unemployment, more restrained policies on wage increases will probably be necessary if a steady rise in wages and prices is to be avoided. Whatever happens, the plans for resource availabilities and uses will undoubtedly continue to provide a useful guide to monetary and fiscal policies as well as a rational program for investment and expansion of output and exports.

Selected Bibliography

This bibliography lists only the source materials on Norway used extensively in this study. It is not exhaustive, and it omits references to a large number of periodical articles in the *Statistiske Meddelelser*, published by the Central Bureau of Statistics; in *Ökonomi*, a periodical published in Oslo by the Naeringsökonomisk Forskningsinstitutt; and in the *Statsökonomisk Tidsskrift*. It also omits the mimeographed memorandums prepared at the University of Oslo Institute of Economics, some of which are in English. The author's mathematics did not permit serious use of these memorandums.

References to parliamentary documents may be clarified by the following comments. The Storting is the Norwegian parliament, and the *Forhandlinger i Stortinget* is the official record of parliamentary actions and debates. A full index or register of parliamentary documents, called *Stortingstidende*, contains references by subject and speaker. The *Stortingsmelding* (*St. meld.*) are numbered reports to the Storting submitted by government departments or by special advisory committees. The parliamentary committee reports are called *Instilling* (*Inst.*). A draft law is a *proposisjon* (*prp.*) and may be referred either to the Storting (*St. prp.*) or to the Odelsting (*Ot. prp.*) for consideration. The Odelsting may refer the law to the Lagting (Lt.), the other house of the Norwegian parliament.

Where possible, reference is made to English sources and to the existence of English or French titles, prefaces, or summaries in Norwegian publications. The author had access to professional translations into English of many of the documents cited and also to translations of daily newspaper articles. These translations were for the use of the American Embassy and the ECA Mission to Norway. In some cases the translations were used instead of the original documents.

The author also relied heavily on conversations with government officials during the years spent in Oslo and in Paris studying the Norwegian economy.

A. BASIC LONG-TERM PLANS, ANNUAL PROGRAMS, AND
   NATIONAL BUDGETS

(chronological order)

All the documents listed here were published in Oslo except for those
published in Paris by the Organization for European Economic
Cooperation (as noted). Short summaries of the annual budgets have
been translated into English and mimeographed by the Finanzde-
partementet, Nasjonalbudsjettetbyraa, Oslo.

*Nasjonalregnskapet og nasjonalbudsjettet, Saerskilt vedlegg nr. 11
til statsbudsjettet, 1945–46.*
Om nasjonalbudsjettet 1947, St. meld. nr. 10, 1947.
Nasjonalbudsjettet 1948, St. meld. nr. 1, 1948.
Gjennomföringen av nasjonalbudsjettet 1948, St. meld. nr. 50, 1948.
OEEC, Report to the ECA on the Annual Program, Vol. II, *Report to
the Economic Cooperation Administration on the 1949–1950 Pro-
gramme,* The 1949–50 Programme of Norway. (Memo submitted
by Norway in October 1948.) Paris 1949.
OEEC, Vol. II, *Interim Report on the European Recovery Programme,*
The Norwegian Long Term Programme. (Memo submitted by
Norway in December 1948.) Paris 1948. Official Norwegian pub-
lication of the same document is *Om utarbeidelse av et langtidsprogram til Organisationen for europeisk ökonomisk samarbeid, St.
meld. nr. 54, 1948.*
Nasjonalbudsjettet 1949, St. meld. nr. 1, 1949.
*Gjennomföringen av nasjonalbudsjettet 1949, St. meld. nr. 39,
1949.*
OEEC, *General Memorandum on the 1950–51 and 1951–52 Pro-
grammes, Norway.* (Memo submitted by Norway in December
1949.) Paris, April 1950.
Nasjonalbudsjettet 1950, St. meld. nr. 1, 1950.
*Tillegg til nasjonalbudsjettet 1950: Om tiltak til aa trygge stabiliteten
i landets ökonomi, St. meld. nr. 42, 1950.*
Gjennomföringen av nasjonalbudsjettet 1950, St. meld. nr. 54, 1950.
*Halvaarsmelding om gjennomföringen av nasjonalbudsjettet 1950, St.
meld. nr. 65, 1950.*
Nasjonalbudsjettet 1951, St. meld. nr. 1, 1951.
*Halvaarsmelding om gjennomföringen av nasjonalbudsjettet 1951, St.
meld. nr. 93, 1951.*

Utbyggingsprogrammet for Nord-Norge, St. meld. nr. 85, September 1951.
Nasjonalbudsjettet 1952, St. meld. nr. 1, 1952.
Halvaarsmelding om gjennomföringen av nasjonalbudsjettet 1952, St. meld. nr. 94, 1952.
Nasjonalbudsjettet 1953, St. meld. nr. 1, 1953.
Om et langtidsprogram for 1954–1957, St. meld. nr. 62, 1953.
Nasjonalbudsjettet 1954, St. meld. nr. 1, 1954.
Halvaarsmelding om nasjonalbudsjettet 1954, St. meld. nr. 95, 1954.
Nasjonalbudsjettet 1955, St. meld. nr. 1, 1955.
Halvaarsmelding om nasjonalbudsjettet 1955, St. meld. nr. 80, 1955.
Nasjonalbudsjettet 1956, St. meld. nr. 1, 1956.
Halvaarsmelding om nasjonalbudsjettet 1956, St. meld. nr. 70, 1956.
Nasjonalbudsjettet 1957, St. meld. nr. 1, 1957.
Om langtidsprogrammet for 1958–1961, St. meld. nr. 67, 1957.

B. PUBLICATIONS OF CENTRAL BUREAU OF STATISTICS
(Statistisk Sentralbyraa)

I. *Special Volumes* (chronological order):

Statistiske Oversikter 1948 (Statistical Survey, 1948). Similar to earlier volumes of 1914 and 1946. Contains all basic data carried as far back as available, full English table titles and headings.

Husholdningsregnskaper mai 1947–april 1948 (Budgets de familles mai 1947–avril 1948), 1950. Table of contents and a list of tables in English.

Konjunkturene i mellomkrigstiden, Norge og utlandet (Inter-war Trade Cycles, Norway in Relation to Other Countries), 1951. English summary.

Tendenser i den ökonomiske utvikling, vaaren 1952 (Current Economic Trends, 1952). Table of contents in English.

Nasjonalregnskap 1930–1939 og 1946–1951 (National Accounts, 1930–1939 and 1946–1951), 1952. Table headings and footnotes in English.

Nasjonalregnskap, 1900–1929 (National Accounts, 1900–1929) 1953. Summary and table headings in English.

Det norske skattesystems virkninger paa den personlige inntektsfordeling (The Effects of the Norwegian Tax System on Personal Income Distribution), 1954, by Helge Seip. Preface and table of contents in English.

Nasjonalregnskap, 1938 og 1948–1953 (National Accounts, 1938 and 1948–1953), 1954. Preface and table headings in English.

Ökonomisk utsyn 1900–1950 (Economic Survey, 1900–1950), 1955.

Nasjonalregnskap, Teoritiske prinsipper (National Accounts, Theoretical Principles) by Odd Aukrust, 1955. Summary and table of contents in English.

Nasjonalregnskap, 1949–1955 (National Accounts, 1949–1955), 1956, a mimeographed document.

II. *Regular Publications:*

Statistisk-ökonomisk utsyn over krigsaarene, 1945. (Apercu de la situation economique pendant les annees de guerre.) Table of contents in French.

Statistisk-ökonomisk oversikt over aaret 1946 (Apercu de la situation economique en 1946), Identical volumes for 1947 and 1948. Tables of contents and lists of tables in French in the course of following years.

Ökonomisk utsyn over aaret 1949 (Economic Survey, 1949), and each year thereafter, published in following year. Before 1952, French tables of contents and summaries; English tables of contents and summaries since 1952.

Statistisk Aarbok for Norge (Statistical Yearbook of Norway). Full table headings in English.

Statistiske Meldinger (Monthly bulletin of the Central Bureau of Statistics). English table of contents and list of tables and French translation of all table headings.

Maandedsoppgaver over Vareomsetningen med utlandet (Monthly bulletin of External Trade). Table, titles, and a general note in English.

Maanedstatistikk over de Norske Aksje og Sparebanker (Monthly statistics for Norwegian joint stock and savings banks). Contains statistics of reporting banks.

Norges Private Aksjebanker og Sparebanker (Norwegian Private Joint Stock and Savings Banks). Annual survey of data for all banks.

C. OTHER REGULAR OFFICIAL PUBLICATIONS

Report on Economic Developments in Norway. Quarterly reports in English submitted by the Norwegian government in mimeographed form under the Marshall Plan Agreement, from December 1948 to March 31, 1953.

Norges Bank (Bank of Norway) *Bulletin.* Published monthly before the war (the English title was *Monthly Report on Economic Conditions in Norway*); published six times a year from 1947 to 1952 (the English title was *Monthly Bulletin* in 1946 and 1947); published four times a year since February 1953 (available in English).

Norges Bank, Beretning og regnskap. Annual reports of the Bank of Norway to the Storting, published as Storting reports.

Arbeidsmarkedet. Monthly statistical report of Arbeidsdirektoratet (Department of Labor).

D. OTHER IMPORTANT OFFICIAL REPORTS AND STATE-MENTS
(chronological order)

Fellesprogrammet 1945: De politiske partienes samarbeidsprogram for gjenreisningen, 1945.

Gjenreisningen program, Vedlegg til Fri Fagbevegelse, June 1945.

Om utferdigelse av lov om engangskatt paa formuestigning, Ot. prp. nr. 25, February 1946 (1945–46).

Om engangsskatt paa formuestigning, St. prp. nr. 18 (1945–46).

Om sanering av pengevesenet, St. meld. nr. 8 (1945–1946).

Statsbudsjettet, St. prp. nr. 1. (The annual presentation of the administration recommendation on the fiscal budget for the coming fiscal year.)

Norges ökonomiske og finansielle stilling. Address of Finance Minister Brofoss in Storting, February 1946. (Published as a separate pamphlet by Arbeidernes Opplysningsforbund.)

Finansdebatt, *Forhandlinger i Stortinget,* April 1–3 and October 9–11, 1946. (The "finansdebatt" normally covers the national budget and the fiscal or "statsbudsjett." Usually there are two finance debates, one in the spring and one in the fall, based on reports on developments under the budget.)

Trontale og finansdebatt, *Forhandlinger i Stortinget,* 1947, March 25–27. ("Trontale" is the annual statement delivered by the government on the main policies to be followed in the next year. Normally the debate on the "trontale" is separate from the finance debate.)

Om saerlige tiltak til trygging av landets ökonomi, St. meld. nr. 43, August 15, 1947.

Om gjennomföringen av fellesprogrammet, St. meld. nr. 45, September 5, 1947.

Trontaledebatten, *Forhandlinger i Stortinget,* February 11–13, 1948.

Finansdebatt, *Forhandlinger i Stortinget,* April 15–17, 1948.

Foreign Currency Problems. Address delivered by Finance Minister Brofoss to Oslo Chamber of Commerce, September 30, 1948. (Unofficial translation of address; unpublished.)

Finansdebatt, *Forhandlinger i Stortinget,* March 22–24, 1949.

Nasjonalbudsjettet og det europeiske langtidsprogram, debatt, *Forhandlinger i Stortinget,* July 25, 1949.

Mellomkrigstid, etterkrigstid, framtid. Address by Finance Minister Brofoss. *Arbeiderbladet,* October 7, 1949.

Trontaledebatt, *Forhandlinger i Stortinget,* February 7, 1950.

Finansdebatt, *Forhandlinger i Stortinget,* March 20–22, 1950.

Om skatter, avgifter, prisregulering ökonomisk stabilizering m.v. debatt, *Forhandlinger i Stortinget,* June 20–21, 1950.

Nedsettelse av bevilgningene til investeringer i statsbudsjettet, 1950–51, St. prp. nr. 129, October 27, 1950. Vedlegg: uttalelse av penge og finansraadet, August 30, 1950.

Om tillegg til skattelovene for landet og for byene av August 1911, Ot. prp. nr. 81, November 1950.

Om tillegg til aksje og sparebanklovgivningen, Ot. prp. nr. 82, November 1950.

Om gjennonföring av nasjonalbudsjettet 1 halvaar 1950 og nedsatte bevilgninger til investeringer, debatt, *Forhandlinger i Stortinget,* December 6–7, 1950.

Retningslinjer m.m for boligbyggingen, debatt, *Forhandlinger i Stortinget,* March 14–15, 1951.

Trontale og finansdebatt, *Forhandlinger i Stortinget,* April 10–12, 1951.

Circular from Ministry of Finance to Joint Stock and Savings Banks. (Unofficial unpublished translation, May 1951.)

Instilling fra Penge og Finansraadet, January 13, 1952.

Finansdebatt, *Forhandlinger i Stortinget,* April 1–3, 1952.

Retningslinjer for penge og kredittpolitikken, St. meld. nr. 75, April 1952.

Prisloven, Ot. prp. nr. 60, as amended, 1952.

Norway's Post-War Economic Problems. Lectures by Commerce Minister Brofoss at the University of Oslo Summer School, 1952. (Mimeographed and privately circulated.)

Den utenriksökonomiske situasjon, debatt, *Forhandlinger i Stortinget*, October 25, 1952.

Om midlertig lov om adgang til regulering av renter og provisjoner, Ot. prp. nr. 55, April 1953.

Finansdebatt, *Forhandlinger i Stortinget*, April 21–23, 1953.

Lov om priser og konkurransereguleringer, debatt, *Forhandlinger i Stortinget*, May 28–June 1, 1953.

Den utenriksökonomiske situasjon. Address of Minister Brofoss, *Forhandlinger i Stortinget*, June 5, 1953.

Finansministerens redegjörelse for statsbudsjettet i Stortinget, *Forhandlinger i Stortinget*, February, 19, 1954.

(*Note: Many of the following addresses also have appeared in the* Forhandlinger i Stortinget *but the author has relied on the sources quoted instead of on the* Forhandlinger i Stortinget.)

Monetary Measures, *Bank of Norway Bulletin*, January 7, 1954. (Contains the text of the July 1953 Rate of Interest Limitation Act.)

Address by Mr. Gunnar Jahn, *Bank of Norway Bulletin*, February 15, 1954.

The Speech of Mr. Mons Lid, Minister of Finance, to the Storting on February 14, 1955, Concerning the Economic Policy of the Government, *Bank of Norway Bulletin*, March 23, 1955.

Address of Mr. Erik Brofoss, Governor of The Bank of Norway, on February 21, 1955, *Bank of Norway Bulletin*, March 23, 1955.

Address of the Prime Minister, Mr. Einer Gerhardsen, to the Storting on June 20, 1955, *Bank of Norway Bulletin*, July 15, 1955.

Statsministerens redegjörelse i Stortinget, October 27, 1955. (Mimeographed copy.)

Finansminister Mons Lid foredrag i Stortinget mandag 16 januar 1956–57. (Mimeographed copy.)

Address of Mr. Erik Brofoss, Governor of the Bank of Norway, February 20, 1956, *Bank of Norway Bulletin*, March 6, 1956.

Finansminister Lids tilleggsredegjörelse om den ökonomiske situasjon i Stortinget, 19 april 1956. (Mimeographed copy.)

E. REPORTS OF THE ORGANIZATION FOR EUROPEAN ECONOMIC COOPERATION, PARIS

I. *Reports on Country Programs* (see Section A):

Interim Report on the European Recovery Programme, two volumes, 1948.

Report to the Economic Cooperation Administration on the First Annual Programme, 1949.

Report to the Economic Cooperation Administration on the 1949–1950 Programme, two volumes, 1949.

II. *Annual Reports on Progress:*

Report on the Progress of Western European Recovery, June 1949 (first annual report).

European Recovery Programme, Second Report of the OEEC, 1950 (second annual report).

Economic Progress and Problems of Western Europe, June 1951 (known as the third annual report).

Europe, the Way Ahead, Toward Economic Expansion and Dollar Balance, December 1952 (fourth annual report).

Progress and Problems of the European Economy (fifth annual report), 1953.

Sixth Report of the OEEC — From Recovery towards Economic Strength, March 1955.

Seventh Report of the OEEC — Economic Expansion and Its Problems, February 1956.

III. *Reports on Financial Stability:*

Report on Internal Financial Stability, October 15, 1949.

Internal Financial Stability in Member Countries, 1950.

Financial Stability and the Fight Against Inflation, 1951.

The Internal Financial Situation in Member and Associated Countries. Report by a group of independent experts, 1952.

IV. *Other Reports:*

A Standardized System of National Accounts, 1952.

National Accounts Studies, Norway, June 1953.

Statistics of National Product and Expenditure, 1938, 1947 to 1952, 1954.

Economic Conditions in Denmark, Iceland, Norway, and Sweden, 1955.

Statistics of National Product and Expenditure, No. 2, 1938 and 1947 to 1955, 1957.

F. BOOKS AND ARTICLES

Bjerve, P. J., and O. Aukrust, *Hva krigen kostet Norge.* Oslo, Dreyers Forlag, 1945.

Bjerve, P. J., "Government Economic Control," *Scandinavia Between East and West*, ed. Henning Friis. Ithaca: Cornell University Press, 1950.

European Recovery Program, Norway, Country Study. Washington, D.C., ECA pamphlet, February 1949.

Galenson, Walter, *Labor in Norway*. Cambridge: Harvard University Press, 1949.

Grunwald, Joseph, "Planned Economy in Norway, A Reply." *American Economic Review*, June 1950.

————— "National Economic Budgeting in Norway." Unpublished dissertation, Columbia University, 1951 (available in microfilm).

Holben, R. E., "Planned Economy in Norway, Comment." *American Economic Review*, December 1949.

Hoffmann, Johann, *Main Features of Norwegian Post-War Housing Policy*. (Mimeographed memo by J. Hoffmann, Director of State Housing Bank.) Oslo, May 1952.

Klein, Lawrence R., "Planned Economy in Norway." *American Economic Review*, December 1948.

————— "Economic Planning Western European Style." *Statsökonomisk Tidsskrift*, Oslo, 1948.

Leiserson, Mark, "Wages in a Controlled Economy." Unpublished dissertation, Harvard University, 1955.

State Housing Bank, *Housing Needs and Housing Shortage in Norway, 1939–1949*. Unofficial translation of unpublished report of the statistical department of the State Housing Bank, May 12, 1950.

Index

Aid. *See* Marshall Plan

Agriculture: dependence on in 1900, 3–4; prewar position, 3–5; investment, 1946 plan, 40; investment, 1948 plan, 97; share of ouput and employment postwar and prewar, 139–40; output in 1952 and 1948 plan, 140–41, 142; investment, 1953 plan, 185. *See also* Farm prices

Aluminum: government-owned enterprise, 75; plants, capital-output ratio, 138

Annual budget. *See* National budget

Aukrust, Odd, 7

Balance of payments: at time of liberation, 1; prewar, 3; emphasis in 1948 national budget, 62; difficulties as of early 1948, 89; goal of 1948 plan for 1952–1953, 90, 142; equilibrium achieved by 1951, 145; equilibrium 1951–1952 and inflationary pressure, 179–80; goal of 1953 plan, 183–84; current deficits 1953–1955 compared with 1953 plan, 185–86. *See also* Exports; Foreign exchange earnings; Imports; Import surpluses

Bank loans: prewar and postwar, 26–27; plan to limit expansion so not inflationary, 33; expansion 1945–1948, 55–56; attempts to limit 1947 and 1948, 56; expansion 1946–1952, 109, 112; attempts to limit expansion 1949–1952, 109–11; moral suasion to control expansion 1955, 189; agreement of private banks to limit 1956 and 1957, 189–90

Bank reserves: at time of liberation, 10; prewar and postwar, 26–27; legal requirements 1945, 30–31; 1945 proposal to freeze substantial part, 31; factors decreasing 1946 to 1950, 108; ratio to deposits by 1950, 108–9; new law on reserve requirements, 109, 111–12; aim to hold constant 1951 and 1952, 10; new requirements imposed 1955, 190

Bjerve, Petter Jakob, 7

Black markets, 52

Budget. *See* Fiscal budget; National budget

Building: controls over, 77; licensing, 77–78; relaxation of controls 1949–1952, 116; investment 1949–1952 compared with plans, 122–23; investment in 1953 plan, 185; actual investment higher than planned 1953–1956, 187; sales tax on building 1955, 192–93. *See also* Building materials; Construction; Housing; Maintenance

Building materials: basic scarcity, 62; allocations, 77–78; and investment controls, 77, 80–81; scarcity of and 1946 plan to restrict consumption, 82–88; and evasion of controls 1949–1952, 123

Bureaucracy, 203

Capital levy: recommended 1945, 22; stiffer one favored, 31; Norges Bank plan, 33–34; law as passed 1945, 34; receipts, 54–55

Capital-output ratio: 1948–1952, 136–38; and output goals in 1953 plan, 184

Central bank. *See* Monetary policy; Norges Bank

Central Bureau of Statistics: study of prewar economy and effects of war,

Date Due

NOV 1 7 1958			
MY 21'68			